RIDING *The* E...

FOR
MARK, MARGERY AND JOHN

RIDING *The* ELEPHANT

Nancy Keesing

Sydney
ALLEN & UNWIN
Wellington London Boston

First published in 1988
Paperback edition 1989
Allen & Unwin Australia Pty Ltd
An Unwin Hyman Company
8 Napier Street, North Sydney NSW 2059 Australia

Allen & Unwin New Zealand Ltd
75 Ghuznee Street, Wellington, New Zealand

Unwin Hyman Ltd
15–17 Broadwick Street, London W1V1FP England

Unwin Hyman Inc.
8 Winchester Place, Winchester, Mass 01890 USA

*Illustrations for chapters I–XII and prelims by Kenneth
McGuire; illustration for chapter XIII by Helen Gundlach*

National Library of Australia
Cataloguing-in-Publication entry:

Keesing, Nancy, 1923–
    Riding the elephant.

    ISBN 0 04 442117 6

    1. Keesing, Nancy, 1923–   —Anecdotes.   2. Women
authors, Australian.   I. Title.

A828′.303

Set in 10.5/12 Garamond by Best-Set Typesetter, Hong Kong
Printed by Australian Print Group, Maryborough, Vic.

Contents

Acknowledgements

My thanks to the Australian Society of Authors; the Mitchell Library; Jill Hellyer, Joyce Scarlett, Meg Stewart, Thelma Afford and Michael Costigan for relevant material and information; Maxine Poynton-Baker for her written contribution; Bryony Cosgrove for her editorial advice and to Reta Grace for her patience and careful typing.

Permission to use the following photographs is gratefully acknowledged.

Charles Loneragan, commercial artist, (Endpapers); David Alcock, 5; The Wunderlich Collection which is housed in the Mitchell Library, State Library of New South Wales, 9; Michael Elton, 10, 11, 12; Photograph 19 has appeared previously in *Southerly*; Ina M Bracegirdle, 20; Quinton Davis, 21; Permanent Trustee Company Limited, Janet Glad, 23.

While every effort has been made to trace copyright for material used in this book, further information would be welcomed by the author and publisher.

Riding the Elephant

I WAS four years old and it happened like this: we had been living in Auckland for a year, where my architect father had become my fisherman father. I too had become a skilful hauler of garfish—called 'piper' in New Zealand—from the harbour to the jetty of Cheltenham Beach. My record catch was seven in one morning.

Dad was not visibly ill and I have no idea why he took this long holiday in the city of his birth. And now we were aboard SS *Wanganui* sailing back home to Sydney.

Also on board was Wirths Circus returning to Australia from its annual tour of New Zealand. In the dining saloon my parents shared a table with the tall man and the dwarf who were great friends and excellent company, they reported. Children ate at an earlier sitting so we did not meet the fabulous pair directly, though we saw them from a distance promenading the deck reserved for grownups, and very incongruous they were, for the tall man was strikingly thin and the dwarf a roly-poly.

The circus animals travelled in holds below deck. The decking above the elephants' quarters had several largeish holes cut in it for, I suppose, light and air but also for the delight of children who, carrying apples and bits of bread, were taken to feed the jumbos. Through each hole elephant trunks, three or four I think, sprouted like strange prehistoric growths. Each tough, leathery, sinuous sprout ended in a gaping aperture, pink and red and runny with mucous—and into this mysterious mouth, that according to my father was not a mouth, but a sort of nose, we thrust our offerings. Holding food the trunks withdrew briefly, to where? To what? I'd never seen and could scarcely imagine, Elephant.

How fortunate the elder daughter of table companions of the tall man and the dwarf. One morning I was escorted (by father? by whom?) to the elephants' hold where monstrous shapes loomed in brown gloom and pachyderm legs rose like vast but flabby tree trunks, supporting flanks like the shapes of old coats that slowly move in a cupboard when an opened door admits a draught. High above me their ear-flaps, and their great docile heads from which trunks uprose to the pinholes of light far away, down which peered the eyes of ordinary children holding bread and apples in ordinary sunlight.

And one trunk snaked down. 'Hold your apple out. See, she's putting her trunk down to your hand. Now place the apple in her trunk and see how she gets it to her mouth.' Her mouth was a smiling cavern, her yellow, sawn-off tusks. . . There is a smell, warm and foetid rather than rank, and of bodies rather than manure. The hold becomes more visible as eyes adjust to its darkness. It is very clean. The elephant keeper and the trainer, with scraping brooms and buckets of water and mops, swab living leather and moist flooring.

The trainer, a saturnine man, calls something to the hugest elephant and oh! horror! her trunk is around my waist. I had never then seen a snake but atavistically I sensed, and invented, boa constrictor. I was too shocked to make a sound. I was twisted away from the floor sideways; nearly upside down. I was near the roof. I was on her back and somehow—ladder? rungs in the wall?—the keeper had perched on her rough, rock rump and held me securely. I rode the elephant.

The face of a child I knew in another life appeared close by through one of the holes in the deck. I returned its stare seriously. This was no moment for poking grimaces. For I am supreme. I am the lord, I am the lord, I am the lord of everything.

The trainer utters another call. His hands guide me back to the trunk. Head upright I am enclosed; lowered; reduced...

Against injustice, failure, sheer laziness. For ever after, for evermore, I say to myself: '*Once* I rode an elephant. *When* I rode *the* elephant...'

'What are you writing?' or 'What's your next book about?' ask my friends. It is difficult to answer. At first I say: 'It's a kind of memoir of my life and good times in Aust. Lit.' After a time I change this to: 'The kind of autobiography I write when I'm not writing an autobiography.' Both answers are truthful. But a friend who has read this work in manuscript asks further questions. 'You keep mentioning Mark. He isn't a writer. How did you meet him?' And 'I know you wrote *Garden Island People* but not everyone has read it and here you refer several times to Garden Island but don't explain how and why you had a job there. You should.'

So here is the kind of autobiography I write when I'm writing a brief, chronological foreword:

My parents were Margery Isabel Rahel, nee Hart, and Gordon Samuel Keesing. They were born in New Zealand, he in Auckland, she in Dunedin. They met, and married, in Sydney where I was born at 22 Darling Point Road on 7 September 1923. My sister Margaret is some two years younger than me.

I was educated at SCEGGS, Sydney Church of England Girls' Grammar School, Darlinghurst and at Frensham, Mittagong. I spent a year as an Art student at the National Art School in East Sydney. In 1942 my parents moved from Darling Point to a house with three and a half acres of bush, orchard and garden at Pennant Hills. I took a wartime job as a clerk in the Department of the Navy and worked in the Accounts Branch until 1945 when I was accepted for the course conducted by the

Board of Social Studies at Sydney University. I was awarded my Diploma of Social Studies in 1947. I then worked as a Social Worker at the Royal Alexandra Hospital for Children for some five years.

In 1947 my cousin Orwell Phillips married Vanda Hertzberg of Brisbane, whose grandfather had migrated from Germany to Australia in 1867. Vanda's brother Mark was a Chemical Engineer, a graduate and medallist of the University of Queensland; he was overseas working for his PhD at the University of London. Mark returned to Australia at the end of 1948 and we met soon afterwards. He took a job with the Colonial Sugar Refining Company (CSR).

We saw each other quite often, usually at family occasions though we sometimes had dinner together and after a concert or theatre drank endless cups of coffee at the Mary Elizabeth coffee shop in Elizabeth Bay Road. Mark was not a writer but an adventurous and well-informed reader and he became popular with my friends in the literary world. He was working very hard at his job and, as he told me later, did not plan to marry until he was earning an adequate salary.

We married on 2 February 1955 at the Great Synagogue in Sydney. Our two children were born in Sydney, Margery in April 1956 and John in October 1957.

And I am still riding the elephant.

Three Ring Circus

MY mother and father were descended from Jews who settled in Australia and New Zealand in the eighteen-forties and eighteen-fifties. On the Keesing side my great great grandfather Hartog (Henry) Keesing was born on the last day of 1791 in Amsterdam to a family who had lived in Holland for over a hundred years. Henry, in youth, was conscripted into Napoleon's army but in 1813 somehow got to England, anglicised his first name and married. He and his wife Rosetta had nine children, two of whom migrated to America before the family sailed for New Zealand (another son left for America later, from New Zealand). According to my father the eldest son, Barnet, suggested that the family should emigrate to one of the new colonies; Henry replied that he could not take the responsibility of leading his family into the unknown like some latter-day Moses, but if Barnet would go first to spy out the land, he would follow.

Official British settlement in New Zealand began in 1840. In 1839 and perhaps earlier Barnet was in the Bay of Islands whose meagre white settlement at that time was chiefly connected with whaling stations. Meanwhile in the 'hungry forties' in England Henry lost his capital in a bank crash and decided to go to New Zealand. He organised some trading goods necessary for his new venture as a store-keeper and took steerage passages for his family on the barque *Union* which arrived in Auckland in March 1843. One of his sons, Ralph, was my great grandfather.

Ten years after Henry's arrival in New Zealand my maternal great grandfather, Moritz Michaelis, landed at Melbourne. He had been born at Lügde near Pyrmont in Germany, but for some years had worked in Manchester for a business that dealt in cotton goods and other clothing. When the Victorian gold rush began his employers decided to trade in Victoria and he and a colleague were sent out to establish that venture.

In those early days the small Jewish populations of Eastern Australia and New Zealand often forged close ties both of business and marriage. My paternal grandmother, Hannah Benjamin, was born to an Anglo-Jewish family long established in Melbourne; she sometimes referred to a fellow student at her school: 'little Nellie Mitchell' who became Dame Nellie Melba. My maternal grandfather, Hyam Hart, came from a family of English Jews several of whom migrated to Australia and America in the eighteen-twenties and eighteen-thirties; his wife, Florence nee Michaelis, had close family ties with the Hallenstein family who in 1879 established a clothing factory and chain of early department stores in New Zealand. Hyam Hart was engaged to work as an accountant for this firm whose head office was in Dunedin and that is where my mother was born. Before 1914 Hyam retired and moved permanently with my grandmother to Sydney, where my mother's two elder married sisters lived.

In 1914 my father returned from his years studying architecture in New York, Paris and London. He joined the AIF soon after the War broke out. He served with the Engineers in France for the duration of the War, was commissioned a Captain, and was decorated—Mentioned in Despatches. After the Armistice he accompanied a party appointed by General Monash to inspect sites of Australian war graves at Gallipoli and to design a cemetery and memorial. He therefore returned to Australia somewhat later than the majority of the AIF.

During his army service there was sorrow at home in New Zealand. His father Harry Albert Keesing (Ralph's son) died and so also did his adored sister Beryl, as well as her husband, John Parker. Their infant son Lindsay Parker who was born in 1913 was put in my grandmother's care. These deaths changed my father's life. He may once have planned to practise as an architect in New York, but now he returned to Sydney, where his mother and Lindsay joined him.

My parents met each other in Sydney, and married in 1922.

Before their marriage they bought an Edwardian house at 22 Darling Point Road near St Mark's Church. It was on a sloping site and two and a half storeys high. They converted the top storey to a flat that was reached by outside steps and was let to a somewhat mysterious family who lived on there during the Depression of the thirties, rent free. This was a typical generosity of my parents who believed in doing good deeds quietly. The tenants repaid my parents by several times allowing their bath to overflow and flood our ceilings and floors. Our house was almost opposite my aunt Brightie Phillips' house behind which, in St Marks Road, lived Granny and Grandfather Hart. Granny Keesing and cousin Lindsay lived in a flat over a mile further down Darling Point Road—too far to walk from the tram so, to my envy, they caught the tiny red bus that I remember like a toy vehicle. Lindsay, however, recalls before that a tiny horse-drawn bus.

My grandmother Hart was one of eleven children, my grandmother Keesing one of eight. My childhood was a bewilderment of aunts and uncles and great aunts and uncles and first and second cousins galore, not only in Sydney but in Melbourne and New Zealand. Neither the Tasman crossing nor the uncomfortable, slow trains of those times deterred many of these people from making visits. I was often geographically and chronologically confused.

Honesty and compassion are paramount qualities but absolute truthfulness is not: for one thing it is impracticable. For another perfect truth can be often cruel, usually more by accident than intention. I strive to be honest but occasionally dissemble; I sometimes withhold the truth, and that can be a kind of lie. Who better than the daughter of an absolutely truthful man better knows the dangers of naked truth?

My father equated absolute honesty and absolute truth and never understood that these absolutes are seldom reconcilable and never equal. If he detected anyone in a lie he immediately assumed that person was also dishonest or dishonourable—synonymous words in his vocabulary. These semantic flaws in his lovable and loving character were a chief cause of eccentricities that increased as he aged, and were also the reason for many of the disappointments of his life and career. They sometimes led this kindest of men to be, unwittingly, unkind.

He made impossible demands of people and set unattainable standards that he imagined were reasonable; he assumed that anyone he liked, loved, trusted met his standards. Consequently, lacking ordinary wariness, he was easily and often deceived—by his family in minor ways but sometimes less harmlessly by business colleagues and general acquaintance. By contrast you had to be up very early in the morning to put one over my mother. Lacking all sense of proportion, Father's outrage, when he detected a lie, was as great for a little white harmless fib as for a scandalous misrepresentation or a major whopper.

From this it followed that he had no tact at all:

Father : *What* am I eating?
Mother: A new recipe, apricot mousse, do you like it?
Father : It is perfectly vile. I can't abide messed-up food. I call it 'mouse'.

Or:

Father : Are you going into *town* looking like that?
Mother: Yes, why?
Father : I've never seen a more ridiculous hat in my life; maroon does not suit you; high heels destroy the natural grace of any woman.

Dad's far-carrying, booming voice was another embarrassment. Whole trams-full of passengers, or rooms-full of people perforce overheard his opinions and home truths. It was useless to pretend to be someone else's wife, child or colleague. He always noticed evasive action. '*What* is so interesting outside the window? I am speaking to *you*.' To a daughter he might add: 'Never trust anyone who can't meet your eye.'

Unfortunately he had no good close friends of his own age who might have laughed at him in kindly fashion and cut him down to size—no man of his own age who had his respect and against whom he might have measured himself. The friends of his early youth were made during his student days in New York and Europe and the Great War cut him off from them for ever. Every friend he made during four years' service in the first AIF was killed. Certainly he was a reasonably popular man—better liked than he always realised—but the men he respected and admired were often older then he. For instance he had a group of luncheon acquaintance at the Imperial Services Club and in Legacy, but seldom met them elsewhere. He had no interest in horse racing, convivial drinking or organised sport. He loathed large social gatherings and noisy groups. He was a dreadful dancer. He considered most of the things other men enjoyed a waste of money or of time, if not positively distasteful. He abhorred 'smutty' talk and jokes. Bridge was safe, its conversation being limited to the fall of cards, the machinations of the opposition, the ineptitudes of one's partner. My parents played a lot of bridge at which my mother was brilliant and he only fair; but she was clever, and untruthful enough, to keep him from realising this.

At the Imperial Services Club, it is alleged by some recent historians, plans for secret armies were hatched and fascist talk was talked. If that was so my father was sublimely unaware of this kind of thing, perhaps because his fellow members respected (or despised) his Jewishness; anti-semitic or racist people would scarcely have sought him out, and no one in his right mind with a guilty or subversive secret would have confided it to this upright, truthful man. For if he thought some truth should be spoken, he spoke it. Loud, clear and fearlessly.

He was proudly a Jew but inconsistent in his pride. Religion was one of the many matters he had been 'put off' at one time or another. He was 'put off' religion by the strictness with which it was practised in his parents' home at all times, and particularly during Saturday luncheons to which, since the family lived near the Auckland synagogue, the Rabbi was frequently invited. The Rabbi was, said my father, 'a dreadful man' without manners and far from truthful. The alleged untruthfulness apparently arose because the Rabbi practised tact and sometimes offered one opinion one Saturday and another on the same topic the next week.

Father was, too, a racist sort of Jew. He had little liking or tolerance for co-religionists from Eastern Europe, or even from Germany, especially if they spoke accented English. When refugees from Nazism flocked to Australia during the thirties my father helped and in some cases employed these distressed Germans to the best of his ability but he found something to disapprove of in almost every one of them who came within his ken.

One of these young men was a highly talented draughtsman who later became a well-regarded architect in Australia. Dad's architectural firm employed him. But his style of drawing, and use of strong colour in architectural drawings were different, more 'advanced' perhaps than

9

those favoured by established local practitioners, and very unfairly my father insisted that he alter his foreign and new-fangled ways, or get out. He got out.

A woman with a PhD in social science was sent to see him. 'You can forget that German degree of yours,' Dad advised her, 'you don't count as "doctor anything" here.' She went away dismayed, and worked for years in a piffling job until someone discovered her qualifications and suggested she apply for a university lectureship. She was appointed promptly.

When he studied architecture in New York in 1910 and 1911 Father decided, in a cool and calculated way, that he would change his religion if he could find one he preferred to Judaism, and set out to attend the church services of as many Christian denominations as possible. For one reason and another he found Christian worship exceedingly unappealing, except for the Unitarian form which attracted him for a while. Unitarians, he considered, were broad-minded and receptive to a range of belief. However when it came to a real point of a decision he could not swallow notions of a god made into man or any brand of triune deity.

A little later, in Europe, the atmosphere of certain cathedrals, as well as of village piety, gave him a feeling of warmth towards Catholicism, and he also admired Catholic traditional ritual. He was irrevocably 'put off' that sympathy one day when he followed a colourful procession of Church dignitaries and worshippers through the medieval streets of a French cathedral city. As the procession mounted the steps of a beautiful gothic cathedral a red-robed cardinal turned aside and blew his nose through his fingers directly towards the onlookers and too close for hygiene. A prince of the Church! Disgusting.

In Paris where he also studied architecture he wanted to attend a synagogue service during one of Judaism's holy days. The concierge of his lodgings gave him the address of a small synagogue nearby. All unprepared and unsuspecting he found himself in what must have been a congregation of *emigré* Chassidim, a sect of whom he had never heard. It was a single-storey room so that the women were not segregated in an upstairs gallery, as he was accustomed to, but sat invisibly behind a heavy screen. Dad thought this outlandish and dreadful, as were the black fur hats worn by the men and their sidelocks and beards. He could follow the service despite what he found a weird intonation of Hebrew until . . . horrors, at a certain point in the chanting the men began to dance, quite vigorously. It was a foreign and distasteful occasion at which he never ceased, lifelong, to scoff and yet, in a strange way, to marvel.

Despite his lack of enthusiasm for religious observance he attended Sydney's Great Synagogue fairly regularly when I was a child and dressed carefully for service in a dark suit, starched wing collar with dark tie, and black bowler hat. My mother did not always accompany him and his daughters were not taken to service until we were old enough to read. We were then supplied with improving books to keep us quiet and interested during the interminable, incomprehensible prayers and to prevent us from wriggling and indulging in other behaviour likely to annoy neighbours and aunts in the women's gallery.

On the other hand Father was active in Jewish communal affairs. Both my parents loved and respected Rabbi Francis Cohen. After he retired they turned to Liberal Judaism and my father was one of the founders of a Liberal Jewish congregation, The Temple Emanuel, in Sydney. He had a number of Jewish friends from his days as a member of the Jewish Debating Society: the one I best remember was Zoe Benjamin, a true dwarf who founded the Kindergarten movement, and Training College, in Australia. There he also met Marcus Hertzberg who was reading Law at the University of Sydney and who was destined to be my father-in-law.

Father believed everyone should know enough about their religion to decide for themselves whether or not they wished to accept and follow it, so he taught us basic Hebrew and important prayers and conducted the Sabbath Eve service in my widowed grandmother Hart's house every Friday night. However it was at my Church of England school that I learned bible stories, got most of the Psalms of David by heart (in lieu of memorising the Anglican Catechism—the fate of Anglican girls) and formed some idea of what religion was all about for those who did or could believe in its requirements and benefits.

Until he was a young architecture student of twenty-two, in New York, my father averred he had no personal experience of anti-semitism. He attributed the New York variety to the 'pushy ways' and unsavoury appearance and behaviour—or so it seemed to him—of many American Jews. However as a boy at Auckland Grammar School he was aware of, and resented, aspects of his religion that made him feel different, and cut him off from many of the social and sporting activities of his school companions. He could not play games or sport on Saturdays, for instance, and I suspect—from a strange, scrambled autobiography he once attempted to write—that he was aware of some kind of social discrimination when he was a boy and youth. Certainly he felt himself to be a 'loner' and added his awareness of early social failure to the catalogue of grievance and dislike that he constructed about his mother. His own father, Harry, was a strictly orthodox Jew who despised and rejected any Jew who, in New Zealand or Australia, conducted a pawn-broking or money-lending business for, he said, if in some eras and countries Jews had been forced by circumstances and prejudice to pursue avocations that had brought odium on themselves and their people, there was no excuse for perpetuating this kind of action in new countries and in more enlightened days.

My father joined the Sydney Legacy Club when it was founded in 1926, regularly attended its meetings and in unostentatious ways helped many children of deceased servicemen. He became the honorary architect of the Returned Sailors' and Soldiers' Imperial League of Australia as it was then called, and designed for the RSL various buildings and facilities in New South Wales and War Memorials in several public parks. He was architect of the Maccabean Hall, the Australian Jewish War Memorial in Darlinghurst Road, and of a synagogue at Bondi, since superseded, whence he was called home by telephone on the day of my birth.

When I first became aware of my father's profession he was working with an architect called Jack Francis Hennessy who had many commissions from the Roman Catholic Church. Father was associated with designing buildings for the Loreto Convent at Kirribilli, and with the final extensions to St Mary's Cathedral which were completed in 1928. Father used to travel to Brisbane quite often because his firm had the contract to design a spectacular Cathedral of the Holy Name that Archbishop Duhig planned for a large site in the Valley sector of Brisbane. The entry in the *Australian Dictionary of Biography* for Archbishop Duhig is in part as follows:

> The cathedral was planned as the largest to be built anywhere in the world since the seventeenth century. It was a work not only of ecclesiastical purpose but of civic pride and State development; for Duhig proposed to pay for it with dividends from his investments in Roma oil-wells. The spectacular foundation ceremony. . . in 1928 was followed by a more spectacular collapse in the Depression. The oil-wells and the cathedral were both casualties. A court action was brought by the Sydney architect Jack Francis Hennessy in 1949 for non-payment of fees for the cathedral plans and specifications; Hennessy was awarded £25,750.

I think the cathedral fiasco was a terrible personal disappointment to my father. It might have been the large achievement in the European tradition that it was his great, and never realised, ambition to design. He would not speak about it—chiefly, as I understood, because he did not want to discuss what might become distasteful litigation.

No large buildings in the European tradition were commissioned during the Depression. However, father did put to good use one of his areas of study: modern kitchen equipment and hospital design, which instead he sometimes incorporated in the building and renovation of hotels and also in factory design. His chief work in those years was as architect for Tooth's Brewery for whom he designed, or modernised, a number of Sydney hotels, large and small, as well as brewery buildings and a large soft drink factory.

He retired early from his profession, in about 1941, chiefly because he became disgusted with the subterfuges of after-hours drinking that resulted from six o'clock closing of hotels and bars. He was appalled when, early in the War, a builder whom he respected, and a brother architect, resorted to bribes and the black market to obtain scarce materials. For his retirement he bought a house at Pennant Hills that was surrounded by three and a half acres of orange orchard, poultry yards and vegetable garden. The actualities of his career never did match his ambition.

My grandparents kept a strictly kosher house in Auckland. The Keesing family were among the founders of the Auckland synagogue where for many years Harry was Honorary Choirmaster. In her widowhood, my grandmother in Sydney was far less strict. I have no idea when Father decided to dispense with many of the Jewish dietary laws which he believed were outmoded in modern times and had been established originally for hygienic reasons. Once I attempted to discuss the dietary laws with him from the point of view of *The Golden Bough* and *Totem and Taboo*—taboo indeed! Pish, tosh and rubbish! My father did not eat butter on meat sandwiches because having grown up under a different regime he disliked the taste, but otherwise would cheerfully mix milk and meat foods, enjoy shellfish and eat bacon for breakfast nearly every morning of his life. He believed that bacon having been cured was wholesome; pork, however, in any shape or form, was unwholesome and strictly avoided.

Dad's story of how he first made the break from his home precepts about food was that in his youth he had a terribly sore throat. Someone recommended warm bacon fat sipped from a spoon as a sovereign remedy. He tried it. It worked. That was enough for him—he was a great man for remedies. Carron oil for sunburn, iodine tincture for cuts and scratches—any worthwhile remedy favoured by Father was bound to smart, sting or taste terrible. That showed it was 'doing good'. For some ten years in his later middle age he swore by alfalfa tea as a cure for, and preventative of, practically everything, and so drank a cup of the horrid infusion before retiring each night. To supply his fad we grew a patch of lucerne whose stems and leaves were cut and hung to dry.

Nearly as bad as lying was any display of 'temperament'. Artistic or any other form of temperament was no excuse for certain forms of behaviour or misbehaviour. You were either completely truthful and celibate if unmarried, faithful to one sexual partner if wed, or you were not—and consequently disgraceful.

Only once during my girlhood did Dad have a good friend of his own age. This was a senior journalist with impeccable Returned Soldier credentials—he had served with the AIF in France during World War I. He was blessedly not a bridge player. His conversation widened Dad's horizons no end. I do not imagine that he said or told much that Dad might not have heard from countless men, but he must have conveyed information and ideas in a way that Dad found compelling and believable. Frequently at the breakfast table we were served a re-hash of his friend's leading article for that day, and sometimes were given its background as recounted by the man over lunch a day or so before. Then this journalist divorced his wife of many years and married another. Dad accepted this situation with some difficulty. He then divorced the second wife and relations between the two men became strained. When the man then re-married his first wife it was too much for my father's notions of propriety. The friendship was not only terminated, but the offender was wiped from the slate of my father's acquaintance. He may have been honest but in Dad's view he was not 'upright'.

I would not know so much of this episode had it not occurred during my first great eavesdropping period: 'Well if he spends so much time with new wives you wouldn't expect him to be upright,' my mother ventured. 'I suppose you imagine that is funny,' roared my father, 'you have absolutely no sense of humour.' He was always accusing my mother of having no sense of humour—but she did, and it was delicious.

Some twenty years after this I met the journalist who asked very warmly about my father and gave me a friendly greeting to convey to him. Dad snorted, dismissed the man out of hand as a complete 'bounder', and expressed the hope that I would have enough sense to curtail my acquaintance with him. That was not difficult because, with a third wife, (the others then being dead) he was leaving Australia to spend his retirement running a small business in England.

The only man I know of who, despite a somewhat chequered marital career, never lost my father's deepest affection and respect was General Monash. Dad solved the problem of Monash's personal life simply by refusing to believe that his idol had even a speck of loam—let alone great dollops of clay—on his feet. The gossip that Dad could not escape hearing was, he averred, put about by envious and malicious people.

When I was a child I thought my father was the most wonderful man in the world. He was handsome and imaginative. For his own daughters and also nieces and nephews, many other children and, later, grandchildren, he devised splendid adventures and expeditions, always by public transport, rowing boat, walking or horseback—he knew nothing of engines. My mother did not ride or row but otherwise gallantly joined in our harbour fishing expeditions; and on little beaches that in those days were virtually deserted, she would help grill our morning catch for lunch. Her tiny feet were not fashioned for very long rough walks but she would accompany us for a while, then find a tolerably shady place on a beach or in the bush while her husband and daughters tramped for miles making discoveries of shells or flowers or seeds to bring back to her.

Both my parents read widely. They borrowed books from Angus & Robertson's lending library each week. Dad had a surprising taste for novels by writers like Faulkner and Hemingway; mother preferred English authors and often, too, re-read books she had bought in her youth, many of which Dad dismissed as 'precious'. The nearest thing to 'modern' poetry on her shelves was Leon Gellert's *Songs of a Campaign* which I found compelling at a very early age, and once knew by heart. I loved the poems of Æ and Francis Thompson and some of her other favourites. Several times a year they took us to the Art Gallery where Dad would expound to us on the glories of Australian painting in his embarrassingly booming voice. Whenever I could sneak away from the Streetons and Gruners, the Syd Longs and the Lamberts I would shiver in front of the painting of the Sons of Clovis. Why Clovis amputated his sons' feet and set the two of them adrift on a barge on the Seine to die I did not know; and that was one question not to ask my father: he never read books of any kind about World War I and would not look at pictures of dead or dying people or go to War films. He only spoke about the War in France if he could not possibly avoid doing so.

As I grew up I became less tolerant of my father's more infuriating prejudices and eccentricities, but he could always surprise me back to adoration because of his kindnesses to other people and his absolute integrity. On the other hand my mother and I became great friends—we had many interests in common, and a shared sense of humour. In 1982 I wrote a three-part poem about her, which was published in 1986 in Susan Hampton and Kate Llewellyn's *Penguin Book of Australian Women Poets*. Part I runs as follows:

> My sharp-brained, tart-tongued mother is old and potty
> At ninety-one. Her hair flies like white cloud,
> (She always wore an 'invisible net'), all spotty
> With milky coffee the front of her clothes no matter
> How kind and careful the nurses. Her fingers fumble,
> Her mouth mumbles and drops burst out in a spatter.
>
> The nurses love her because she does not cry out
> But sings them French songs I'd never heard her sing
> While the other old mad creatures rant, weep, shout.
>
> Nothing perturbs her. Not news of death nor sorrow
> Within her family. She thinks we've come from New Zealand
> By the old *Wanganui* and will sail back there tomorrow.
>
> She who bought Streetons, two Turners and a Rembrandt etching
> Does 'Painting' at Occupational Therapy.
> Colouring-in it is; she adores it. Watching

Her thin hands holding the brush I think I will die
On the spot. Such pity I have for her. She's lived
Past what she would ever have wished. How can one cry
For an ancient baby who sings French songs for the nurses?
'She's always so full of fun,' they say. I could kill them.
They're turning my mother into a three ring circus.

My mother was a delicate, thin child and young woman. 'Canary legs'
was her family nickname. She was also the blue stocking and plain Jane of
the handsome family whose 'afterthought' she was—being ten years
younger than the elegant middle sister, and thirteen years junior to the
eldest one who was a great beauty. My mother was the daughter with the
wicked sense of humour, the one her elderly father 'spoiled', her sisters
said. I cannot even guess where that sense of humour, or her subtlety,
came from; both qualities were wasted on my father who relished a joke
only if it was plainly labelled with a capital J and not 'smutty'.

In about 1911 Mother returned with her parents from the last of their
hitherto frequent trips 'abroad' (meaning Europe) or 'home' (meaning
England). Her sisters, who were married women by then, waited on the
wharf at Dawes Point to greet the travellers. The gangway for first-class
passengers cranked down and one of the first to descend it was 'little
Margery', her hair 'up' for the first time in her sisters' vision of her,
fashionably more resembling an inverted plate than anyone yet wore in
Sydney, tripping precariously on outrageous Louis heels. Her *outré* hobble
skirt stopped scandalously above her ankles, and she flaunted a black
Sobrani cigarette in an emerald shagreen holder. Outrage focused on the
Russian cigarette.

'For goodness sake, Marge, put that out!' hissed the sisters. 'What will
Father say if he sees you?!!!'

But Marge flicked the holder towards them and smirked:

'Father gave it to me.'

The balance of power in the Hart family was never the same again. In
Alnwick House, their beautiful home at Darling Point, 'little Marge' had
her own upstairs drawing room in whose luxurious privacy she 'worked'
and entertained her friends. She decorated the walls with Raphael prints
in gilt frames, covered the chairs in dark rich velvet, kept a Florentine
papier maché writing set as brilliant as a bird of paradise on her mahogany
desk. Her books filled a large bookcase. She wrote an article for the
Bulletin about Gilbert Murray's translations from the Greek, read and re-
read Ruskin and bought all the 'new' novelists—Arnold Bennett, Sinclair
Lewis, J. B. Priestley, Thomas Burke, Lord Dunsany, Rose Macaulay and
the poets her family alleged to be incomprehensible: Æ, W. B. Yeats,
J. B. Thompson...

That return of the prosperous Hart family in 1911 was about a year later than the departure of the impecunious architectural student, Gordon Keesing, who travelled steerage to New York with £40 to face the world because he did not wish to be beholden to his family. Part II of my 1982 poem about Mum is to be found in the last chapter of this book. Part III, however, is as follows:

> My grandfather's old-age child and youngest daughter
> Was frail and skinny and 'spoiled' her sisters said.
> And now she's ninety-one and they are dead.
>
> Before she was out of the schoolroom her sisters were married—
> The great beauty, barren; the elegant mother of three.
> My mother put up her hair and travelled. She tarried
> Bemused by Ruskin in Florence. In gay *Paris*
> My grandmother decked her ugly duckling like a swan,
> My mother went overboard for Gilbert Murray
> And made herself classical swathes of white chiffon.
> And her old-age father said 'Charming' and didn't worry.
>
> She smoked cigarettes in an outré shagreen holder.
> Her sisters cried, 'Heavens! What will Father say?'
> 'It is his gift,' smirked my blue-stocking mother, grown older
> Than her envious older sisters. 'Well, put it away,'
> They snapped. 'You're back in Australia now, for good
> And your flaunting fads will not be understood.'
>
> Misunderstood she languished for London and Venice.
> The *Bulletin* published her essay on the Murray translations.
> My grandmother took her calling. Her nemesis
> Was delicate teas and drawing-room conversations.
>
> Grandfather grew doddery old. She, dreadfully bored.
> Her sisters said: 'We told you you'd be sorry,
> The way you dress and talk, men are over-awed.
> Come down a peg and we'll find you a catch to marry.'
>
> My mother laughed, blew smoke in their eyes and, teasing,
> Snared the catch of the year, a hero from the war,
> The artistic, eccentric puritan, Gordon Keesing,
> And found she had got herself more than she bargained for
> Or ever quite came to terms with: my complex father
> Not to be wheedled or twisted to anyone's whim.
> They dearly loved, but did not understand each other.
> In her second childhood she never speaks of him.

In Melbourne my mother's youngest aunt, Alice Michaelis, lived with her brother Ernest in the house their father, Moritz Michaelis, had built at St Kilda. 'Linden', one of the most beautiful houses in Australia, was at the centre of a large garden that produced fruit and vegetables as well as flowers and green lawns and is now a National Trust building. Grandmother Hart and her daughter visited it every year whether or not Alice—or Dal as she was called—was home (often she was travelling to outlandish places like Outer Mongolia). Ernest, who was 'delicate', was always in residence—except for the times he visited my grandmother in Sydney. In Melbourne my mother renewed her friendship with her first cousin, Frank Michaelis. She had become friendly with him during one of her stays in England while he was a schoolboy at Harrow and with him she had experienced the delights of drifting in a cushioned punt screened by romantic willows, although probably the delights were sampled no more than once or twice. She was in love with Frank but I doubt he realised this. He married a slightly more distant cousin not long before he left Australia with the AIF for World War I and died from pneumonia.

My mother's feet were small as a child's, size two for shoes; her unreliable ankles were prone to twists and turns. But she agreed to visit Jenolan Caves with her cousin Dorothy Theomin from Dunedin who was ten years her senior. Dorothy, like my mother, considered herself a 'new woman' but of a different stamp; like Aunt Dal, Dorothy was an adventurous traveller, but unlike Dal who was small and daintily built Dorothy was tall and rangy and looked like an amiable horse. When she spoke she neighed, and when she laughed she whinnied.

Dorothy, as if equipped at any time to climb a mountain or cross a desert even in Sydney drawing rooms, wore practical coats and skirts, ghillie brogues and sensible velour hats.

During the expedition they stayed at Jenolan Caves House, then a quite new hotel from which tours started daily. And, as today, tours of the caves were of different lengths and duration. But then, unlike now, there were relatively few properly cut steps or handrails in the caves—and no electric light. Instead the guide shone a carbide lamp to indicate pathways and disclose beauties and strange formations.

They took a couple of the shorter, easy tours. But Dorothy was keen to go on the longest and most arduous walk to visit the largest and most beautiful, but also most remote, caverns. Mother said, very well—she'd go too. Dorothy tried to put her off. Mother supposed that Dorothy's objections were based on her usual offensively patronising attitude—but to be fair to Dorothy, who was really a very kind woman, she may truly have been concerned and have understood better than my mother what was involved. Dorothy argued and even finally offered to relinquish her own adventure—but this made Mother more obstinate.

In the event Mother was terrified but with profound determination she followed her cousin. She kept her eyes as best she could in the gloom fixed on Dorothy's large sure feet and she put down her own small shoes in those confident steps. She saw practically nothing of the caves and heard barely a word of the guide's explanation. The long journey in darkness seemed almost without end but at last the party emerged to daylight.

'Bravo! Well done Marge!' neighed Dorothy. 'I never thought you'd get across that plank over the underground river without help!'

'What plank? What river?' gasped my triumphant, exhausted mother.

Two lots of our cousins were really rich and had nannies. They governed large nurseries—children's separate quarters really. Their uniforms were not much altered from the illustrations to Christopher Robin, but in Australia they wore white dresses and navy blue felt hats for their afternoon perambulations with their charges—else surely they'd have been jeered off park benches by the general populace.

We were not really rich; we had no huge nursery; we had 'nurses' who in domestic protocol were a cut above the maid but, unlike nannies, quite definitely beneath the family mother. During the year we had lived in New Zealand my mother managed with Jean Jenkins who was a 'general', which meant a woman who was a maid of all work but capable of banging together a reasonable breakfast and who, with luck, could produce acceptable cakes and dishes for the other meals too. The women of my family at least all cooked well and were often in the kitchen themselves.

A general who could don a parlormaid's cap and apron in the afternoon, and answer the door with aplomb to visitors (usually Mum's friends arriving for a game of bridge or mahjonng); who could clean house efficiently and who also liked cooking and did it well, was a 'treasure'. (Heavy cleaning and laundry was done by women who worked by the day.)

From the point of view of 'littlies' a genuine treasure was one who did not chase you out of her kitchen, allowed you to cut out little pies and popovers from pastry scraps, and baked them for you to eat, and who would sometimes invite you into her own room to show you family snapshots and other treasures, or dab your wrists with a bit of her scent: a kindness not appreciated by Mum, who hated the smell of it. Jean Jenkins was a married woman with school-aged children of her own who, I imagine, slaved and saved for some special project, because no one could doubt the closeness and affection of her own family.

Before Jean, when I was two or so, there had been Ida, dimly remembered as a loving and loved presence. After Jean came nurses who slept in the Nursery so called, the room behind the balcony where we had our beds in the lovely fresh air of all weathers, though in true gales a cumbersome roller shutter could be pulled down. First was elderly 'Goldie' or 'Nursie'. Miss Golding was an elderly Englishwoman who was saving to return to her family 'at home'. When she did so she wrote to us on charming postcards to which we replied for years until, no doubt, she died. Clump, thump, and the last of her tribe in our family was a rough young woman who told Margaret and me to call her 'Chucks' which is the only name I remember her by.

Chucks probably only lasted a short time. She was a sadist. In 1977 I described in my collection of poems *Hails and Farewells* one of the awful things she did to us, and the last, for its evidence could not be hidden:

Marathon Steps, Darling Point

1929

> A sadist nursemaid broke my sister's doll
> on an upright post of this metal-piping handrail.
> A stucco house called 'Condover' by its gate
> watched all with shining eyes and made no protest.
>
> Sister and I, hot, tired, whining, breathless,
> *we* protested, though scared witless; and the girl
> rough, shabby, hating us, hurled the china baby
> harder and harder—its pink head shattered to powder.

Either we kept quiet about Chucks' other misdemeanours or our parents failed to believe what we were trying to tell them.

1970

> The eyes of the house called 'Condover', vacant, filmed
> with cataracts of dust, stare blind this morning
> and wait its demolisher. Unit buildings glitter
> strong eyes across Double Bay. The steps climb changeless,
>
> steep, twisted; weed, moss, stone. Each hollowed surface
> speaks to my feet, my soles—my soul remembers
> the bulging toy-box in our unsafe nursery,
> clutter of snakes and ladders and broken joys.
>
> The stone treads know, I know, blind 'Condover' knows
> the pink doll wasn't broken—it was murdered.
> Four decades on, steps stained by powdered china,
> accuse the sky with two fringed, blue glass eyes...
>
> and what I am, and do, began at Marathon

When I was five I was taken each day to a famous girls' school only a stone's throw from our house. The kindergarten there, unusually for those days, and daring too, was co-ed. Too daring. A little boy exposed his little self to me; I unwisely mentioned this interesting event at home along with my accustomed recital of the day's doings, and my parents removed me from that convenient establishment and found another. But not before I'd acquired a taste for Kipling who wrote about elephants.

20

The kindergarten teacher, with explanations and necessary paraphrase, was some half way through the Mowgli stories when I was whisked from corruption leaving even the current tale unfinished. Never mind, I'd noticed a long row of slim Kipling books in red leather bindings on the home shelves—they were slim because printed on rice paper—so I decided to find and read that story for myself.

Granny Hart had taught me to read the previous year, but Kipling proved more difficult than *Three Little Kittens*. Never mind. I was confident of finding Mowgli in whatever book he inhabited and so, logically, began with the volumes on the left and slowly ploughed through successive books towards the right until at last, one day and many months later, my quest was successful. Goodness knows what I made of *Plain Tales from the Hills* at the age of five, but I did perfect my reading. I had not asked Mum to help me because I'd got it into my head that everything to do with that first kindergarten was tinged with disgrace, shame and mystery. Questions about Kipling might no more be answered than enquiries about a juvenile flasher. How awful if, like me from a beloved teacher, Kipling were to be removed from the bookcase. Silence was wiser.

My second school was SCEGGS at Darlinghurst. My father took me there by tram and on foot each morning on his way into town. My mother, with baby Margaret in tow, called for me every afternoon. My first year there was unhappy and gave a warped shape to much of my childhood.

In some ways Mum, so sharp and witty, and also so obsessed with theories about raising babies according to Truby King, and older children according to every up-to-date theory, was a perfect fool. Probably some of her blind spots were due to her own education with a governess. She had no personal experience of a large school. I was a shy and awkward child for as long as I remember and everything that happened to me seemed to compound my problems. My first school venture had ended abruptly through no fault of mine, yet the way the episode was handled left me with feelings of guilt and failure. I'd absorbed through the pores of my skin the Australian eleventh commandment which ordains: 'Thou shalt not dob anyone in.' I kept harmless secrets for a maid who pleaded, 'Don't tell your mother', her secret being usually some trifling matter like an overlong back-door conversation with the grocer's delivery man, or a chipped cup. Unintentionally I'd dobbed in a five-year-old flasher. And was I not fascinated by what he had to show? Yes, and for reasons I did not comprehend it proved how sunk in wickedness I must be.

Mother sent me off to the new school before my tiny uniform was ready and I, arriving in a cotton print in mid-term, long after everyone else had settled in, was a figure of curiosity and, I felt, of scorn. Even the cotton print was disaster, at school. Mum couldn't sew but she had a few good ideas and had invented for her daughters what would later be called a playsuit about ten years before those garments were commonplace. It was an eminently sensible one-piece garment combining shirt and flared shorts, and buttoning from neck to waist. My aunt's maid Clennel who was an enthusiastic dressmaker had given shape to Mum's design and the result, both practical and pretty, was a great success. Understandably my unusual dress aroused comment and, from teachers and other kids' mothers, considerable admiration, but it was my badge of shame, of difference; also, though I could easily manage the large buttons by myself, it slowed me down in the lavatory and that caused jesting comment I could have done without.

My much less comfortable uniform must have arrived after only a few days, but by then the damage was done. I loved my teachers, hated and feared most of the other girls and, at home was increasingly sly and secretive—because by then I had no idea what I might, or might not, safely confide.

III

The Laughing Cavalier

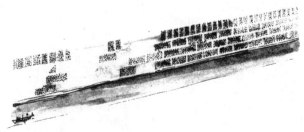

I DIDN'T care for Miss Fuller and am sure she found me a pain in the neck, but she was a marvellous teacher and to her I owe much of the basic education that has sustained me lifelong. Miss Fuller was stocky and ungainly with leathery greyish skin of the same colour as her short springy hair. I thought of her as old but she was no more than middle aged. She wore drab jumpers and skirts and clumped about in golf brogues. My sister, when very small, itemised animals she'd seen at the zoo and coined a beast called 'hippamopotamus' which I used as my private nickname for Miss Fuller. Her little piggy eyes were hooded by wrinkled flaps; they didn't miss much so it was silly of me, aged nine, to open a storybook beneath the desk during a history lesson, and positively tempting providence to chew a toffee.

'Nancy Keesing. What *are* you doing?'

'Nothing Miss Fuller.'

'Well, nothing to do with Catherine of Aragon I agree, but what are you hiding in your lap?'

'Oh, just a book, Miss Fuller.'

'Your history book?'

Gosh, I hope she doesn't ask to see that, for I've embellished the portrait of Catherine therein giving her a slick black curl over each coifed cheek.

'Well. . .' I say.

'And what are you swallowing?'

'Gulp. . .'

Miss Fuller ruminates. She has an excellent sense of timing, and even perhaps a mite of sympathy because interminably poor Betty (probably retarded as I now realise) has been unable to understand the lesson. At last, and not severely, Miss Fuller gives me a chance—which being me, I miff. She says:

'Put your storybook away. Sit up straight and pay attention. And remember, no one can do two things at once.'

'Oh, *I* can Miss Fuller.' Brightly.

'Aren't you clever!' I should have been warned.

'Perhaps you will explain what you mean to me and the class.'

'If I have to stir gravy I whistle and read a book too.'

'You are thoroughly impertinent. Half an hour's detention!'

Detentions after school for me were doubly awful, triply awful because, oh the shame of it, unlike *everyone* else, I was not allowed to go home on my own, walking with friends. I had to meet Miss Slarmie after school, who was employed to see my *younger* sister safely home. If my misdemeanours delayed them Margaret would get fretful and Miss Slarmie very cross, so that later she would tattletale to my mother, who would tell my father, who then wished to know all the sins of commission and omission that had led to my detention, and who then *reasoned* with me. I'd have much preferred a sharp smack.

The gilt-framed picture over the fireplace of the junior detention room was a large black and white print of Frans Hals' *The Laughing Cavalier*. According to *The Children's Encyclopaedia*, the cavalier's twinkling eyes look out so directly his gaze follows one everywhere.

I had many opportunities for testing this amazing fact for, from the age of about eight onwards, I was frequently in the detention room. The reasons for my atrocious behaviour were legion. In some lessons I was bored because I finished my work long before Betty and others and fidgeted while they tried to understand. I was hopeless at sport and consequently denied the fame that from early ages was conferred on the playing field. Forbidden to walk with my friends through the back streets of Darlinghurst to the tram I felt miserably out of much of the real fun of the day. I was Jewish and had to learn three verses of a Psalm each week for scripture instead of a jolly hymn, and no matter how word perfect I was would never be chosen to help the school chaplain don his stole and surplice for chapel services. I hated being different, though in private I thought the Psalms of David were not boring but beautiful—they were challenging and infinitely preferable to most of the hymns in *Hymns Ancient and Modern*.

Also, although no one noticed this until I was about twelve, I was seriously astigmatic and short of sight, so I missed important things like catching and hitting balls or really seeing what the flasher, who often lurked near the lower gate, actually did that so fascinated some of the girls. I missed nuances of expression on many faces, and many instructions on a blackboard.

I was good at most lessons but that was another occasion for shame. The only acceptable thing at which I shone was inventing wickedness, and wicked nicknames for teachers, and advanced forms of cheek. I tried very hard to improve my record. My classmates began to respect my excellence in these pursuits; they dared me to do this and that, and increasingly egged me on.

Old Mrs Mifflin who teaches Latin, whatever arcane subject for the future that may be, limps a little and waddles as she walks. She waddles across the school's immense main hall towards the staff room, unaware of being followed by mimic-waddling me and my pet cronies of the moment who follow discreetly, giggling.

Madame Paisley exits from the staff room:

'Nancy Keesing, what *are* you doing?'

'Nothing, Madame.'

'I see. I think you werrre being unkind.' My audience has sloped away.

'And now you are untrrruthful. Half an hour's detention.'

This was a disaster, for I truly adored Madame and if there were one person at that school whom I would wish to please, it was her.

And she was right, for I was often unkind.

I ceased my prankishness eventually a year or so later when I realised precisely how beastly I was. Miss Fanny Fenton occasioned my change of heart. She was probably less than ten years older than the girls of ten or so whom she had to teach. She was fat, so with accustomed subtlety I dubbed her Fat Fanny. She was shy. She blushed easily, not just over her face, but with a wave of red that spread from face to neck to upper arms. Those arms! They had double-jointed elbows so that when—as was a habit of hers—she discoursed she placed her hands palms down; and, facing outwards on the table, her elbows angled outwards too. Her Arts degree was no doubt impeccable but she had no skill for teaching, and no experience. Nevertheless she had wide blue eyes and pretty fair hair and might have been acceptable to a class of girls most of whose teachers were middle aged and dowdy, except that she dressed very badly in homemade clothes that accentuated all her unfortunate features and her floppy bosom.

I did not know at that age that Miss Fenton was a victim of the Depression. Her father was an impoverished clergyman in a poor parish and SCEGGS was employing her more from compassion than a need for another English teacher. She had one defect that doomed her beyond everything. She lisped.

She lisped the form of my name I most dislike, 'Nance', and called me 'Nanth'. Naturally I kept some of my friends in fits of giggles as I mimicked Fat Fanny, Fatty Fenn, ringing various changes until someone dared me to state my objections to her face. Next time she called me 'Nanth' in front of the class I shot my hand up smartly. Anticipatory giggles became audible from around the room.

'Yeth Nanth?' responded Miss Fenton with her rather sweet ingenuous smile.

I stood. I said: 'Mith Fenton. My name'th not Nanth.'

She blushed to those elbows. 'Then what ith your name?'

'Nan–cy,' I said. 'Two syllables.'

Right there she burst into tears. She rushed out of the room.

I did not know what to do. No one could think what to do. The class captain looked as if she *should* know, but did not. We sat in dismayed silence, and no one, after the first moment, could bear to look at anyone else.

Miss Fenton returned quite soon and said, 'I hate teaching. I hate thith job.' She collected her books and papers and went through the door again. Until the school bell signalled the end of that lesson we sat like stunned mutes. She did not dob me in. She turned up for her next appointed lesson with us as if nothing had happened except that she called me 'Nancy' with emphasis whenever she was forced to address me by name, which was as seldom as possible.

I longed to hear 'Nanth' again. But no one gets a second chance at innocence.

Madame Paisley, who had failed when I was a bit younger to save me from myself, taught French. Very sensibly she taught girls when they were seven or eight and just beginning, and not again until they were senior students studying for the Leaving. By then I was at another school and so, to my sorrow, missed her advanced lessons and could not profit from her love and knowledge of the French classics. Her lessons for little girls were marvellous because as soon as she thought we were restless, or when she suffered too much from the pain of listening to us mangling her language, she allowed herself to be deflected into wonderful discussions about anything at all. On the last day of term, traditionally, she would tell us one of her famous ghost stories.

Madame held herself so rigidly straight that she looked very tall, though her height was average. She wore the clothes of a bygone era—always black and (I later realised) the corsets of a bygone era too. I have no idea whether some of her shiny black dresses and high collared cardigans were new or whether, having entered middle age slim, and keeping her figure, an old wardrobe served her eternally. She wore high buttoned black boots. Her hair, more jet black still than grey, was frizzed into a style to suit the clothes—just like Queen Mary's hair, as our mothers often remarked.

Madame was 'a Countess in her own right', we knew. And we knew that this had something to do with the French Revolution or perhaps Bismarck. One of her godmothers was Queen Victoria and, as a baby, she was 'dandled on the old Queen's knee'. Her only fortune after the Great War was jewellery, all of which she wore every day of her life in loops and chokers around her high collars and in rings that crusted every joint of all her narrow fingers on each hand but not her thumbs. Any other woman who wore a fraction of Madame's jewellery at one time would have been labelled impossibly common and ostentatious by my mother. Whenever I encounter the phrase *grande dame* I think of Madame Paisley.

Her wonderful stories often concerned her youthful adventures with Mr Paisley. We simply could not believe in him. Mr Paisley was an explorer of the Amazon, which is the largest rrriver in the worrrld.

'So there we werrre, hiding below decks, for the Indios lined either bank. Where we werrre the side crrreek was quite narrow and we did not dare show our heads. We had barely enough water to drrrink and believe me, children, the teacupful of water, one teacup only, that was allowed for washing each day, was prrrecious.'

'Excuse me, Madame.'

'Yes, yes.'

'You had a bath in a teacup!'

'I did. It was prrrecious.'

None of us could envisage a young Madame. So our twelve brains wrestled with some sort of Alice in Wonderland magic by which a dignified, stately Madame...or else a fragile Sèvres china cup...

Another of her reminiscences also had to do with a bath. She admired Sir something MacRobertson even more than we admired his famous gold-paper wrapped chocolate; and she had known him, too, in some other age or life. 'He rrrose from the rrranks by his own effort and genius. He was so poorrr he made his first chocolate in his bath!' I cannot answer for eleven other brains in this instance, but mine invented a pudgy old pink-skinned man wearing a kilt, and only a kilt, as he sat in his bath full of melted chocolate...

What *do* Scotsmen wear under their kilts? One of my mother's risqué jokes which I was not supposed to have overheard, and certainly failed to understand, ended with the triumphant phrase: 'Only a tilt i' the kilt, lass.' I took a fit of helpless giggles which I would not, and frankly could not, explain to Madame.

'Half an hour's detention.'

Looking back it seems so sudden, like a southerly buster, or a thunderstorm that alters the aspect of the world. One moment we were a group of reasonably sane young girls, except for a steamy cloud called Sandra 'n' Patricia that hovered near us, and the next moment we were all mad. One moment we worked at knots or camp cookery for Girl Guides' badges; or learned to follow knitting patterns and make complicated jumpers in complicated stitches or helped to scrape and paint the family boat; or dived from higher and higher boards. At the next instant we were seized with fervour for religion, art, ballet, poetry, boys, life.

I hadn't much noticed Jeanette McIntosh until then; suddenly I envied her. Her father was a suburban general practitioner and a widower. He could seldom attend school sports-days and events; not much to envy there. A paid housekeeper ran their home—Jeanette said she was all right. Now we noticed that Jeanette was allowed to buy and eat what she fancied from the school tuckshop every day. And even better...she was allowed to choose and buy her own clothes.

Our mothers clucked about Jeanette. Had she no aunts? No female relatives? Poor child. Down the long slope of time, and envious no longer, I wonder what she *did* look like. I remember her at a GPS sportsday. She tottered on immensely high-heeled court shoes and wore a slinky clinging dress whose gored skirt swirled about her stout, silk-stockinged legs. Her slabby Scots face was heavily powdered and she wore a lot of cyclamen lipstick. A group of boys clustered around her exotic presence. She giggled continually and the boys said things to her and brayed like hounds or snorted like stallions. I envied that.

Then, oh lucky Jeanette, she came to school with her left arm in a sling, her hand heavily bandaged. No ordinary broken arm. One evening each week Dr McIntosh had a bridge game at his house—always the same cronies, a doctor friend, a solicitor neighbour, a real estate agent. While they played they sipped 'Scotch'—how glamorous. Jeanette stayed up 'till all hours' to serve their supper when they were ready for it. She did her homework at the kitchen table. The wireless was in the living room and, as she couldn't listen to that on bridge nights, her father gave her a gramophone. Lucky Jeanette. She also answered the telephone.

The bridge game was sacrosanct. She was supposed to judge whether calls were real emergencies or not, and real emergencies were very rare. Most patients had to leave messages or ring again in the morning. So Jeanette must decide when a birth or a death was imminent or hours away. The things she *knew*. Most of us had only the haziest notion of what a midwife might do, but Jeanette often had to phone the one her father employed.

One evening she was cutting crusts off a stack of supper sandwiches; the knife slipped and deeply severed an artery between her thumb and first finger. She tried every remedy she knew. She held her dripping hand under the cold water tap. But blood still spurted—so she wrapped her hand in a tea towel and went into the living room.

'Oh Dad, I've cut my hand badly.'

'Then put it under the tap. Three no trumps.'

'I have. It won't stop bleeding.'

'Sorry partner. I missed hearing your bid. Don't be tiresome Jeanette. I'll look at it after this rubber.'

Despairingly she raised her bloody towel and fainted at her father's side. Crisis. Remorse. Sutures. Oh lucky Jeanette.

Then even Jeanette, and perhaps especially Jeanette, together with about half of the rest of my class, 'got religion'. Religion at our strict Church of England school had always been very much a part of life. Chapel every day first thing in the morning, and a full-fledged service, with sermon, taken by the school chaplain once a week. (He was Canon Langley from St John's Darlinghurst, a jolly cleric who adored Psalms and read them with intonations of joy: 'The valleys grow so green with corn they laugh and sing, they laugh and sing!') When we were smaller a dessicated, prudish woman of great piety, and by my reckoning no real religion at all, had taken Divinity, but that was behind us and now she was no more than an irritating part of the teaching background, forever pulling us up for crooked seams in our stockings, or too much wrist poking out from our long-sleeved cotton blouses. Now Divinity lessons once a week were taken by Miss Dorothy Wilkinson the headmistress, who was a fine teacher—I enjoyed those as much as chapel.

Girls who got religion joined a group called 'The Crusaders', and there no Jewish friend could follow them. They dashed up to the chapel to pray at all kinds of hours. They studied their bibles. They signed the pledge. They got faraway looks in their eyes and envied Catholic friends who might decide on the veil. They went off to a camp, lucky things, because so did a large group of Crusader boys who slept in a hut downhill from the girls but joined them for meals and stirring hymns and soul searching round the camp fire.

At our Girl Guide encampment of five bell tents pitched on a remote private property, the only male *I* ever saw was an old man called Ted who came over from the dairy shed each morning, hoisting a dixie of milk in one hand and a can of cream in the other.

'Oh Mrs Parsons,' we warbled. Mrs Parsons was our Guider.

> Oh Mrs Parsons you are a wonder.
> And when we are old and grey,
> We will sing: 'By gosh, by thunder,
> You were some girl in your day.'

But even Guides, many of them, had brothers, knew boys. *Talked* about boys even, as we constructed intricate fires that would catch alight from no more than two matches, and *no* paper permitted.

It was a cruel world for a brotherless girl whose male cousins were ten years older and practically grown up; whose immediate boy neighbours were ten at the oldest; whose parents didn't know *any*body. The shame of going to the Double Bay flicks with father and kid sister. Jeanette, wearing a pill-box hat with veil, would be in the back row chewing gum and holding hands, with boys.

Smart young men, like the sons of one nearby family who were in their magical twenties, now wore pork pie hats, usually with a natty little feather in the band. 'Never seen anything so ridiculous,' opined my father who tramped each morning to the tram snorting to his crony, a judge who wore a monocle. *Their* headgear was unchanging. But now the wilder lads of Sydney Grammar School were bashing and folding their high- and dented-crowned hats into approximate pork pie shape, and wearing the results at a jaunty angle. This innovation of theirs caused nearly as great a shock horror, as when their own sons and grandsons grew, some forty years on, their hair to shoulder length.

Not to be out of a hat battle, and, naturally, to attract girls, meeker boys pork-pied their hats too. Eventually Sydney Grammar School bowed to the inevitable and had its uniform hats blocked à la pork pie. We still wore thick ribbed stockings and long sleeved blouses with starched collars to hold our ties rigid, in the hottest weather. Those of us who took proper pride in our appearance also wore serge gym tunics all year long—cotton ones crushed too easily.

Sydney Grammar boys were dreadfully 'fast' it was said. King's boys were stodgy, stuck-up imbeciles; Shore boys were perfect—was not Shore our 'brother' school? How should I know? If even a despised Cranbrook lad—Cranbrook was not a GPS school—had looked my way I'd have been pleased enough. None did.

At about this time when we were thirteen or fourteen and in our last carefree year before the dreaded Intermediate exam, Sandra 'n' Patricia, inseparable cronies, turned fourteen (the school-leaving age then) within a few days of each other—and left school. Many girls would leave as soon as the Inter was over, but to finish school before that was almost unheard of.

Rumour flew. They'd been 'asked to leave', but not expelled. Rich Sandra was going to a Swiss finishing school. But Patricia could not do that, and we decided to feel sorry for Patricia who was Sandra's besotted follower. What would happen to *her*?

(Patricia went to a Business College and became quite a nice young woman despite her continuing 'fast' life, which we followed disapprovingly—and enviously—in the social pages of newspapers and magazines. Sandra's mother took her daughter 'home' to England where she was, we heard, supposed to 'come out' but instead disgraced herself in some way, and never did. Sandra then returned to Australia and seemed, according to those same infallible social pages, to spend most of her time at High Society events in the remoter countryside. She was back in Sydney for most of the War, however, and became the Senior Society Slut of Sin City.)

Until Sandra 'n' Patricia vanished we had not quite realised what a strange, steamy cloud, lay over us. It had lurked and hovered for three or four years. Now the air was extraordinarily clear.

When those two had come to the school we had been more or less innocent little girls of ten or eleven or so. On cool days we'd still occasionally play chasings or ball games in the garden at lunch time. We quailed before Sandra's supercilious look. We knew she'd been expelled from two schools before SCEGGS took her on. What had she done? She sat with us to eat her sandwiches and said very little. She was everlastingly combing her longish blonde curls. She smiled a crooked smile towards Patricia who until then had been best friends with Maxine Johnston. All at once we sounded awfully silly to ourselves.

Maxine Johnston walked out of chapel and suddenly noticed that two buttons of her flannel blazer were missing; squares of material where they had been sewn were cut out, with a sharp razor blade it would seem. Maxine's mother raised Cain but no culprit was ever actually identified and punished, though Sandra was her neighbour at prayers that day. Sandra was also sitting next to Pip Smith when, one day in the middle of Canon Langley's weekly sermon, Pip suddenly screamed. What a flurry. She screamed, stood up, brushed past her neighbours and rushed towards the row where, against the back wall, the teachers sat. Miss Wise and Miss Price grabbed Pip and escorted her outside. Matron said the red mark on Pip's thigh must be the bite of an insect of some sort and treated it accordingly. We, who were later invited to inspect the lesion, were sure, as Pip was sure, that it was caused by a long needle or pin being pushed into her leg. Pip's parents spent a long time interviewing the headmistress. Did they, too, believe some extraordinary insect had bitten their daughter? All they would say to Pip later was that they were sure no such thing would happen again.

Sandra, with Patricia, sat at lunch time, or in chapel, or at school concerts, inside an invisible, steamy cloud of avoidance. Their life away from school was barely imaginable. They went to country races and polo-club meetings, and adult dances. They seemed immensely older than the rest of us, and infinitely separate. The cloud of steam shifted, changed shape as we too did, but it was ever present. Did some, or many, girls speak of it to their mothers—or was everyone as impermeably secretive as I was? Often I've wondered what was really happening at that very well run school. Did parents enquire? What were they told?

Only Madame seemed to speak to the two in a normal way, to send them off to tidy up a corner of the garden, or put away a tennis net, or do any of the ordinary things that anyone else might be told to do. *We* 'did not speak' to Sandra 'n' Patricia, but some of us must have. Else how were we so certain they 'did it' with boys? Did what? We were not so certain. How were we so sure Sandra had first 'done it' with her parents' gardener when she was nine or so?

It was, and still I think is, a matter of pride for 'good schools' that they can succeed where others have failed; keep on students whom others have expelled. But how could, or did, that school help Sandra 'n' Patricia? At what cost to the rest of us? It would be nice to think that clouds of steam no longer swirl about adolescent children.

I doubt it.

Most of our mothers were sufficiently enlightened and modern to tell us about menstruation in advance of its onset. We cut up frogs and dissected their ovaries. We discussed poetry and art, religion and history. We became young women in a fathomless fog. 'But what do you *do* if he kisses you *that* way?' What do you do to find one to kiss you at all?

At SCEGGS, by the time I began studying for the Intermediate, I had the good fortune to be taught by Vera Newsom, a fine poet herself though I did not know that then. Nor did I realise how young she was because to me all teachers seemed venerable, and many of ours were. She must have been less than ten years my senior, recently graduated, keen on introducing us to poets who were modern then—particularly the Georgians, many of whom were still at the peak of their careers—though she also fostered our appreciation of the great poets and writers of the past. In one aspect she followed the fashion of her day and held Australian bush balladry in scorn. She encouraged talented girls to write beyond set compositions, and to attempt verse.

All the efforts of Vera Newsom or her predecessors had been unable to make me comprehend the simplest rules of formal grammar. By luck I was an excellent speller. I wrote grammatically because people about me spoke grammatically and I had a good ear, 'However', said my headmistress, Miss Wilkinson, who had called me into her study, 'it is absolutely ridiculous, but if you fail the grammar question in your Intermediate exam, you will fail in English. *I* am going to teach you enough about the principal parts of speech to last you until after the English exam next week—you will think it very babyish but I'm afraid it's the only remedy.' So she drew a train engine which was noun, pulling a succession of carriages which were adjectives and adverbs and other arcane things, in due order. She clearly labelled them and commanded me to memorise the train, which I did. Thanks to Miss Wilkinson and her train I passed with an A in English.

The following year, 1939, I went to Frensham at Mittagong. I'd had ten years at SCEGGS and in every way was ready for change. Again I had an inspired and inspiring English teacher. Esther Tuckey was Australian—rare at Frensham in those days when most of the staff were English. Now for the first time I also had a splendid history teacher, Lena Curd, who was English. Miss Curd was a friend of Winifred Holtby. She read *South Riding* aloud with us on Sunday evenings. She and Esther Tuckey wrestled with T. S. Eliot poems as they were published and explained to a few interested girls their tentative interpretations; they traced most of the allusions in the *Wasteland*. Esther Tuckey presented English literature with a broad historical sweep as well as in the detail demanded by the curriculum—indeed from her I first learned to value learning for its own sake. She also read recent Australian poetry. I owe my introduction to the poetry of R. D. FitzGerald to Miss Tuckey.

There were two youthful teachers at Frensham who taught younger girls, but in that small school everybody knew everyone, particularly when their interests were similar. So I soon came to know Rosemary Dobson and Joan Phipson. Rosemary was a very recent 'old girl' whose mother, Marjorie, was on the staff. Fairly soon she left for Sydney and, in a year or so, was working in the editorial department of Angus & Robertson. Rosemary's poetry both delighted and inspired her contemporaries— hers was obviously talent of high order. She was a tallish, thin, quick-moving girl but, unlike many of us, she knew how to listen to others, how to be graceful in repose, and she was beautiful. (We became close friends for many years in Sydney. Joan I knew less well, until years later when she had become a distinguished writer of books for young people.)

Fostered by Esther Tuckey and other interested staff, Frensham had a flourishing 'Pen and Ink' club which met regularly, sometimes to discuss the original writing of its members, sometimes to talk about writing techniques or forms, sometimes to attempt (as a group) a set exercise of some sort. The school magazine, the *Chronicle*, did not publish 'original writing'; instead *Pen and Ink* appeared annually, its typewritten roneoed sheets stapled between covers designed by talented art students. The Art mistress, Ruth Ainsworth, was another creative teacher who enlarged our vision and technical skills.

I wrote my only play during my last year at school, but at least it was produced! It was a highly symbolic verse drama set inside a huge bell which, at the moment of dénouement cracked and broke. It could not have been staged more than once because the bell scenery was on sheets of newspaper glued together and painted grey. It took me, and a few obliging friends, hours and hours to construct; when the bell cracked—that is when the paper was ripped to pieces with great vigour by helpers standing behind it, that was the end of the bell, and the scenery. The only notable thing about the production was that Winifred West, the school's founding headmistress, spoke the main part in her marvellous voice.

Drama was very much a part of Frensham life and there was a beautiful open-air theatre, in bush near a creek. Miss West's sister, Frances Kennedy, produced memorable plays both classical and recent. The school had some outstanding acting talent, including Patricia Connolly, but excluding me, for I was abjectly self-conscious and poorly voiced. I think my only stage appearance was as the back legs of a horse in some farce or other. I was scarcely involved in school acting at any age, and this may be the reason for one of my life's regrets: my inability to read contemporary play scripts. I simply do not have the knack of producing a play in my head. If I have seen a play staged I may read the text with pleasure, though I then cannot imagine it being acted or spoken other than as I saw it produced. I do enjoy reading plays that rely a great deal on language and poetry, and I enjoyed writing dramatised documentaries later.

I passed the Leaving Certificate with rather spectacular results in English and History, and scraped through a bastard susbject called Qualifying Maths that enabled the innumerate to matriculate. I could have gained an exhibition to the University. But I had decided to study Art with the blessing of Ruth Ainsworth and my parents.

IV

The Sydney Short
Story Club

BANJO Paterson must have walked along Darling Point Road quite often, though he did not live there, for when we were small children he was frequently pointed out to us by accompanying adults. I gathered that this grumpy-looking gentleman, who wore his hat at a slightly rakish angle, was immensely famous and important but was not sure why until a little later, when Mrs Trim OBE recited the works of Paterson, Lawson and Adam Lindsay Gordon to Margaret and me (by heart) and introduced us to other bush balladists too, and to some of the more hilarious verses in the *Coles Funny Picture Book*.

Mrs Trim took a few guests into her Church Point bungalow on a hillside overlooking Scotland Island and a great stretch of Pittwater. It was called 'Glencairn'. There we spent our Christmas holidays for five years from 1929. When Margaret and I caught whooping cough, we and Mother put in our weeks of quarantine there, the sufferers throwing up over convenient verandah railings. Church Point then had no road connection with Terry Hills and the North Shore. The car-less Keesings reached it by a service car from Dee Why that made the trip twice a week. And we got suitcases, fishing gear and all to Dee Why by ferry and tram.

Mrs Trim was a retired hotel-keeper from Tamworth and the OBE was awarded in recognition of her mighty fund-raising efforts to send parcels to the AIF during World War I. She was a tall, comely woman whose long hair was always neatly dragged back into a bun. She wore striped blue and white cotton dresses of bygone style with high starched white cotton collars; and by day, long, starched aprons—and very shiny, well-polished, black, high-buttoned boots.

I early formed an opinion that Mrs Trim knew everything and I was probably not far wrong. She could extract ticks from one's hair, discourse about farming and regret the smallness of her Church Point place where she could only keep some chooks, a pig and a cow. She was a good stern Christian: after one of my frequent quarrels with Margaret, she warned me, 'She who calleth her sister a fool is in danger of hell-fire,' which worried me a lot. The huge central room of her cottage, used for dining and sitting, was dominated by a rectangular table covered by a thick fringed woollen rug, and then a white cloth. Its high walls were hung with framed mottos: the first stanza of *Home Sweet Home* prettily surrounded by pink roses; 'I groaned because I was lame until I met a man who had no feet' or words to that effect; 'Lives of great men all remind us/We can make our lives sublime/And departing leave behind us/Footsteps on the sands of time' which was her favourite; and many, many more.

Money is no indicator of 'class' or of brains. Paradoxically I, at two famous girls' schools whose fees were high, probably had a wider experience of many kinds and classes of girls of my age than I would have done if attending a Selective High School of that era. For instance I had to share teaching time and classroom space and facilities with some extremely dull if not retarded children. This was so right through to the final year because some of these girls had parents who were determined they should finish the whole school experience, even though many of them could not and did not sit for the Intermediate and Leaving. Many private schools, but *not* selective high schools, provided such students with alternative and stimulating activities, and no one questioned whether this was peculiar, or a waste of time and resources. My friends who went to high schools had a more elitist education than I did, and were often more aware of themselves as an elite thereafter.

Certainly, at the time it was often frustrating and irritating to share lessons with perfect fools, though perfect fools often proved to have non-academic skills and gifts that sometimes put the rest of us in the shade. If we were reasonably successful at school work we usually had parents who could accept, and expect, that we would sit for the Leaving and 'do something' when we left school. The great battles for girls' rights to higher education had chiefly been fought and won among the Australian middle class before our time. Still, few parents expected their daughters to work and marry, or rather, to work after marriage, and few girls expected to do so either. No one seemed to contemplate the enormous waste of every kind that was involved in providing training that might be put to use for no more than three or four years. Girls vaguely wanted to 'do' nursing, or Art, or Music, or to study for a degree, after they left school at about seventeen. Then they expected to work at what they had 'done' for some five years, marry, have families, look after houses and perhaps find some charity or voluntary work to fill in chinks of spare time.

These assumptions, and indeed these dilettante situations, must have contributed to the perpetuation of appallingly low rates of pay for women, by comparison with the salaries earned by men doing similar work. Bad luck for young women who genuinely wanted to pursue chosen careers and for less privileged girls whose parents and families had scrimped and saved to forward their ambitions! No woman could live well, and few more than marginally, on the rates of pay then offered. (This is why so many of our school teachers were shabbily dressed. I still squirm when I reflect how my splendid education was essentially subsidised by selfless, high-minded but misguided women. Male teachers also had atrocious pay, but it was princely by comparison with what women took home.)

But if it was taken for granted that girls who qualified might embark on University or other tertiary courses, it was not by any means universally agreed that they should join the workforce eventually. As most tertiary or post-secondary education was paid for privately, poorer students sought scholarships, cadetships or entered a bond arrangement as did trainee teachers—or else they missed out on further education altogether. Parents who paid for daughters to 'do' a degree, or nursing training, or whatever, and waste it, seemed not to regard the situation as wasteful. Nor did the community question this erosion of its resources.

When middle class girls qualified for their chosen job or profession they blithely accepted the appallingly low wages and salaries. For one thing few well-off parents ceased giving their daughters some sort of allowance once they had paid work. Thus the young women who might have agitated for higher pay and conditions were effectively muted by custom. Less privileged girls whose parents had made great sacrifices to educate them had to manage as best they could on the prevailing wage scale. They too usually lived on in the parental home because their income did not rise to respectable independent living. Feminism was very much the preserve of a few well-educated upper middle class women. There was little effective contact between feminists and women in the mass.

For my generation the War brought much change as to jobs for women, and yet little change in the conditions—in that those jobs were still paid for at rates that did not allow true independence. Patriotism and a sense of adventure led many of my counterparts into areas of work that would have been unthinkable in peace time. One of my school friends who was not academically inclined was 'manpowered' into a factory production-line job despite the protests of her rich and conventional parents. She had to leave her upper North Shore home at six a.m. winter and summer to get to her factory in South Sydney on time. She became a forewoman and acquired status and self-respect that no one would have predicted for her. Numbers of my friends joined the land army, and then the women's services, and were trained as drivers, signallers, cipher clerks and for other unexpected tasks. Their mothers, busy working for Red Cross, or Servicemen's Canteens, wondered how the girls would settle down again when all the fervour and excitement was over.

Most of the girl friends I had made at school married eventually, but those of us who trained for skilled work or the professions on the whole married later than had our counterparts of a generation or so earlier. In any case many women of the World War I era were bereaved of their men by the horrendous casualty lists of the Great War and simply did not ever marry. It must also be said that at a time when marriage still seemed the 'normal' state for women, World War I had provided some unmarried ones with an acceptable excuse for either unconventional choice, or sad failure to be 'chosen'. World War II had an effect on the marriage pattern of my generation also and so did what I can only call social class, though it is never easy or accurate to assign class in Australia. To some extent I have in mind a sort of family acceptance of ideas of gentility. There were countless young girls in my youth who spent every penny and wartime clothing coupon they could save, on household linen for their glory box —their literal, sandalwood glory box; and every hour they could spare on embroidering that linen or on making underwear for themselves to wear when they should marry. Some of them were very skilled at the paid work they did, and some of them were able and willing to accept seniority and responsibility (though usually at a minor level) in their jobs. But it never entered their heads that when Mr Right came along there might be conflict between him and their careers—they had jobs, not careers. Moreover, and wartime notwithstanding, they hoped to be debutantes at a ball, and to be launched upon a middle ground of society according to all the rules and mores of that society.

There are affinities between those girls—they are comfortable grandmothers now—and the daughters of some migrant and ethnic groups today, who really, because of peer and family pressures, do not have valid choices between marriage and career. Few people are effectively more blind in their bigotry than those ardent feminists who continue to advocate ways and choices that simply are not available to many girls.

In 1941 I enrolled at the Art School at East Sydney Technical College where I rapturously adopted the prevailing uniform of paint-smeared smocks, which made all the girls look pregnant, arty colour combinations as to other clothes, and sandals. Had it not been for the deteriorating course of the War, I might have persisted as an art student beyond my first year—instead I felt I should make some more positive contribution to the war effort. I'd never 'got religion' as many adolescents do, but instead contracted patriotic fever, and went to work as a clerk for the Department of the Navy on Garden Island.

During long train journeys to and from work during the War I knitted countless pairs of socks in khaki wool, and seaboot stockings in greasy wool—the Red Cross supplied the yarn. When I could get wool I also knitted jumpers and stockings for myself. Most young women worked at embroidery, or knitting or sewing in transport and at lunch time. Some women knitted during films and even concerts—there were complaints about the clicking of needles. Many of the girls I knew were assembling trousseaux. Others made gloves from un-couponed chamois leather and summer blouses from un-couponed scarves.

Women's craftwork was not innovative. The stencilled designs on mats and doyleys were constant: flowers, loops and leaves. Crochet designs were usually traditional. (When I married in 1955 a woman presented me with a crocheted cover for a tomato sauce bottle!) Taste in craft or needle-work varied from the stereotyped to the abysmal; girls who dressed as smartly as was possible in wartime, contriving the latest fashions from rationed materials, filled their sandalwood glory boxes with objects that might have been made by their grandmothers in their youth.

Costume jewellery was scarce because most of it used to be imported from central Europe and Japan, so substitute ornaments were devised. You could set plaster of Paris in a greased teaspoon, inserting a safety pin on the flat side, and later decorate this 'brooch' with poster colour, as your fancy dictated, and lacquer it. Or you could buy 'barbola', a sort of patent modelling paste from which, with copper wire, all kinds of earrings, brooches and hair ornaments were made. Barbola too was painted and lacquered.

Silk stockings were hard to find and rayon substitutes atrocious. In winter it was smart to wear hand-knitted, intricately cabled stockings in bright wool. In summer, leg paint was the answer. There was considerable art in applying this paint smoothly; tips and hints circulated about preferred methods. If you were dressing up, you finished the paint job with a back 'seam' of eyebrow pencil. The end result was messy stains on the hems of slips and, if you were careless or weary about washing it off at night, on pyjamas and sheets.

The result: suddenly the word 'allergy' was loud in the land. Girls developed blisters and rashes from wartime cosmetics, and from substances used in factories. Barrier cream was very new, and very 'in'.

One girl I worked with operated a hefty ancient Burroughs adding machine with immense competence. How she kept her long and beautifully manicured fingernails intact and their expertly applied polish unchipped was a mystery. She had slender fingers and very white skin, and took to applying barrier cream seductively throughout the day. In her spare time she modelled her hands for a commercial photographer. (Contemporary jewellers' advertisements displaying ornate, built-up filigree and diamond engagement rings featured those hands of hers.

Just as we accepted miniscule wages, so we accepted other expected and accepted roles. Girls not only expected to be sex objects: they also dressed to be sex objects and failure to be somebody's sex object at least in working hours could be a cause of considerable chagrin. Men in the workforce were often middle aged to elderly; or medically unfit for service in the forces; or, by peacetime standards, pretty unattractive. Also, most of them were married. They were fair game for the girls with whom they worked—during working hours.

Few workplace flirtations continued outside for, like most games, they were conducted according to rules and conventions.

Nowadays I reflect that, by our fairly innocent acquiescence in the prevailing modes and mores, my generation set the stage for the sexual harrassment debate of today. From my own work experience, I can only think of two instances that might stand up as genuine complaints of harrassment. Girls did put up with a considerable amount of double talk; every workplace had its known 'bottom pinchers' but the nuisances were usually at more or less the same job level as the victims and issues of actual advantage or disadvantage seldom arose. In fact I look back with some sympathy for many of the men. Kittens sharpen their claws on what is available—and not all men welcomed, or responded, to arch or blatant behaviour. I can well understand the somewhat puzzled reaction of older men in the workforce now whose accustomed, lighthearted and often perfectly genuine compliments to a girl are regarded as offensive, or at least suspect.

1941 and the Art School of East Sydney Technical College, remain memorable for many reasons, and not least that among our many excellent teachers was William Dobell who had just returned from Europe and who taught us a great deal about creativity—in conversation rather than with a pencil. I did make a decisive step forward towards a writing career, though I scarcely recognised it at the time. The Art School had a shop selling art requisites. Its manager, Gwynneth Williams, made it a friendly place and the only centre where students from different years ever met. She got to know many of the students better then they did themselves. As a child Gwynneth had travelled widely in the countryside with her father, a friend of Augustus John, who worked as an itinerant painter, travelling from station to station with his two daughters. He painted portraits of pastoralists, their wives and families and, on occasion, their prize-winning animals.

Gwynneth took considerable interest in Robert Hill, son of Ernestine, who was in my year though much younger than anyone else and who, because of the war, was one of the very few men studying art. Robert really did not fit in with most groups especially as we were young and heedless. It would not have occurred to us to make his spare time or lunch hours sociable, but Gwynneth was always glad to see him and talk, and sometimes he helped her in the store.

She was a shortish, quick-moving, intense woman with fly-away hair, a 'cast' in one eye, and a persuasive, sometimes passionate, manner of speech. Gwynneth was my first communist, and the first acquaintance I ever had who led me to question the ultra-conservative political wisdom that was gospel in my family and taken for granted at my schools. I now know that several of my school teachers were far from politically conservative, but they never overtly discussed their convictions with students. I suspect we occasionally had a signal that I missed, as when, for instance Lena Curd read *South Riding* and told us about her friend Winifred Holtby; or in some of her modern history lessons.

Gwynneth learned of my poetry writing and invited me to 'The Sydney Short Story Club'. From 1941 for several years I attended its regular evening meetings though whether these were held weekly or monthly I cannot now recall. The club met in one of a number of rooms in the premises of the Psychical Research Society, which must have been quite a large concern to judge by its imposing decor. Our meeting room was a library, lined with thick books behind glass doors but, in the adjoining room, seances were often held and the Short Story Club's deliberations were liable to be punctuated by weird moans, screams, sighs and gabbling (speaking in tongues, perhaps).

I don't think the term workshop had been coined then, but essentially that is what the club provided, and I still think its methods could be a useful model. When I first joined I was alarmed because if one wished to have a story or poem discussed, one had to read it aloud and for weeks I was too bashful to contemplate that.

The victim read his or her piece and every member wrote a short opinion on a piece of paper, and signed it. These strictly un-anonymous comments were given to the author to read later. Then the 'experts'—Gwynneth herself, her sister, her man Fred Green and Gertrude Scarlett—led a verbal discussion. Anyone might join in this but some people are chary of speaking their criticism and I do think those written notes were a good idea. The experts kept the level of criticism constructive and friendly; I do not recall anyone trying to score points or being conceitedly clever, or hurtful, though some hopefuls read pretty terrible stuff.

There was a good local market for factual sketches and short stories with trick endings in the O Henry manner. A great deal of the work presented was of that order, and many of the beginners who benefited from the advice given found regular publication either in magazines or evening newspapers. Several of the members were talented—Thelma Forshaw used to belong; several were rather engagingly potty; most were competent people learning a hack trade as best they could; a few were hopeless.

Sometimes the club invited a guest speaker; the two I chiefly recall were Michael Sawtell who as well as being a writer was a splendid raconteur, and Henry Lawson's widow, Bertha. Often the speakers were experienced magazine editors.

After a year or so the only opinion I really valued was Gertrude

Scarlett's. Some of my poetry and stories were insufficiently 'realist' for the other assessors, and I was not about to alter my whole nature as a writer to suit theories. When I could not attend meetings because of the overtime exigencies of the Department of the Navy I would send Scarlett a poem with a letter. Thus began a friendship chiefly conducted by correspondence that lasted some twenty years until she died. We *could* sometimes have met, and in later years often did, but the correspondence we established was ideal for each of us. Over the years meetings between people who live far apart in large cities become hard to arrange and even harder between people of very different ages. Had it not been for letters we would probably have drifted apart.

Scarlett, as I always called her, was a kind of writer who no longer exists—because the necessities that impelled her, and the markets that supported her, have vanished. I cannot regret that. Had she lived in a later era when financial support is available for people of talent, she may well have written and published lasting works. As it was, her immense body of printed or broadcast writings were all ephemeral.

She was about my mother's age. They met once or twice and Mother liked her very much—it would be hard not to. Later, though, my mother became rather jealous of Scarlett for she knew that I, who always was, and still am, secretive about work in progress, confided to Scarlett draft writings and personal concerns that I denied her.

Late in her life Scarlett asked me to burn any of her letters I might have kept because she did not believe in keeping personal letters. Stupidly, and to my great regret, I did as she wished—hundreds of pages in her spidery, legible, loved hand went up in smoke. Fortunately, being untidy and unsystematic I have since found—and treasure—a few survivors.

We exchanged news of books, of everyday and family doings, and confided sorrows and joys. She was a kind, but toughly honest, critic of my work as a rule and I was glad of that. At a later time I could not always agree with some of her notions and reasons—or accept, sometimes, her increasingly over-rapturous praise for my poetry.

It was Scarlett who lent me Christina Stead's *Seven Poor Men of Sydney* long before she was well-known in her own country, leading me to read anything by Stead I could get hold of. And it was Scarlett who directed me to all kinds of books from all over the world that I would not otherwise have heard of.

She was a pretty, plump woman with a lot of laughter lines wrinkling a face made alert and expressive by bright brown eyes. Her voice was breathy and pleasantly Australian. She was immensely proud of her two sons, and their families. Graham and Hubert were overseas with the AIF when I first knew her, so she was constantly anxious. Then they returned safely. Well may she have been proud: her freelance writing had paid for their upbringing; and (this does not always follow) they too were proud of her—a truly loving family. Graham was disappointed all the same, because he'd had to leave school at fourteen and take a job in a bank. After the War, under the Commonwealth Reconstruction Training Scheme he did an Arts Course at the University of Sydney, and had a successful career as an academic.

Scarlett's husband was Dr Dalley Scarlett, a notable figure in Australian music. She was a musical girl and had married when she was very young, having received her first kiss from Dr Dalley on the steps behind the organ pipes of Sydney Town Hall. They went to live at Grafton where he was organist of the cathedral and taught students. In Grafton itself she had many friends and interests. She was wonderfully happy in her home, with her two babies. She loved her husband wholly. 'Everyone' knew, though, and no one gossiped or prepared her for the completely unexpected day when he up and left town with another woman. Her shock and grief, as she often wrote to me, were devastating.

Scarlett refused to be devastated for long and determined to bring up her two sons herself. She would accept nothing from her renegade husband though I think her love, in a way, lasted life long, and that she missed him. She had a very observant eye, a good ear, a sense of beauty, a sense of humour and no literary snobbery at all, so she began to write anything and everything saleable. The *Bulletin* and the *Woman's Mirror* and other journals used to publish vast quantities of contributed 'pars' at rates varying from 1d to 2d a line as well as sketches, short stories and other material. Scarlett, using a galaxy of pseudonyms, wrote pars about anything and everything from natural history, humorous incidents seen or overheard, recipes, household hints, child care and gardening. She sent some fifty paragraphs to magazines every week. Unused pars were not returned, so the writer could never submit apparently unwanted material elsewhere—it just might be printed eventually by the original recipient. Writers had to claim payment for paragraphs and it was not worth a stamp, or trip to town, until a fair number of published pieces made a claim worthwhile, so her system of records had to be efficient. For a range of magazines she also wrote short stories varying from 'true love' to adventure. She wrote a great deal for early radio; lyrics for one of the community singing groups popular in the Depression; and a few book reviews. She regretted that, during the toughest years of her career, few books were noticed in Australian magazines and newspapers, and that reviews were usually written by staff people. In the early fifties when I began writing review paragraphs for the *Bulletin* and other journals—for I too furiously freelanced then to finance the research for the ballad and bush song collections I was making in collaboration with Douglas Stewart—Scarlett was immensely pleased: to her, a Red Page, unsigned par was a real achievement. When a poem of mine appeared in the *Bulletin* she was quick to write and praise.

In all her working life Scarlett never sacrificed her integrity. She held strong ethical views about public and personal morals and several times refused commissioned work because she could not approve the circumstances in which it was offered. But she had far more tolerance than was usual for women of her age and background and also a lively appreciation of the comedy of life, including that part of the comedy that results from sexual fun and games. She who was no Bohemian knew many Bohemians and a lot of randy early broadcasters, and she herself told some strange and funny tales. One of her talents was reading teacups, which she spoke of as a bit of a joke but which in fact she took fairly seriously though she was never accurate about mine.

There was one curious exception to Scarlett's tolerance that was important to me because, later, it enabled me to understand a segment of Australian history that would, otherwise, have mystified. Scarlett had friends of all religions and none: she accepted Gwynneth Williams and her communist friends although she greatly disapproved of Communism, but she firmly believed in, and related in letters, a cluster of canards about convents and nuns. . .about the bodies of newborn babies bricked up in convent cellars or found mummified under wooden staircases; about raving, shrieking mad nuns incarcerated for years within thick stone walls; about depraved priests. It was one of the last lingering echoes of the dreadful sectarian bitterness, Protestants versus Catholics, that bedevilled many communities in nineteenth-century Australia.

I gradually drifted away from the Sydney Short Story Club. It folded up in the manner of many small clubs, though Scarlett swore its demise was caused by its modest funds being somehow improperly diverted to the Communist Party coffers. Gwynneth Williams had begun working in the Party bookshop in William Street, but she also sold the *Tribune* near Woolworths in Darlinghurst Road, Kings Cross and that is where I most often saw her, increasingly ill and frail, selling her papers in all weathers. In between her spieling we had friendly enough talks for a time until she made it increasingly plain that if I would not join the Party I must forfeit her acquaintance. Later she taught English to Indonesians who were in Australia because of the revolution in their country. As I heard it she contracted tuberculosis, and died of it.

In 1943 I sent some poems to an ABC programme conducted by R. A. Broinowski, and several of them were read. I earned my first payment for writing—it was insufficient to turn my head. Broinowski was thus my first editor, and one day he rang me up and invited me to his house, on the North Shore, for afternoon tea the following Sunday. I was tremendously surprised and overcome.

His instructions were full, but anxious. After alighting from the train I would have to walk for half a mile or so. Could I manage that? If I couldn't he'd bring his car to the station. (Petrol rationing was in force then.)

I was a healthy girl of twenty. My family lived at Pennant Hills, a good mile, mostly over a clay road, from our house to the railway, and to reach the Garden Island office where I then worked I walked another mile every morning and evening, let alone all the other walking I did, one way or another. I was mystified first by this invitation and then by his editorial solicitude and it suddenly occurred to me that he might be mistaking me for someone else. Diffidently I said something to this effect, but no, he assured me, his concern was because I was a poet, and some poets were ethereal.

Really. That had not occurred to me and I worried as the day approached that he would be dreadfully disappointed at the appearance on his doorstep of a strong, tall, linen-suited poet wearing platform-soled shoes (good for walking).

There was no awkwardness. Mr and Mrs Broinowski were nice elderly hosts—he looked like an amiable teddy bear with white hair except for being tallish; she was an active, dark-haired woman. Their daughter was about my age. I cannot remember the conversation which was overshadowed by their Australian paintings. Elioth Gruner was a great friend of R. A.'s and some of his magnificent misty mornings, with cattle or mountains, hung on their walls.

For some time I had also been sending poems to the *Bulletin*, which was where I really hoped to publish. The *Bulletin*'s column 'Answers to Correspondents' was where disappointed contributors looked for reasons and comment on their rejected efforts. The comment was often cutting, sometimes facetious, but frequently encouraging and kind—and fortunately I attracted the latter variety. (The column, as I later discovered, was most often compiled by W. E. 'Bill' FitzHenry who several years after this became a friend—but more of Bill later.)

My family and friends, especially Gertrude Scarlett, were delighted about the ABC broadcasts, but absolute rapture emerged from an unexpected source: my boss in the Garden Island Accounts Branch, Bert Bootle. (I called him Tim Tapple in *Garden Island People*.) Bert was a Liverpudlian of middle age who carried a couple of hefty chips on his shoulder. One of these, until recently, had been me. For my first eighteen months on the Island he detested and/or despised everything about me— my accent, my handwriting, my private-school background, my existence, and I returned much, but not all, of his intolerance and ill-feeling; I always respected his ability and energy. Then, gradually, our relationship altered. First we accepted each other, then a rather weird sort of liking, not far from affection, developed. Bert had the worst and most volcanic temper of any man I've known and was a mighty though uninventive swearer. His range was predictable. 'Stone the crows' signalled an outbreak—a succession of 'bloodies' chiefly saw it through.

After he heard from someone about the ABC broadcasts he was annoyed—hurt really—that I'd not told him about them. 'All the same, girl, if you write poetry the *Bully* is the place.' I explained my efforts and rejections. 'Stone the bloody crows! What's the bloody *Bully* bloody thinking of. . .?'

Just about the time I left Garden Island the *Bully* did accept a poem, and Bert embarrassed me dreadfully by spreading the great news in every workshop, store, and department of the Island, with the awful consequence that storemen, naval policemen and typists would call on me to instantly supply lines of Paterson, Lawson, Omar Khayyam that they couldn't recall and that I did not know.

Then the War was over. During the next few years many young Australians set off for England to further their training in careers or to find 'life'. By then I was finding Sydney life, one way and another, and a journeyman career as a freelance writer, stimulating and entrancing. Otherwise I would have gone too; sometimes I've regretted that I did not, for having missed that chance of travel in a youthful fashion, there was no other opportunity until middle age. I was never fated to explore 'overseas' in any footloose and casual way.

Travel apart, many young women now wanted to live independently, and independently of their families. Many struck problems. Some fond, affectionate parents could not comprehend, or accept, a daughter's wish to live alone, or to share accommodation with another girl rather than continue in her pretty bedroom with hot meals cooked by Mum and baked dinner at the weekend. 'I'd have thought,' a puzzled and anxious mother might say, 'that after three years living in AWAS [or WRANS or whatever] Barracks you'd be only too thankful to settle in here again.' It was hard to explain that it was precisely because of those wartime years that family life seemed constrictive and restrictive; that jolly Jack Davey every night on the wireless drove one mad; that one had become accustomed to a somewhat spur-of-the-moment social life, accepting casual invitations freely; that one enjoyed a drink with friends after work and it was a dreadful drag to rush home instead for six-thirty 'tea'; that one (in some cases) wanted a place where one could make love, even if not married.

A further difficulty was the poor standard of rental accommodation. Flats were expensive and so was the almost universal demand for 'key money'. Many owners and agents did not want single women as tenants, not so much because they feared the girls would necessarily exist in a steam of moral turpitude, but because women were fussy about dirt, vermin and appalling plumbing. Exasperated young men more often tackled dreadful plumbing and rotten joinery in their spare time and at their own expense, and were less persistent with complaints to agents. Also young men on decent wages could in any event afford higher rents. The few women I knew who lived in nice flats or houses were usually older, holding reasonably senior jobs and some had private incomes from deceased parents or deceased or divorced husbands.

The concept of sharing houses, as young people understand it now, did not exist. In the late forties and early fifties the process of 'recycling' old houses in inner-city suburbs had not begun except in Paddington. The term 'slums' was still used in a wide and inaccurate way to describe square mile on square mile of older streets and houses; but some of these precincts, after decades of neglect by owners and agents, during first the Depression and then the War, were undeniably slummy and unsavoury.

In Sydney we sought places to live in areas that were traditional for young single people, especially those whose pursuits were in the arts or professions. We chose the Cross and Potts Point, but not Woolloomooloo; parts but not all of Darlinghurst; Elizabeth Bay, Rushcutters Bay and near-city areas like Kirribilli or North Sydney. We did not own cars and relied on good public transport from the city and well-lit streets for reasonably safe walking at night. We ate in cafes a good deal, for the cooking arrangements in our rooms were usually awful. I do not recall having to select eating places from the point of view of respectability. When I first lived at Potts Point the nearest pubs were at the Cross itself and one practically never saw or heard a drunken person; nor did louts come into the Cross to gawp at its low life, which was not particularly colourful before sex shops, sex films and other changes that happened much later, in the sixties, and which accelerated during the Vietnam War when US troops flocked to the Cross on R & R leave. Prostitution was blatant in parts of Darlinghurst (and long had been) but around Potts Point it was discreet, off the street and often conducted by 'call girls'. Call girls operated, sometimes by themselves, sometimes in organised groups, from flats with telephones, and by appointment. Many homosexuals lived in these areas where overt homosexuality had long been tolerated, but there were no notorious gay bars in those days (except for a hotel at the Cross where lesbians congregated) and if there was homosexual prostitution it was as discreet as the heterosexual kind.

'Bodgies' and 'widgies' clustered at a milkbar in Darlinghurst Road and were sometimes boisterous, though seldom alarming or objectionable—which is not surprising since their tipple was milkshake or coke. It was known that drugs could be bought at the Cross but there was no overt pushing. There was a wicked witch at the Cross though, and she'd been notorious for several decades. She and her coven certainly debauched a few young people I knew of but they were deliberately looking for adventures in depravity and had to seek her out.

I was fortunate because my parents did not oppose my desire to live near the city. For one thing their house at Pennant Hills with its mile walk from the railway was undeniably remote; for another I chiefly spent weekends there and still entertained a good deal at tennis parties on the court Dad had built for us. I was fortunate too because I had a retreat that for several years was a virtual secret, though by the fifties everyone including my parents knew of it. This was a studio room in an old sandstone building, since demolished, in the centre of the city on the northern corner of George and Bond Streets.

I really cannot remember exactly how I first came to share this room with Kate, who was much older than I and on the periphery of my real friendships, though we contrived our sharing cordially. The arrangement began in perhaps 1945 or maybe in 1944, when I still worked on Garden Island. Kate had rented the studio for many years since before the War. Until she took a wartime clerical job she'd had ambitions as a painter and sculptor and had worked as a commercial artist. Her artistic ambitions had diminished and soon after I met her she enrolled as a Physiotherapy student at Sydney University. Presumably her income then fell to zero and she was pleased to share the rent, low as it was (memory says 12/6 a month but could that really have been so? I paid it at the Perpetual Trustee Company's office in Hunter street).

Kate was my chief reason for being secretive about the studio, but another was that I was entranced by the notion of having a bolt-hole, a place of my own that no one knew of. I'd shut the door behind me and say to myself, 'No one in the whole world knows where I am,' and this gave me immense satisfaction. I wrote a lot of poems in that room. Then, for the two or three years that I shared with Kate I always acknowledged her senior claim when she wished to use the room, and consequently I was frequently uncertain whether, or when, the room was free. To explain this to most of my friends would have been complicated enough; to explain it to parents, unthinkable.

Kate was divorced, had no children and lived affectionately in a cottage at Artarmon with her widowed mother. Her reason for retaining the studio after she had ceased practising Art was her lover. He was a senior public servant, a man whose face was known far and wide in Sydney. He had a wife and young adult children. His affair with Kate had lasted for years when I first knew of it and was that rare thing, a truly well-kept secret. When Kate's lover could see a short time clear of commitments he would contact her to wait for him at the studio.

They never went anywhere together, or had a meal in a restaurant or took a room at a hotel because he might be recognised. One proof of their love, I suppose, was that they had not yet tired of each other's sole company in, to be honest, fairly grotty surroundings.

If Kate and her man were in the studio she signalled to me by placing, in one of the George Street windows, a large bent wire in the shape of a human that was known to us as 'Joe'. In her sculpturing days she had fashioned Joe as basis for a clay model that she had never completed. I'd always glance up to that window before I entered the building for Joe might be visible at various hours of day, though most often in the late afternoon.

But then, as Kate's Physiotherapy lectures and practical work became more demanding, and also lessened her access to a telephone, the affair with the senior public servant gradually ended. Sometime later Kate's lover turned up late one afternoon saying he'd seen the light on, and for old time's sake... So I poured him a glass of the dreadful cheap sherry we used to drink and he explained how and why his wife did not understand him, and then offered to transfer his affections to me. I was probably more cruel than necessary, and laughed him out of the studio for ever. About twenty years later I read his Obituary in the *Herald* and marvelled at what eulogies manage not to say.

Kate's studio furnishing was a stretcher bed with a bright felt patchwork cover, a canvas deckchair, and Joe. I added a cheap wooden table cum desk large enough to take a typewriter, a wooden chair, a set of bookshelves and a kerosene heater. When Kate withdrew she left the deckchair and the stretcher, which I attempted to transform into a settee under many cushions. She also left Joe behind. Somehow I could not bring myself to throw him away, so I pestered her until she came one day and collected him. Gradually I acquired folding chairs, a mat to partly cover the bare board floor, and pictures and prints for one of the party walls that was lined with nice wood panels.

The old stone building had small shops on its ground floor. A huge and heavy wooden door opened from Bond Street to a wide, and maybe once a gracious wooden staircase that led to the first and second floors. The cold-water-only women's lavatory was on the second floor, men's ditto on the first. Any cleaning of washrooms and passageways was done by the tenants as fancy or hygiene inspired them—a non-system that worked surprisingly well for the place, which was dingy, shabby and grubby but not filthy. Most of the top, or second floor on the George Street side was rented by the Players' Club, a little theatre group. On the Bond Street side Stanley Clarkson, a well-known singer and teacher of singing, had a large room next to the studio of an elderly and eminent water-colour painter. The first floor was a mosaic of smaller rooms except for one larger one facing Bond Street that was the studio of Robert Klippel the sculptor.

My studio was on the George and Bond Street corner and it was surrounded by huge sash windows set in deep stone embrasures.

Next to me on the George Street frontage was a room with two big windows whose occupants one never saw—they used it for storage for one of the shops. Later this room became the well-furnished office of a small import—export business owned by a husband and wife who worked together there and were very friendly neighbours, though they never quite came to terms with their raffish surroundings. The room that adjoined mine on the Bond Street side was eventually, in the early fifties rented by Ray Price and his Sydney Jazz Group. It was also used for teaching, the noise of the saxophone being loud in the land.

But when I first had the studio that room was mysterious. Countless men seemed to have keys. They came and went at all hours and gave no greeting or civil word to anyone they might meet in the maze-like passageway that led to it. One was an elderly man I'd known on Garden Island and whom, indeed, I'd met before that—because he was the lover of a woman who early had recognised my writing ambitions. Both were active members of the Communist Party. The man had pretended not to recognise me and after a couple of blank looks I respected his evident wish.

For some weeks I gave no thought to these neighbours or to the room that, for most of the time on week days, was locked of door and dark of window. Then, one Saturday afternoon for some reason I was reading in the studio, which I did not visit as a rule at weekends. I could hear voices next door but gave them no thought until I went to my shelves for some object and realised much of the conversation was fairly audible. The shelves on my side of the party wall were set in a deep embrasure that reached from the floor to near the ceiling and perhaps had once formed an archway between my studio and its neighbour. I had curtained this recess and kept cups, glasses, and cleaning materials on the shelves. It may be that from the other side the wall looked solid.

That Saturday I really did not set out to eavesdrop. But overhearing some parts of proceedings was unavoidable, and at last I pulled a chair over near the wall and yielded to temptation. It was plainly the meeting of a Communist Party cell. 'Mumble mumble mumble. OK Bill?' 'Sure Jim, mumble.' Then passions rose and suddenly formality was remembered. No more Bill, Jim and Harry but 'Comrade this' and 'Comrade that'. This amused me. When they were friendly again given names were resumed. Then I decided that the little I could hear properly was not anything I understood, or any of my business; so, a bit ashamed of myself, I left the wall.

At about this time, through the WEA I came to know Bob, a strange character who was a fine if minor writer and a good critic. He was also a trades union organiser on the moderate side of Labor politics who, just then, was at the centre—indeed the dramatic and even dangerous centre—of an acrimonious and violent 'takeover' of a union whose offices were a couple of blocks down George Street near the Quay. Bob with his wife came to the studio a few times when other poets and writers were there. Then, one afternoon he knocked at the door in a somewhat breathless and agitated state and asked if he could leave some packages with me until the next day. His truck was in the street below, he said, but he wanted to get it away as soon as possible in case it was recognised. Impulsively I said yes and went downstairs to help him. The packages, hastily wrapped in brown paper and carelessly tied with string were bursting at the corners, and the least curious of people could see that they were ledgers and files. He dumped the lot and departed. Next morning I went into town early and at seven-thirty as arranged, Bob returned to retrieve his bundles. I asked no questions, though it did occur to me that I'd probably been harbouring a major trades union time bomb overnight. However I did mention my comrade neighbours to Bob and he spent a couple of Saturday afternoons glued to my shelving. 'I've got them!' he said on the last occasion. Not long afterwards the union concerned was wrested from its left wing control and into moderate hands that steered it for decades thereafter. Bob, who sometimes feared for his life, died fairly young, but in his bed. Not long after these episodes conspiracy disappeared from Bond Street and jazz took over. The noise could be terrible, but the atmosphere was more salubrious.

After Kate had left and for several years thereafter, until I could find and afford a place to which I could invite friends for a meal or drink, the studio was the centre of my social life. The rented rooms where I lived were not suitable for entertaining. Another advantage of the studio was oddly, its almost total lack of facilities, for I could only serve the simplest and cheapest food there—sandwiches, wine, and in winter tea or coffee made from a billy of water constantly bubbling on top of the kerosene heater. Many people called and my income did not run to much hospitality.

In about 1946, having by then published quite a number of poems in the *Bulletin*, I took it into my head to visit the poetry and Red Page editor, Douglas Stewart. I can't remember now whether or not I made an appointment or simply wandered to 252 George Street. I was a ridiculously shy and self-conscious, socially inept girl—prone to blush and easy game for bullies. (One reason Bert Bootle disliked me so much early in our enforced acquaintance was simply that he could reduce me to a nervous pulp without exerting any real effort.)

I made my way down an immense room past a long, polished counter, towards the editorial department at the back of the building, under the painted gazes of Henry Lawson and J. F. Archibald. I entered Douglas Stewart's dark and uncomfortable office. (All *Bulletin* offices were uncomfortable and most were dark. The place was none too clean either.)

Douglas stood up. He was short, thin, intense looking, nervous in his movements—and shy. He spoke in short bursts. He was serious—also funny, and I managed a laugh. I have no idea what he said about poetry, my poetry, or anything else. All I recall is that our interview reached its natural limit and I had no more idea how to stand up and leave than he to get rid of me. How we finally managed I've forgotten, but my immediate great liking for him was not because he was a poet I admired beyond anyone else writing in Australia, but because nervous agitation spoke to its counterpart.

In 1945 I began the Diploma Course in Social Studies at Sydney University, but I kept up some WEA evening classes that interested me. The first I had joined was an introductory course in Australian Literature given by H. M. Green, whose massive *History of Australian Literature* remains one of the most used reference books on my shelves. Kylie Tennant's *Ride on Stranger* had recently been published, withdrawn, re-issued, and was enjoying a *succès de scandale*. Green, who was an excellent lecturer, identified characters and incidents from that novel, and Scarlett too was able to add some identifications and amplifications. I began to realise how enjoyable it is to read novels about one's own city and its people. Oddly, my parents—who much admired, and sometimes bought, the works of the country's leading painters—seldom looked at an Australian book of any kind.

However I discovered that the really 'in' group of younger WEA members sat at the feet of Donovan Clarke, BA, himself a minor poet and the kind of lecturer who struck sparks from a lively audience. He was, I am sure, less reliable than Green and I'm glad I started with the bread and butter before I embarked on the cake. Don Clarke was greatly given to enthusiasms that were very catching. When the enthusiasm was W. B. Yeats, about whom he lectured movingly and perceptively, that was fine; some of the figures he and we spent a lot of time on, however, were shooting stars rather than lasting planets—but a lot of fun.

Clarke's most notable feature, after a fine voice, were his fly-away eyebrows; often one could judge his state of mind by their angle. He and some of the group dined more adventurously and sumptuously than I was accustomed to. Where, in those days, I found the money to accompany them to very good restaurants I cannot think now—but I learned more on those occasions than about food and wine. The pleasures of crackling conversation that veered from frivolity to deep seriousness and avoided malice were new to me.

With Don Clarke and his entourage and at the University I was meeting really congenial people, many of them writers or hopeful writers and people involved in drama, in Music and in Art. I made many friendships, some lasting. But, distant fields being always so inviting, I wished almost more than anything to see more of Douglas Stewart than during my occasional forays into his office with offerings of poetry. Meanwhile, through Don Clarke I met Peter Hopegood.

Dear Peter, apart from my father, was my first true eccentric. Very early in our acquaintance I learned from that unusual poet the difference between deliberate or self-styled Bohemians and people who absolutely are genuine non-conformers. Then in his fifties, Peter did not look particularly eccentric. He always wore a very clean shirt, open at the neck, and flannel trousers. In winter he added a brown tweed jacket. But he never wore socks and always wore white, or white-ish sandshoes. This was long before sneakers or running shoes were thought of. He had a battered face, short brown hair and lively eyes. As his poetry makes plain he had great humour and wit.

Beyond those qualities he was a mystic. While Robert Graves pursued the White Goddess, Hopegood followed the Hare and the Stingray through Europe and Asia, in Art and Literature, from pre-history to the present. He read Graves as we all did, and respected his ideas, but considered the Hare and Stingray far more interesting, all embracing, wicked—and threatening. He once showed me his immense illustrated manuscript about them that was never finished because he continued to add to it. Who knows whether he ever tried to get it published, or where it is now.

Peter was a sort of shaman, and a magician too. He said he had decided not to use his mystic powers because he found them terrifying. I did, and do, believe him. Once we stood in Don Clarke's garden when a flock of migratory birds, ducks perhaps, arrowed towards us. 'Look,' said Peter. He gazed intently upwards and suddenly the flock wheeled and took a direction at right angles to their original line of flight. Maybe it was coincidence, maybe I am credulous, but Peter said he willed the birds and I remain convinced he did. Then he told me that, had he wished, he could have killed one of the birds in flight and caused it to drop at our feet; also that, if clouds blew up, but did not yield rain, he could will rain from them. He said he relinquished his powers, or no longer chose to use them, after he had willed a man to die and the man died.

There were other mysteries about Peter. No one knew who his family in England were. It was suspected that Hopegood was not his real name—though his ex-wife, Olive, a poet in the Jindyworobak circle, used it. His tantalising half-autobiography, *Peter Lecky by Himself*, gives hints but no information. Yet, whenever I read of the anointing of monarchs, of the divine right of kings, of the charisma that attaches to chosen people, to true nobility, I think of Peter. And I wonder. Only 'charisma' in its true and mystical sense explains the incident of our dinner in style.

Peter worked for a newsagent rolling newspapers for early morning delivery. He was far from rich. But once he arrived at my studio room in Bond Street and announced we were going to dine that night at the Hotel Australia. The Hotel Australia's dining room was very grand, and in the evening its patrons were beautifully and formally dressed. The waiters were even more formal than the diners. Peter was dressed as usual and I in whatever clothes I'd worn to the University all day. Yet I accompanied him as a Hamelin child must have followed the Pied Piper, trustfully, up the long hill towards the hotel. The head waiter, so it seemed, completely failed to notice Peter's tie-less neck, sockless feet, sandshoes. He escorted us to an excellent table, we had a splendid meal, and he solicitously enquired several times if Peter found all to his satisfaction!

On many afternoons Peter called at Bond Street carrying a bottle of gin. If I was working he'd read a book; otherwise we would talk, and he'd tell me about the Hare, or he would show me his latest, beautifully illustrated letter from his friend Hugh McCrae the poet, but he seldom spoke about his life. Gradually over an hour or so the gin, which he drank in sips from the bottle, disappeared. Yet Peter seemed not in the least affected, his speech never slurred and, when he left by a steep, badly lit old staircase, he never faltered or stumbled.

One day while Peter was visiting, a celebrated writer of the day called in—he must have had an introduction from someone, or given some reason for his coming that I've forgotten. Goodness knows, indeed, why he descended on a very unknown poet. I had not met him before. He had recently been sentenced to prison in Melbourne for the alleged obscenity of a novel that nowadays seems a harmless, if overrated book. The man seemed sober. No doubt I offered him a sherry—the only drink I could afford to keep for friends. Understandably and justifiably he talked obsessively about his unjust treatment, his prison sentence, his present financial straits, for he could get no work, and of the novel he planned to write next—which, although it would have the same sort of seafaring setting, would not deal with female sexuality but rather with male drunkenness. He kept talking about his typewriter, which he called 'black bitch' in colourful and increasingly sexist terms. Then he used an expression that might seem pretty rough even now, and that Peter considered unpardonable then.

Peter carefully put down his bottle on the bare floor boards next to his chair. He stood. He grabbed that much younger man by his collar and belt (the only time I've ever seen this done) and frogmarched him out of the room, along the dark twisting passageway outside. Scared stiff I followed. If there was a fight, what to do? Those terrible stairs! At the top of which Peter released his captive and gave him a hefty push. The notorious novelist did lose his footing. He rolled to the dusty landing, got to his feet, and stumbled down the next flight to the street door. I rushed after him and was reassured because, though limping, he was negotiating the foot-path down towards Pitt Street.

Back in the studio Peter calmly sipped gin, and breathed as easily as a contented cat. 'Peter,' I said, 'thank you, of course, but you shouldn't have. You could have hurt him badly. Or yourself.'

'He is,' said Peter, 'the coarsest and most vulgar bounder I have ever met.'

And that was that.

V

Lyre Bird Writers

IN about 1943 I had been introduced to Pakies—a sort of club that became a centre of my life for seven or eight years. Rose, a member of the Sydney Short Story Club, first took me there and seemed reasonably familiar with the place. But strangely, as I then thought, though I became a regular habituée, Rose scarcely ever turned up at Pakies again or at Short Story Club gatherings either. For some time, after story and poetry discussions, she had tried, usually in Repins George Street coffee shop, to convert me to Numerology—which she firmly believed in. She worked out all kinds of generous numerological prophesies based on my name. But it was, of course, her professed admiration for my poetry that won my heart.

Rose was perhaps my first experience of the sort of lonely heart that hopes, usually with little probability of success, to find a like-minded soul in small groups and associations. One reason for my becoming a chronic non-joiner of such groups of enthusiasts was that I increasingly found lonely hearts distressing, also tiresome. Rose was a pretty, heavily-scented middle-aged woman with a squashy figure, given to prods and pats and kisses that I found distasteful. At Pakies after we had eaten our dinner, a man came to our table and asked me to dance. I agreed—the newest newcomer could see that this was a custom of the place. When I returned to Rose she was agreeable, but distant. Innocent days! Not till years later did it occur to me that Rose was attempting a lesbian seduction.

Pakies occupied a narrow, three-storied building at 219 Elizabeth Street, near Bathurst Street. Pakie and her husband Duncan McDougall, during the early years of the century, had been figures in Sydney's theatrical life. They had established the Playbox Theatre in Rowe Street, which brought to the city experimental or controversial theatre, especially contemporary American drama. When the McDougalls separated, Pakie's friends, the architect Walter Burley Griffin and his wife, helped her to find accommodation at Castlecrag, the suburb Burley Griffin designed. Then, together with a woman friend who had been involved with the Playbox, the Burley Griffins urged Pakie to start some sort of congenial undertaking on her own, and the woman friend financed Pakie to set up her club.

The building she found had been a clothing factory. When Burley Griffin set eyes on it he scraped off layers of paint and kalsomine and revealed ancient bricks which had been hand made at the Brickfield Hill pits and which he left bare. Other more modern brickwork used for later additions was painted. Pakie picked up second-hand chairs and tables and those were painted, each in separate bright colours as suggested by artist Roi de Mestre (who later spelt his name Roy de Maistre).

Pakies was always said by those who remembered it in past years to be beyond its great era, when nearly all the famous art, writing and Bohemian figures of Sydney used to go there. Some of course, still did. But during the War various Europeans, many of them refugees from Hitler's carnage, or young men serving with the Free French, Free Dutch and other forces, found the atmosphere congenial—and its patrons greatly interested me. Liquor was not allowed on the premises: that law was strictly enforced. Pakie's son Robin who, though tall and athletic might have appeared the mildest of men, was a determined 'bouncer' and could rely on back-up from other friends. Nor were people admitted who arrived more than moderately tipsy. This was one reason why I felt perfectly happy about dancing with strangers, and talking to anyone and everyone. The dance music, on records, was unusual: South American and European bands were far more often played than the prevailing American and English 'swing' with accompanying crooners, which were more usually heard in wartime Sydney.

Again before my time, art exhibitions had often been held there: Grace Cossington Smith, Roi de Mestre, Elaine Haxton and, in a different category, George Finey had all exhibited at Pakies. Eric Saunders, a fine painter who died young, dominated one wall in my day with a huge portrait of the chess champion Kochnitsky—who himself dominated the chess group on the second floor. Paul Frolich, a Czechoslovakian who had reached Australia with his parents and brother Walter, often arranged evenings of recorded music; and though I am not musical I enjoyed listening to the pieces and to Paul's explanations and the discussion that followed some of them, especially if they were experimental.

Kylie Tennant no longer went to Pakies in my time. People were always saying what a pity it was that I had missed knowing Kylie—and so it was. Years later we became by chance next-door neighbours for two decades, and I found an Eric Saunders portrait of her in her ardent youth dominating one wall of her house. Dulcie Deamer and her companion (known as Syd the Shag) and their entourage still occasionally turned up. I was young, ignorant and intolerant enough to find them repellent. The spectacle of such people, who looked ancient to me though they were only middle aged, carrying on routines perfected in the, and their, flaming twenties—dancing on tables, doing the splits (Dulcie's famous act) and dressing up like Bohemian mutton masquerading as Bohemian spring lamb—was, I thought, horrible. Yet soon I would meet Bill FitzHenry of the *Bulletin* who belonged very much to that group and era, and find in him a dear and generous friend who furthered my writing aspirations more practically than anyone else had ever done.

In earlier times Pakie served her delicious dinners nightly; only on Friday nights in my day. As I understood it she began providing meals partly, at least, to help out-of-work actors and artists during the Depression. Kylie Tennant, however, said that while she felt Pakie 'conducted a kind of combined restaurant and soup kitchen', she also thought 'a lot of the people there exploited Pakie rather unscrupulously. The people who were in work paid, and the people who weren't in work didn't pay. . . I don't think she ever made a profit. . .because there were so many free-loaders about.' Kylie remembered a frequent visitor: Bea Miles, when she was young and lovely. So, as it happens, do I—but not at Pakies. When I was a schoolgirl catching a daily tram at the Darling Point stop in New South Head Road, Bea used to hop on and off the bonnets or running boards of cars along that stretch of main road, travelling only a short distance on each car. Most drivers (and there were comparatively few of them then) knew and tolerated her. She was, indeed, a splendid-looking young woman, nothing like the flabby wreck covered in sores and dirt that she became in later years.

Of Pakie, Kylie said to Meg Stewart: 'She was just herself, she was the most genuine person I could meet. She had great integrity. She never pretended, she was never anything other than she was, and she was able to create some kind of eye of the cyclone, of calm and constructive and creative peace, in the middle of all the turmoil that was going on around her.' The Pakie I remember was small and very energetic in her kitchen. She had slightly frizzy, or very wavy, grey-fair hair cut short. Her face was wrinkled by life and liveliness. She was not a person I ever confided in, but many people did; and although she was skilled in hearing what garrulous people had to say while she (as it were) was on the run, when she really did listen to someone she was as still and receptive as a deep pool.

The food was chiefly huge and delicious salads.

The obvious 'king' of Pakies in my day was James Meagher who kept his Friday night table of family and cronies in fascinated conversation, or shrieks of amusement, during dinner. To attain to James' table seemed to me like aspiring to Olympus. The first good friends I made at Pakies were John Duloy and Ray Simmons with his fiance, Barbara. John and Ray were scientists with the CSR company; and both, though perhaps more particularly John who was intensely musical, were keen to shed daytime pursuits and enjoy talk of art, writing and music after work. These friends introduced me to Chinese food. Once a month we had a table at the Nanking in Campbell Street, a restaurant run by a family of very tall, pale-skinned, handsome Chinese whose food was superb. I still wish I could find a restaurant among Sydney's or Melbourne's excellent Chinese establishments that can serve Duck in Five Courses (*not* Peking duck) in the manner of the Nanking.

It was John Duloy who subjected me to one of the most embarrassing experiences of my youth. He invited me to a Town Hall concert whose main work was to be Mahler's 'Song of the Earth'. We took our seats as the orchestra entered. John told me he was a republican and never stood for the customary rendition of God Save the King with which every Australian public performance, including picture shows, then began. Misguided loyalty to my host induced me to relinquish loyal respect to my monarch. Red-faced I sat beside John through what must have been only one verse but seemed to me like the entire interminable anthem. I loathed the 'Song of the Earth', and still cannot endure any composition by Mahler. These days, I too would prefer a republican form of government but I could no more sit through the national anthem than wish it changed in favour of tinkly *Waltzing Matilda* or dreary *Advance Australia Fair*.

John married a woman called Maisie and Ray married Barbara. I lost touch with John but Ray and Barbara remained friends for years. I kept falling in and out of love, often with men I met at Pakies, always hoping to meet my twin soul, who would be a writer with whom I could share writing ideas and to whom I could confide work-in-progress. I had my twin soul of course in Gertrude Scarlett and never did fall in love with a writer—for which I am now profoundly thankful, having seen too much of the jealousies and strains involved in many marriages of people closely engaged in similar pursuits. A few such marriages work marvellously; but most do not, or else one partner comes to overshadow the other—often to the artistic detriment of both.

In the *Bulletin* in October 1949 I published a poem called 'Old Men':

Old men

Today I have been thinking of very old men,
So old that death, standing just at their backs
Wears no disguise for them but is exactly
As each of them has come to think death looks.
I have been thinking of withered static bodies
Tattered end-papers guarding wonderful books

And it has appeared to me also that they resemble
Cities shrouded by a grey, sweeping rain;
They are simplified, they are like shapes reduced to angles,
The lowest common denominator of all they are and have been.
Dim trees in the park had that aspect this morning
Their colors even reduced, greyed down, not green;

Trees merely forms, as much of the city as mortar,
Bound to the streets or the spires by the sheets of rain,

Or like old men with a common cover of years,
Removing their age from their youth, making them wise
Or lending illusion of knowledge, making them seem
Marvellously sage. Old men blink tired eyes.

Move cracking lips with effort and hesitation
Muttering softly (dead leaves wash to the grass),
They discourse, not of today but of other time
While constantly that shadow which unnoticed stole
Behind each man, his final simplicity,
Waits the last wisdom, the merging of part with whole.

The following Friday night, at Pakies, James Meagher beckoned me to his table and said he hoped I would not be offended, but here was his reply:

Young girls

With all due respects to Nancy Keesing

Today I have been thinking of very young girls,
So young that their birth lying in front of their faces
wears a disguise for them that is partly
As each of them thought that birth ought to look.
I have been thinking of lively moving bodies,
Delicate covers adorning a commonplace book.

And it happened to be that they also resemble
Villages basking in sunshine, glittering gay:
They are so complex, all circles converting to squares;
The highest common factor of all that they are or will be.
Bright shrubs in the park had that aspect last evening,
Their colours even brighter made wine-like, not tea.

Shrubs merely forms, much less of the village than limestone
Bound to the lanes or the roofs by the glare of the sun.
Or like young girls half naked for wanting of years
Combining their youth with their age to make them seem fools,
Or shattering illusions of knowledge making them seem
Absurdly stupid. Young girls eyes wide as pools.

Move luscious lips with effortless ease
Call loudly (green leaves are bright on the boughs)
They scream not of memories but of time far ahead
While fitfully that image which briskly upstarts
Before each girl, her primal complexity,
Anticipates foolishness, the taking of whole from its parts.

James Meagher looked middle aged when he was young and also when he was old. (As did another friend, Walter Stone.) There is a good deal to be said for premature white hair. Meagher was a Dubliner, a friend of James Joyce, who in the 1920s had come to Sydney and established a flourishing law practice from offices in Liverpool Street, near the Court of Petty Sessions. A good deal, and perhaps the best-paying part of James Meagher's practice, was among criminals—he was Tilly Devine's lawyer. But he also was the lawyer of countless respectable businesses and businessmen and of cultural societies such as the English Association and May Hollinworth's Metropolitan Theatre. He was a great Latinist, and translator of latin poets.

He was the first absolutely civilised man of my acquaintance. I have recently learned that some of the tales he spun, and that he said happened in Sydney, are a part of Irish lore; but he was so compelling I never doubted him in life, and wholeheartedly now forgive him for allowable deceptions in the cause of conversational art. He was immensely kind and had a collection of clients for whom he acted for no fee. In essential matters people, even people as unworldly as my father, trusted James in quite extraordinary ways. On one occasion, later on, my father (correctly for once) decided that an American friend of mine was a crook. He consulted James and James, in less time than it takes to tell, confronted the offender, scared him stiff, and put him on a plane back to his own country. He was a great friend for a gullible girl to have in her background.

Often his wife Angela, son John and daughter Margaret (then a schoolgirl) came to Pakies with him for dinner. He was not kind to Angela who was, admittedly, a difficult woman, but far from as tiresome and foolish as he sometimes made her seem in front of other people. She was from Glasgow and spoke with a thick Glaswegian accent. Sometimes her sister joined the group, a nice woman who gave the Meagher children support and security. James was Catholic but not as pious as the women of his family, whom he teased, amusingly as I thought then. Now I am less sure. I cannot recall most of the talk we enjoyed, the frothy or serious give and take. I value James' memory as much for the people I met through him as for what once seemed the most important acquaintance of a year or two. All the same, though I forgive Angela much and deplore much on her account, I cannot forgive her for burning a manuscript of James' life in Sydney that he left when he died. He wrote splendidly, published almost nothing while he lived, and has been cheated of what he meant to be his lasting memorial.

And so with James Meagher I attained a permanent seat on Olympus. But before I scale those heights I want to write of the closest friend I made at Pakies, Barbara Trollope.

Barbara was a granddaughter of Anthony Trollope and of Sir Edmund Blackett, the architect of some of this country's most beautiful nineteenth-century buildings. She was about some ten years my senior—a thin faced, vital, unconventional, amusing, immensely intelligent young woman and. . .a frail hunchback. There is really no substitute for the word 'gay' in its non-sexual meaning. Barbara was the gayest, gallantest girl I ever knew, and the most widely popular. She even managed to find drama and interest in her job as stenographer for a soft-drink manufacturer. She was a superb typist. Her employer was a sensitive man, and well before it became common to employ the 'handicapped' he was understanding when the constant pain which she tried not to acknowledge got the better of her.

Although I lived in town through the week I spent most weekends at Pennant Hills, and Barbara often came to us then. My mother loved Barbara, and she my mother.

Barbara lived in her parents' home at Asquith, not far by rail from Pennant Hills. Her parents were hard up; her own job was poorly paid; otherwise she would have preferred a flat of her own. The Asquith household was uncongenial to her. Mrs Trollope was a tall, proud, thin, handsome woman with a disapproving expression. Fortunately she had a son she was proud of, and satisfied with. Barbara's crippled state and raffish Pakies friends were an affront to her. Mr Trollope was a nice, small man but, by anyone's standards, a failure. In fact the Trollope baronetcy is a hereditary Norman one, but he did not use his title, and nor did his famous grandfather. Mr Trollope, as I was told, dropped Barbara when she was a baby, and crippled her for life.

His other terrible failure was a book, which he had written over many years, when he worked as a wool-classer on NSW properties. It was, I think, a sort of autobiography. It was massive, handwritten and he had kept no copy. Near the beginning of World War II he sent his manuscript to an English publisher; the ship carrying the parcel was sunk by enemy action. That was one of the things Barbara's mother did not let him forget. Barbara, 'Bar', was fond of her ineffectual father.

For a few years Bar was a sort of extra daughter in our home, and my mother a sort of surrogate one for her. They achieved this unlikely equilibrium by playing the game of You-Know-And-I-Know-What-We-Know-and-Prefer-To-Disregard. Dad, who seldom saw what was directly in front of him, simply accepted Barbara at her good actress's face value, but often found her presence and mannerisms (she was a giggler) irritating.

Mother was no fool, nor had she come down in the last shower of rain. She knew perfectly well that Barbara, denied marriage and motherhood by her physical handicap—which no one noticed as a rule, being too absorbed with her lively facial expressions, her gift of the gab, and her own refusal to acknowledge difference—was given to brief love affairs Mum could not approve. Moreover they were the kind of love affairs she feared I too might indulge in, and hoped I did not. My mother was far too loyal to me, and too loving, and perhaps too nervous of answers, to ask Bar directly about my city life and behaviour. But she would speak to Bar as to someone much nearer her own age and opinion than I was, which Bar was not. And this implied that Bar was far more sensible and able to moderate her emotional life than I was, which she also was not. They played their kind of game while I, on the sidelines, enjoyed their deliberate skirmishing at cross purposes.

Dad had by now retired from his profession early, and was growing increasingly out of touch with a changing world—one in which he was to live, half-blinkered, for another quarter of a century. He made a few good friends in Pennant Hills but they were not his intellectual equals and never challenged his statements. One of these friends was a young man whose mediocre intellect seemed outstanding to Dad. As so often with my father he had first met this man and his wife through their children. All children adored my father, and he adored most children.

The marriage was rocky, though Dad did not realise that. The man met Barbara at our house, began seeing her in town, and treated her with lies and great unfairness. For the first time in her life, she really believed she had a firm proposal of marriage from him—after he divorced his wife, which he said he would do. Then, during Barbara's inevitable winter bout of bronchitis, he dumped her most cruelly. My mother experienced a rare crisis because for once we told her all. Should she explain to my father and cause him to lose, not just a man friend, but a whole family of friends? Sexual misbehaviour was Dad's absolute anathema. And then, if Mum did tell him, he might well not wish Barbara ever to come to our house again. Yet if she said nothing, Dad was bound to chatter about Barbara's ex-lover, and thereby cause her terrible if unwitting pain. Finally Mother, Bar and I had a discussion, into which I was, for the first time, admitted as an equal by my mother. Barbara decided it was best to say nothing to my father, and nothing was said.

When Barbara died comparatively young, and mercifully before her afflictions made her vital ways of life impossible for her, my mother said 'She was a true lady'. No one can better that.

In 1949 I caught mumps. The tiresome childish disease kept me in bed at Pennant Hills for three weeks in great discomfort. The weather was hot and humid, my face and neck swelled till I looked for all the world like a well-known caricature of Louis Phillipe depicted as a pear. My mother produced strips of old sheets to support my sore and wobbling chins. Exuding sweat and frustration I must have been an infuriating patient.

After I was pronounced cured and not infectious, quite stupidly I persisted in believing I looked like a freak and would not go out of doors. The first appointment I simply had to keep was with Beatrice Davis at Angus and Robertson. On my way along Castlereagh Street a street photographer snapped me—the print was reassuring.

From childhood I had been familiar with Angus and Robertson's cavernous shop and lending library. That day for the first time I climbed a wooden staircase to the gallery floor of the editorial department where my friend Rosemary Dobson had worked for some years, and was introduced to Nan McDonald whose fine poetry I'd long admired in the *Bulletin*. I already knew Beatrice Davis slightly, at the English Association. I recall, because of the mumps, feeling particularly clod-hopperish beside Beatrice who is small, dainty, graceful and very pretty. My unease was compounded by nervousness—the manuscript of my first book of poems lay between us on her table. Like almost every editor before or since, to every young poet, Beatrice spoke of hard times in publishing and the problems of publishing verse...

A few days later Beatrice phoned to say Angus and Robertson would publish the book if the Commonwealth Literary Fund would agree to subsidise it. Douglas Stewart had selected most of the book's contents for *Bulletin* publication. He thought well of my poetry. I was optimistic.

After a few weeks Douglas asked me to see him in his office. Bad news. The CLF had enlisted an outside reader for an opinion, and the opinion was that the book ought certainly to be published, but as it might be expected to return its costs a subsidy was not recommended. Doug was disappointed too, for he was convinced Beatrice would not change her mind. He had, however, a constructive suggestion: I should get in touch with Roland Robinson and see if the new cooperative venture, Lyre Bird Writers, would consider publishing the poems. He had only a cursory idea of how the cooperative functioned, but Roland would explain. I admired Roland's *Bulletin* poetry. We had not met. 'An odd fellow,' said Stewart, 'but a real poet'.

Leonine Roland with a mane of tawny hair sat in the studio deck chair, hands clamped to his knees and looked at me intently from beneath massive eyebrows. He had a pleasant voice but a truculent turn of phrase, and a suspicious, needling manner. He had read my poetry. He would allow that, objectively, it was quite good of its kind, and up to standard for Lyre Bird Writers; but for his own taste he did not care for that sort of verse. However, with Stewart's recommendation he was prepared to discuss publication. He seemed to dislike me and I was ready to return the compliment. Lyre Bird Writers, Roland explained, had been founded by himself, Nancy Cato and Kevin Collopy. Each had put in an amount (£10 I think) sufficient to publish one book. Roland's *Language of the Sand* (a paperback) had appeared. Collopy had withdrawn, and his poems *The*

Splendid Hour were published by the Australian War Memorial in 1951. So the next Lyre Bird publication was to be Nancy Cato's *The Darkened Window*, due out soon. Nancy had wished to design her own book in a hard cover decorated with motifs from Aboriginal art and had contributed the extra money necessary to produce it. In principle, however, the scheme was that each new book would be published when its predecessor returned its cost. The time of waiting for Cato's book to replenish the original kitty seemed impossible to calculate and likely to be some months, so I asked whether I could contribute sufficient money to allow earlier publication for my manuscript. Roland said yes, provided Nancy Cato agreed. So began a long series of letters beginning 'Dear Nancy' and ending 'Love Nancy' between Sydney and Hope Valley in South Australia, and a long friendship. The two Nancys have occasionally been mistaken for each other—I am not the successful novelist she has become.

Norman Lindsay, because of his close friendship with the Stewarts and his interest in new literary projects, offered to draw a pen-and-ink frontispiece for my book. This was long before I met Norman. The naked girl, asleep beneath a tree, that illustrates the title poem, 'Imminent Summer', is not my likeness. The frontispiece was not a favour to me, but to Lyre Bird Writers; it was Lindsay's generous way of lending support to a new venture that he approved of. (Because of its Norman Lindsay frontispiece that small book *Imminent Summer*, when it appears in secondhand catalogues, has a price out of all proportion to comparable publications.)

It has always seemed to me that Lyre Bird Writers remains a good model for modest cooperative publishing. If its original scheme was followed without modification no one could lose more money than their original contribution. We made it adaptable to suit our needs. Each successive title we published benefited those published earlier, because it made the venture more widely known through reviews and other publicity and because collectors wanted whole sets. Its success depended on a good deal of hard work by those concerned; it was very much a venture for people with time and enthusiasm. Had we been more experienced we could, perhaps, have costed our books to repay us at least in part for our time, but that did not occur to us in our inexperienced youth.

2a Bond Street became the virtual distribution centre for Lyre Bird books. Perhaps in those days envelopes that fitted odd-sized articles were not procurable, or maybe were too expensive. I (and later Ray Mathew) wrapped endless slim vols with paper and string, and kept records. Obviously Nancy Cato in distant South Australia could help only with publicity and support in other ways. My efforts as a packer were quite enjoyable. For one thing often I had to visit Edwards & Shaw, who printed and designed the books so well, to pick up stock from their printery in Sussex Street. There was always good talk there with saturnine

Dick Edwards and Rod Shaw, whose teasing took me some time to come to terms with. I liked walking along the 'Dukely' streets—Clarence, Kent and Sussex. They can still reveal Sydney's origins, but there were more old buildings standing then and none of them had been tarted up as shops and showrooms let alone restaurants and liquor stores. When I read Leicester Cotton's *The Sydney Assassins/A Mid Victorian Mystery* (Lansdown 1964) I felt sure the building from which the killer rowed his victims to death was the Edwards & Shaw one, for it had once stood on the waterfront of Darling Harbour. I tried, in a desultory way, to confirm this—Edwards & Shaw could not help and I was not inclined to undertake detailed research so I let the matter rest. Some things about a much loved city ought to be true, and should be taken on trust.

Roland's great contribution to the Lyre Bird venture was in arranging publicity—chiefly readings from the books. He enlisted a well-known elocution teacher, Grace Stafford, who several times lent her rooms for these events. Once Ruth Cracknell was a reader; she is one of a handful of professional actors who is able to read poetry superbly. Roland is a magnificent reader of poetry, his own and other people's. New young poets were keen to join and share in the work. No doubt the CLF would have continued to subsidise at least some projected books—but each man kills the thing he loves, and Roland killed his Lyre Bird.

The bank books and records were in his name. The bank manager very understandably found Lyre Bird's ad hoc and casual arrangements unsatisfactory, especially after the concern reached a point where transactions were frequent and sums of money, comparatively small but regular, were being deposited or paid out.

The bank's requirements were perfectly usual ones: we should have a constitution, a regular annual meeting, audited accounts, and office bearers properly authorised to sign for using the accounts. Roland, a convinced anti-capitalist, would not agree to any such repugnant procedures. Nor would he yield *his* dream, in the shape of those bank books, to anyone else. Perhaps Ray Mathew and I could have been more persuasive or persistent. But after some three years we were somewhat sick of being storemen and packers. So the venture ended, though it was never officially wound up. Roland changed his address and for years thereafter the bank would contact me to point out that their annual charges were depleting the amounts deposited. Once, when Ray Mathew in London was hard-up, I tried to persuade Roland to at least take steps to wind the thing up and get what money remained to Ray, but he would not be persuaded.

Some twenty years later my husband Mark and I were invited by a young poet called Patrick McKee Wright to a poetry reading in a Balmain waterfront garden. I'd met him at an Adelaide Festival Writers'

Week. We were told to bring something to drink, and took along a couple of bottles of beer. In fact we never did have our beer because we hadn't thought of an opener, and no one in that wine-drinking household could find one that tackled a crown seal. Not that we thirsted—the poets and their friends were generous in sharing the wine they'd provided for themselves. Mark and I sat on a sea wall, with our feet just above the harbour. It was a hot night. I kicked off my sandals and dabbled my feet in the rising tide, listening to poetry while small fish gently nibbled my toes. After the readings several young poets complained, in the immemorial way of young poets, about the difficulties of finding publishers for their slim vols, the unreasonableness of the CLF and so on and forth. At last I said that the price of the wine consumed that evening would have paid for at least one, perhaps two, slim vols. Why, I asked could not something akin to Lyre Bird Writers be established? *The Flagon Press* would, I suggested, be a splendid name for it.

I don't think my idea bore books, but in justice to Balmain poets many of them did, and do, combine to publish one way and another. The incident is recorded rather differently by Frank Moorhouse in *Days of Wine and Rage*: 'Nancy Keesing, when chairperson of the Literature Board, once visited a reading, looked around and said, "What they're spending on alcohol and drugs would publish a dozen books." ' It was, in fact, long *before* I was Chairman of the Literature Board and I can only hope I did not sound so patronising as Frank suggests.

Until some time in the sixties most women, young and old, wore hats and gloves not only for formal daytime occasions but when they 'went to town' to work, to shop, or for a lunch date or theatre. Milliners' shops were as ubiquitous as, today, are shops selling handbags. (Who ever *does* buy the hundreds of thousands of handbags on display in Australia?) Women of my mother's generation clung to their hats and gloves long after the rest of us abandoned them. In picture shows considerate women without being asked to do so removed their head-gear in order not to impede the view of those sitting behind them. Truly rude women declined to take off their hats even when politely requested by those at their backs. I remember my last hat very well—it was of green silk and my friend and neighbour Ruth Dircks and I shared it when either of us had to attend a funeral, or other rare event where hats were still in order. Perhaps the burgeoning of suburban shopping centres and car-driving housewives played some part in the demise of the hat. How to account for a current renaissance of hats I do not know, but I never see gloved hands these days unless the weather is cold.

It is, then, a minor mystification that when people recall Miles Franklin they often remark that she wore a hat. Kylie Tennant writes in

The Missing Heir (1986): 'I met Miles Franklin. "You interest me," the little bird-like lady in a large hat told me. She had big flashing brown eyes.' In 1963, in a letter to *Nation* Jill Hellyer wrote of Miles as 'a small gentle person who sat near the back at meetings of the Fellowship of Australian Writers in her rose-trimmed hats'.

Perhaps an awareness of Miles's hats is to some extent a measure of her energy, and of the fact that most of us who knew her (at least by sight) saw her chiefly at meetings. By contrast Mary Gilmore wore a hat when she went out (as many photographs of her prove) but I, and other people of that time, chiefly visited her at home in her flat and remember her white, fine hair. Douglas Stewart in *Writers of The Bulletin* (ABC 1977) tells how 'once Miles Franklin brought Mary Gilmore in [to his office] for some mysterious purpose, two grand old ladies like high priestesses of the Australian religion'.

Norman Lindsay in *Bohemians of the Bulletin* wrote:

> I met Miles Franklin only once in the early days and that in one brief and glorious vision of young girl. . . *My Brilliant Career* had just been published and we were all reading it, and lavishing appreciation on it.
>
> She was very short, but pleasingly plump, and she wore a large flowered hat, a summery ankle-length frock, and a superb mass of black hair in a cascade that reached her pert rump, to match a pert nose with fine eyes and arched black eyebrows, and an alluring pair of lips.

The most remarkable literary hats were worn by Ethel Anderson who was very deaf and carried a silver ear trumpet into which a person speaking to her was invited to shout. The ear trumpet's stem was always decorated to match the trimmings of the hat of the day. If the hat was decorated with pleated magenta and pink ribbons, so was the trumpet, or both might sport flowers, or a feathered circlet. I think I was only once invited to 'converse' with Mrs Anderson at a luncheon at the Lyceum Club, but I saw her several times and watched her with interest from afar because she was a writer I did, and do, admire greatly.

But Miles Franklin. . . I too had seen her from time to time at writers' gatherings, but had never met her. I did not greatly care for her writing, either as herself or as the rumbustious Brent of Bin Bin, and what I knew of or heard about her scared me stiff—she always *sounded* so redoubtable, despite her usually gentle appearance and demeanour. So many half mysteries (such as the silly Brent of Bin Bin personification) seemed to surround her.

Then, not long after my first book *Imminent Summer* appeared in 1951 and while the affairs of Lyre Bird Writers were still my dominant interest, Rex Ingamells, who then lived in Victoria, visited Sydney. Since 1949, when R. G. Howarth was its editor, poems of mine had appeared in the annual Jindyworobak anthology whose pages (and editors) were not limited to poets who necessarily belonged to the Jindyworobak movement, or subscribed to its ideas and ideals. I was no Jindyworobak, a fact that Roland Robinson frequently and forthrightly deplored. Roland had an immense admiration for Ingamells and a real friendship with him. Ingamells and I at this time, and on one of his later visits to Sydney, had fairly long talks. I tried to enlist his help in persuading Roland to see sense in the bank's requirements to formalise Lyre Bird Writers. At another time Rex confided to me his anxiety about Roland's somewhat chaotic personal affairs, chiefly because he very much deplored the unhappiness Roland sometimes caused others. Roland once told me that Rex was his good influence in many ways. Rex died untimely in 1955 in a car accident and was mourned for reasons often unconnected with nationalistic poetry. He was a kind, clear-sighted man and I am sure that, had he lived, several personal disasters among people in the poetry world, and at least one appalling marriage and its sequel, might have been avoided, or at least ameliorated.

My first real acquaintance with Rex came about on an evening when he and Roland were to visit Miles Franklin at her house in the southern suburb of Carlton. They discussed the arrangements at my studio where we had met to talk about Lyre Bird affairs. Rex thought it absurd that I had never met Miles. I demurred and probably aired a few of my ill-informed opinions of Miles' life and work which Rex, rightly, pooh-poohed. We had a quick Repins sandwich and then set forth in an electric train rattling through a very wet and cold night. I felt distinctly a second-class citizen while the lords of nationalistic poetry discoursed on arcane Jindyworobak matters.

Miles lived several wet streets away from Carlton station at 26 Grey Street, a small brick Victorian cottage. Roland and Rex dashed up the front pathway to the two or three steps that led to a tiny front verandah cum porch. I, increasingly aware of being superfluous as well as uninvited, stood behind them as one of them rang the bell, and both greeted our tiny hostess with enthusiasm. My background presence was then explained and she exclaimed: 'But why are you standing half in the rain?' She added the warmest of welcomes. An irresistible woman. I became very embarrassed because she turned on Rex and Roland, gave them a lecture about their bad manners and ordained that her hallway was too small to accommodate three wet persons wishing to remove their coats and dry off a little. She said the men could manage on the verandah, pulled me inside, and shut the front door behind me. She darted off somewhere for a towel, and insisted I unpin my long hair (which I wore in a chignon) and dry it. She led me into her small, warm living room, darted back to the front door to admit Rex and Roland to the hall, and told them to stay there till she called them. She reappeared. While I towelled, combed and re-pinned my hair she gave me a lecture I have never forgotten.

She seemed to know quite a lot about Lyre Bird writers and accused me of being a doormat. She'd noticed me on a few occasions, she said, and deplored my shyness and lack of confidence. 'You'll overcome *that*, but you must *never* be a doormat!'

When Rex and Roland were allowed into the living room she deferred her talk with them while she showed me some of her treasures. I chiefly remember, on her mantelpiece, straight-sided jars containing layers of variously coloured earth that she had collected or that friends had given her from different areas of Australia. They made colourful and beautiful decorations and glowed with a passion beyond electric light.

Supper was formal. There was tea in a fine service, delicate bone china cups, saucers and plates, sandwiches, biscuits, an iced cake. Before Miles poured tea she explained her ceremony for her first-time visitors. The cup that was to be mine was the Waratah Cup. It was a fine Doulton cup decorated with a waratah. It was, said Miles, a prototype. I cannot remember how or where she had acquired it, but for its beauty and symbolism it was her great treasure. Later she asked me to write briefly in her Waratah Cup book—everyone who was so honoured did so. When I opened its pages a galaxy of fame confronted me. She sensed that I was about to protest my unworthiness. 'Remember what I said to you,' her brown eyes glared. So I found something to write and then sipped my tea, without tasting it, in a condition of sheer fright. How awful to drop the Waratah Cup that I held tight in literally trembling fingers.

After that Miles and I met sometimes. I was now disposed to read her early books, particularly *My Brilliant Career*, with more sympathy than I'd accorded them before. All the same I think the film of *My Brilliant Career* was a rare instance of a movie being far better than its book in almost every way. At its preview Beatrice Davis said, 'Miles would have loved it.' Beatrice had a long editorial association with Miles and had much of her confidence so she may have been right—I felt less certain. In truth I do not find her style of writing congenial, but as to Miles as a person, I almost loved her. Her conversation was fun. Occasionally she wrote a note to me: one I recall was when the *Bulletin* published 'Because of the Rusillah' by Mena Abdullah and Ray Mathew and Miles wrote a few lines to share her delight.

Miles died in September 1954. Her best-kept secret was her will, the details of which did not become public until 1957. Colin Roderick in *Miles Franklin/Her Brilliant Career* (Rigby 1982) wrote: 'Literary circles learned with astonishment that she had made provision for an annual award...to be made to the novel of the year which the panel of judges considered of the highest literary merit of all works entered... The winning novel must present Australian life in any of its phases.' Miles Franklin had herself nominated the first judges: Beatrice Davis, then fiction editor, and Colin Roderick, then education editor, of Angus and Robertson; her accountant and friend George Williams, who was intended to represent 'the man in the street'; Ian Mudie, poet and historian of South Australia; and the Mitchell Librarian 'for the time being,' notes Colin Roderick, 'to ensure that books entered fulfilled the relevant conditions of her will'. Not the least part of the surprise felt, when the Award was announced, was a general realisation of the determination and frugality that must have been necessary for the saving of so generous a sum for so generous a purpose.

In 1963, nine years after her death, Angus and Robertson published her book *Childhood at Brindabella* which she wrote towards the end of her life, in her seventies. Thelma Forshaw not only rubbished the book in a 'review' printed in *Nation* in October 1963 but slammed into Miles too, speaking of 'the truculence that was her trademark'. Thelma Forshaw then made an extraordinarily inappropriate comparison with the work of Colette. I quote from this peculiar, perhaps malicious review because it prompted three letters that between them give a good picture of Miles:

> I recall reading many years ago the young and bitter howl of *My Brilliant Career*. Even then, it seemed to me like the roar of that greatest of all egoists—the spoilt baby. Miles obviously felt she was not getting the attention due to her. And the adored pampered infancy she recounts in *Childhood at Brindabella* makes clear how Australia's indifference and lethargy must have shocked her when she emerged from the familial hothouse into its harsh, impartial weather. Australia failed to dote to hear the imperious voice of 'genius' in the utterance of the family pet.
>
> I remember seeing her at a meeting of the Fellowship of Australian Writers some twenty-two years ago. . . The long, truculent upper lip, the scorn for makeup and dress, the earnest, dominating voice propounding—such an aggressively unvarnished personality I found forbidding. A little artifice would have helped humanise her. Still, she conceals more effectively than any artifices. Only the inveterate crossness of tone, the assumption of infallibility points to a something concealed—the thorn in the lion's paw.
>
> A primitive, she writes like a young self-educated coal miner. Polish is for sissies. Artificing for phonies. Miles would have scorned both. . . She shares with D. H. Lawrence a remarkably similar cantankerousness and naivete. *Childhood at Brindabella*, by its subject and by its hymn of praise invites comparison with Colette's *My Mother's House*, but if art is artifice, Colette wins hands down. While photographs are employed to give body to the people Miles Franklin has only pressed between her pages like flowers, one feels that photographs could only have destroyed the magic of the world Colette summoned to life with her pen.
>
> In the end, there is nothing so revelatory as letting people speak for

themselves. It is what Miles Franklin dared not do, and, while loyalty and dignity are admirable in a person, it takes a greater art than she had to make them serve a writer as triumphantly as they served Colette.

The letters that followed on 24th August and 7th September 1963 were from Anne Rodaway who wrote, in part:

> We must accept life as it is and comes to people—and it was brave of Miles to write and give us ten years of hers. In the preface, the publishers note—there is a charming picture of her:
>> 'What a shy, wild creature Miles Franklin was for all her outspokenness, slight, breathless, her quick utterances flying away from her like birds, and her brown eyes, even while they sparkled with vivacity, glancing this way and that all the time like birds on the watch for a hawk.
>
> How well the writer sums up Miles Franklin—and here she is—being attacked by the hawks. She did well to be afraid—spite has sharp claws.'

And also from Dal Stivens, who said:

> I read Thelma Forshaw's description of Miles Franklin in 1941—'the long, truculent upper lip, the scorn for makeup and dress, the earnest, dominating voice propounding—such an aggressively unvarnished personality I found forbidding' and I did not recognise the Miles that I knew and loved. It's a pity Thelma Forshaw did not see more of her. She was shy, gentle, generous. True, she was a feminist. But she was never a battleaxe. She used an Italian rapier.

And finally from Jill Hellyer, who wrote:

> May I add my protest to those of others in regard to Thelma Forshaw's description of Miles Franklin? I can only hope that those who did not know her personally were not impressed by this distorted vision. I remember her as a small, gentle person who sat near the back at meetings of the Fellowship of Australian Writers in her rose-trimmed hats. She carried out many kindnesses to friends in the most retiring and unobtrusive manner.
>
> Her reticence to speak in public at all was brought to light on one occasion when she was requested to move a vote of thanks. There was gleam of humour in her eyes as she told the president with gentle emphasis: 'Young man I don't know who you are, but you evidently don't know that I never stand up and speak in public.' However, she did move that vote of thanks most charmingly.

In his book *Knockers* (Cassell, 1972) Keith Dunstan describes many of the most celebrated 'knocking' events and reviews in our literary history. Early twentieth century victims include Shaw Neilson, Henry Lawson and D. H. Lawrence. Dunstan discusses—often with quotation—some of the notorious early and wrong-headed reviews of Patrick White's novels *The Tree of Man* and *Voss*.

Some writers disregard poor and/or unfair reviews; others are distressed and even damaged by them. Some people believe that adverse reviews lead to poor sales of books and, conversely, that appreciative reviews sell books. Both views are debatable. One thing is certain. Down the perspective of time the good writer and fine work triumphs over knockers, inept reviews, and reviewers who display apparent malice.

Thelma Forshaw (in her article quoted in this chapter and also in an article quoted by Dunstan in which she slams Germaine Greer and *The Female Eunuch*) and reviewers akin to her are the real losers.

As my chapter shows and as Dunstan also makes plain, unfair attacks attract hot defences. Many wrongly denigrated authors and their works benefit greatly, and often very quickly, from the publicity generated by episodes like this.

VI

Saints of Sorts

WHEN I gained my Diploma of Social Work from Sydeny University I had no settled idea about a job. I was certain I did not wish to embark on the additional year's study needed to qualify either as a Psychiatric or Medical Social Worker. I intended to apply for a job in the Child Welfare Department eventually, but had to wait to do so until the end of 1948, when I would be twenty-five. Meanwhile Anne Priestley, my Brisbane friend and fellow graduate, asked me to stay with her family over Christmas and into the New Year, so I shelved decisions. Soon, though, I'd have to earn some income. I was also eager to use my new skills.

Early in March 1947 Norma Parker, head of the School of Social Work, phoned to ask me a favour. She was already one of my favourite people so my agreement was taken almost for granted, and I did not quail when in her quiet voice she straightforwardly elaborated. Anyway the job she described was only 'temporary'—say for two or three months.

Stella Davies, the Almoner at the Children's Hospital—medical social work departments were then still called Almoner Departments—urgently needed an assistant until she could engage a fully qualified person to replace a long-time second almoner who had now left to be head of her 'own' department elsewhere. Miss Davies had engaged two people since then, Norma explained; one had lasted no more than a few weeks and her successor had resigned after four months. The trouble, said Norma diplomatically, was that many recent graduates found it difficult to submit to Stella's 'settled' ideas and methods. As I continued to listen, Norma became unequivocal: few social workers could relate to Stella or her famous terrible temper. 'Yet,' said Norma warmly, 'she *is* nice, she *is* good, people who *can* relate to her think the world of her, and it's an important hospital, which simply can't afford to be in such a difficulty. What's more, you'll learn a lot.'

I had not met Stella Davies but I had heard about her notorious bad temper and her rudeness from fellow students who had suffered periods of practical work under her supervision. Well, I thought, for three years I'd worked for the Department of the Navy on Garden Island and my boss was the world's worst tempered and rudest man. We'd ended up as great friends. I felt sure I could cope with the world's rudest and worst tempered woman. I told Norma I'd agree at least to an interview with the dragon, but with no firm commitment.

Miss Davies was little and frail and gently spoken. Her eyes were blue, but faded and slightly rheumy in late middle age. She wore her dusty-half-grey brown hair in a very sparse bun and wisps of it flew around her head. She had a sweet smile that was pathetic because so uncertain—as if she were not sure I'd accept her smile. She wore a shapeless linen uniform, understarched and rubbed thin, over a nice but obviously old teal blue jumper and skirt. Her shoes were worn to the shape of her feet but once they'd been expensive, I thought. Her hands were wrinkled and fleshless, rather like bird's claws. She spoke softly with an Anglo-Australian accent a little more Anglo than Australian; her voice sounded tired.

She explained what my share of the work would be. She said until I found my feet she'd make sure no medical problems of a kind that I was untrained to tackle would reach my desk. I'd have to provide myself with two white uniforms, but the hospital would launder them. She questioned me about my family, my home, my friends, my hopes—and before her intent gaze, and swift smile, I somehow found myself revealing a current love affair with a man who lived in another city that I had previously discussed with no one and had certainly not intended to confide to a stranger.

But, she said, if the man was coming to Sydney in a week or so, surely I'd want some time with him. Well, yes, for his impending visit was one of my reasons for not seeking a job until the end of March. Oh, she said, this *must* be arranged; it *can* be managed. Her air of harrassed certainty made me want to hug her warmly and say: 'No, no. I couldn't let you down.' I would learn that to Stella almost nothing was as important as love.

Stella's carefully preserved navy blue Morris was the joke of the Hospital and the wider Social Work world. She drove confidently, competently and slowly, yet dreadfully because she paid no heed to the huge increase in road traffic in the era of euphoric prosperity that followed World War II. Nor did she properly comprehend the consequent difficulties of modern city parking.

She would arrive for an evening meeting in, say, a building at the corner of Martin Place and Pitt Street. For countless years she had driven to meetings in that building and parked at, or nearby, its front door. Now, aggrieved and frustrated, she was compelled to drive around several blocks seeking a parking spot that was often some distance from where she wished to go; say half way along Phillip Street in the block between King Street and Martin Place. Dramas began when she left her meeting to go home. She knew exactly where the car was—half way along Elizabeth Street in the block between King Street and Martin Place. But no shabby little blue Morris was there. Damn and blast (her favourite expletives): her foes, 'those joyriders', had been at it again.

In those days policemen on the beat were plentiful in city streets and she'd find a cop without trouble. The city police by now knew Stella.

'Probably joyriders again, Miss Davies. I'll come with you and we'll see if we can find the car.' It was not difficult as a rule because her memory of the East-West roads concerned was usually correct, and all they had to do was discover the cross-way of the grid. So there was the Morris in Phillip Street.

'Oh, thank you very much constable.'

'No trouble Miss D.'

'Fancy stealing a car just to drive around a couple of blocks. It doesn't even go fast.'

'Makes you wonder don't it Miss D. Hopeless for a getaway vehicle or anything like that.'

'What is the world coming to?' in practised unison.

One morning an officious young constable driving a newly introduced patrol car noticed Stella as she drove across the Harbour Bridge from Cremorne where she lived. She would, as usual have been sitting grimly upright, her hat lopsided at a queer angle to keep the morning sun out of her eyes, her gloved hands holding the wheel firmly in case the Morris should display some improbable will of its own. She attracted the constable's attention when she wove across following traffic, as if no car but hers was on the road, so as to reach an exit that would lead her, by her accustomed maze of back streets, to Pyrmont Bridge Road. Sydney's back streets were a book to Stella.

Where that fish cafe had just opened, the Slattery family lived in '29, 1929, that is. She'd never forget the day five Slattery children were admitted to the hospital, all with diphtheria, or the night that followed after which three of them would live, or the funeral of the other two at which grieving Slattery turned up drunk and hung a shiner on one of his wife's tear-swollen eyes. She'd driven them both—not in this *new* car, but its Ford predecessor—back to the Hospital and wangled coffee and a hot meal for them, and got Slattery bedded down to sleep it all off on the back porch of the old laundry, and... My goodness! There's Betsy McGloin as large a life and not a day different from when she was eleven except she is now presumably the mother of those two lovely children. So she slowed down and honked her horn and Betsy waved with her 'good' hand—the other had to be amputated after that dreadful scald, when she was nine and had been left alone in the house in charge of the baby.

Stella did not notice the new patrol officer who had kept on her tail all this time. He was now convinced that, early morning notwithstanding, the old girl was drunk as Chloe. He decided not to pull her over until he saw a space where she could stop safely. Never know what the silly old chook would do if he gave her a fright.

Before he could act she turned abruptly into a side entrance of the Children's Hospital. He followed her down the drive and, by a side track, across a grassed area past one wooden building to the back of another. She parked there and got out of her car. He loomed at her side. 'See your licence lady, please.'

While, rather puzzled, she worked the clasp of her handbag Miss Flew, one of the younger physiotherapists, dashed down from the verandah of the building: 'Oh Miss Davies, I've been watching out for you. Could you spare a moment for. . .?' 'Sorry, didn't realise you were. . . Is everything all *right* Miss Davies. . . Can I. . .?'

'Of *course* everything's all right,' said Stella a bit snappishly because she was fumbling to extract her licence from her wallet without first taking off her gloves. 'This young man wishes to see my licence. He has, of course, every right to do so. Would you be so good, dear, as to tell Kath Kitchin that I may be a few minutes late for my first appointment.'

Just as she got hold of the licence, Dr McSwingle or rather *Mr* McSwingle (Stella was most particular about the correct titles for surgeons) who was the Senior Honorary Surgeon—and looked exactly like his celebrated caricature by Wep—came along the pathway at the head of a group of students who, in deference to the great man all looked suitably grave, important and pompous. The great man boomed: '*Good* morning Miss Davies. So glad to see you. Could you spare ten minutes after ten o'clock, dear lady, to discuss the final arrangements for. . .'

As he explained, the constable drew back discreetly to the cover of the patrol car, and was thankful for a few minutes to revise what he'd intended to say. When McSwingle and entourage processed onwards to Isolation, the constable came forward. This time he touched his cap. He glanced at the licence and handed it back. 'I followed you through town, ma'am because I, er, thought, er, your near front tyre looked a bit, you know, like worn. But I can see now that it is quite OK.'

Stella took back her licence, gave him a winsome smile, thanked him for taking so much trouble and asked:

'Is your name by any chance Bransom?'

'Why, yes.'

'I thought so. I never forget a face. You are the spitting image of a lad called Fred Bransom who used to work here in the boiler room.'

'My father, ma'am.'

She and the constable chatted for five minutes, long enough for her to catch up with the life history of Fred Bransom and send him her good wishes. Then she waved Constable Bransom on his way. He started up his car in a thoroughly confused state of mind. Until now he'd have sworn he could spot 'em.

What triggers it? She arrived at the office looking exactly as usual, but a little late because she had made a home visit to the home of a polio

patient on the way. She talked amiably for a while with Kath, the head
steno-secretary, who had a folder of letters for signature. She complimen-
ted Beth (Kath's off-sider) on her altered hairstyle. She thanked me for a
vase of garden flowers atop the filing cabinets. From her corner desk she
phoned the Medical Superintendent, Dr Ratcliff: they had a longish
conversation at the end of which she laughed at some remark he made.
She interviewed a mother about a routine matter and noted some good
news about a baby's recovery.

She picked up her black fountain pen to make a note on a file. It had
run dry. She muttered 'damn and blast it' under her breath and filled the
pen. She sat forward to peruse some notes of interview with the parents of
newly referred patients.

'Damn and blast it to hell!' she exclaimed loudly and with conviction.
Kath missed a beat on her typewriter and looked at Beth. They both
glanced at me, in my corner, and looked relieved when the axe fell there.

'Please come here Miss Keesing.' Her tone was imperious. I stood beside her desk. 'Sit down, sit down,' she snapped. 'Not there, you're in my
light.' I moved the chair six inches.

'Now,' she said, pointing to a page on the file, 'can you explain this?'

'Oh yes, Miss Davies, I interviewed Baby Benson's mother the day
before yesterday. She was here for a good half hour and...but it's all
there in the record.' The record, dictated by me immediately after the
interview and typed by Beth, was clearly set out. She glanced at it
muttering. 'Will that girl *never* learn to spell.' She jabbed at 'disirable'.
Her pen spattered. 'Damn and blast it to hell' she exclaimed. I could see
Beth's plucked eyebrows disappearing towards her hairline—her mar-
tyred expression. Kath, who chiefly typed for Stella, and almost never
made a mistake, looked expressionless.

'Now Nancy. Please read this section here and explain to me
why...and how...and who said that? how...and when...'

I explained. She gave an exaggerated sigh of exasperation.

'Do you seriously stand there and tell me...?'

'No.' I could snap too. 'I'm not standing here. I'm sitting beside you
explaining as best I can about...'

'Oh, damn and blast you to hell,' she shrieked and blew her nose
furiously because her tantrums seemed always accompanied by a flow of
mucous. Her voice would choke at any moment.

'Good God!' she cried. If I can't get any sense in my own office I'll have
to speak to...' Through our ever open door and window we watched
as she dashed up the long path to the main building, clutching the
offending manilla folder, her white uniform billowing around her, a
pathetic, tiny figure. We saw her brush brusquely past a family, great
favourites of hers, who were walking downhill in our direction.

Kath, Beth and I exchanged shrugs but said nothing. The family arrived on the doorstep. 'Come in,' I called, 'Miss Davies signed all your papers. They're ready for you.'

'What was biting her?' asked the puzzled father, 'she never even had a word for the twins.'

'Oh dear,' I lied, 'she was in a frantic rush. Some crisis in Casualty, I believe.'

'Poor soul, she works too hard,' said the mother forgivingly. 'We shan't wait to take up her time when she's so busy; the twins can leave their parcels on her desk.' The twins, beloved ex-patients, placed two clumsy parcels, each with a hand painted card, on Stella's blotter. They looked dejected. Kath cheered them up with a choc bar apiece and a promise that Miss Davies would write to thank them for their presents. When the group left we shrugged our shoulders and sighed. The twins' disappointment, her rude behaviour to their parents on the pathway, would exacerbate Stella's invariable, inevitable remorse.

She returned to her desk in time for a busy orthopaedic follow-up clinic. Then she took herself off for a hot lunch in the dining room. I truthfully excused myself; Miss Flew and I had arranged to dash down to a Grace Bros sale at lunch time.

'Well get yourselves something to eat,' she grumbled, 'you girls can't work properly on empty tummies.'

At the end of a demanding afternoon when the last child on crutches and last baby in splints had gone home, she came across to my desk. 'I got all that settled,' she said, 'and on the whole you were quite right. But why didn't you *tell* me you'd discussed it so fully with Sister Hopkins?'

'It was all written up in my report, Stella.'

'Reports!' She blew her nose, and glanced at the clock, which showed some ten minutes short of five o'clock. To Kath she said: 'You girls put on your coats and be off. It's been a long day.' And to Beth, 'If you find a dictionary in your Christmas stocking it will be from me.' Laughter.

Next morning she stopped at a newsagents on her way to work to buy pretty cards for the twins. She asked me, 'Why do you stay on with a bad tempered old woman like me?'

'Goodness knows,' I replied. One day I could give her a small fraction of the answer, but it would not be complete because I could not imagine myself ever saying directly to Stella Davies: 'You're a great woman, I admire you enormously. I'd do practically anything for you. I think you are dreadfully under-appreciated and under-estimated in the Social Work profession, but I'm afraid that is chiefly because you are your own worst enemy.' Nor could I ever ask her: 'But Stella, what *triggers* it?'

To seek triggers for Stella's bouts of irritability was not the same thing as pondering their cause. Had one known what might bring on a bout of evil temper, one might have been able to avoid or avert it. Sometimes for weeks on end the office was peaceful, at least from her quarter, though our chronic overwork and inevitable crises did not abate. Then, perhaps twice or three times in a month she'd hit the roof with a vengeance. Beastly Sister Smith would say, with her sweetly sanctimonious smile, that Miss Davies was only fit to be certified. Miss Davies, though loathing Sister Smith, somehow took care never to overstep the further bounds of propriety and language in set-tos with her. In rational discussion she was usually calm and she could conduct a quite acrimonious ordinary disagreement with taste and reason, and be justifiably furious without becoming frenzied.

I'd worked for a year at the hospital. The job had extended into permanency. Then my twenty-fifth birthday came and went. I scarcely gave a thought to my erstwhile plan to join the Child Welfare Department, though with the experience I now had a successful application would have been certain. Nor had Stella, or the Hospital powers-that-be, given any obvious thought to my future after the agreed trial period of my 'temporary' employment. I simply stayed on and got a small increment to my meagre starting salary of £400 a year. Then two fully qualified medical social workers joined the Department. Stella was jubilant. 'See,' she said, 'you made a go of it and they can too.' They did. The department was reasonably harmonious and usually took her rages in its stride. Stella simply decreed that I was senior as to time of employment, but not as to qualifications, and that I should retain my corner in the front room while the newcomers had desks and files in a back room formerly used by Physiotherapy.

We were all still overworked because a polio epidemic filled not only the Polio Ward, but others too and lasted for a long time. Two of my school friends, both mothers of young families, were permanently and severely handicapped during that last appalling siege before Jonas Salk almost miraculously freed the world from the scourge poliomyelitis. I do not use the word 'miraculous' as a cliché. There *are* modern miracle workers and modern miracles. My parents worried about my working so close to such massive infection but I felt inviolable and, in the event, the worst illness I contracted at the Royal Alexandra Hospital for Children was, as I have mentioned, mumps.

Stella continued to argue with her staff and with Social Work students doing practical work at the Hospital, but gradually some of the heat dispersed. She, being honest, learned to respect good results from methods that she once despised though she never fully accepted newer ways. One of the basic problems between Stella and her staff was philosophical. She was English trained by some of the great social work 'saints' of the early twentieth century. But the mantle of 'sanctity' had shifted to America and by my day Australian training was chiefly based on American and Canadian models, theories and textbooks. Our casework philosophy, theory and training was 'non directive'—we hoped to steer our clients towards making their own decisions. Stella was frankly bossy. I'm not sure that results differed greatly.

Many of our clients, men and women, almost worshipped 'Miss Davies' though a few hated her; but the children concerned were her paramount concern. The term 'battered babies' had not been coined then and incest was a crime we scarcely heard of unless, perhaps, we worked for the Child Welfare Department, or as an occasional reason for closed Children's Courts in the country and outer suburbs. For one thing flagrant instances of child abuse were usually reported directly to the police by the medical staff, and thence to the Child Welfare Department.

All the same I now think I sometimes missed noticing obvious signals of abnormality and distress, whereas Stella must have saved the lives of countless battered babies. She would work, and counsel, as hard and best she knew the first time the parents of a suspiciously injured child were referred to her. After that, no quarter; she called the police. And after that the child was usually placed in the care of a children's home, perhaps, eventually to be fostered.

'But,' protested we, her younger, more recently trained colleagues, 'the family is *all*. Almost *any* child is better off in its own family, no matter how terrible the home life may be.'

'Nonsense,' snapped Stella in effect. 'Almost any child is better off alive than dead. Almost any parent is better off free than serving a sentence for murder.' First and last she was a realist.

Bill FitzHenry was a brown gnome emanating from the brown gloom of the *Bulletin* office whose floors were covered with brown linoleum, desks and counters were brown wood, and windows brown with city grime. He was the 'memory' of the office where he had worked since boyhood. Normally W. E. FitzHenry was the librarian and in the library had his neatly kept Cutler roll-top desk surrounded by shelves filled with brown, perhaps once red, bound volumes from the magazine's first issue in 1880. When a special number needed an article about *Bulletin* history Bill usually wrote it, and very well indeed.

Most of the office odd jobs, like making a first selection of the verse contributions and writing some of the weekly 'Answers to Correspondents' (a sometimes fearsome, sometimes funny substitute for rejection slips) and sending replies to idiot mail, fell to Bill who also often got the job of interviewing garrulous callers or more welcome visitors who dropped in at inopportune moments.

Most of Bill's roles and tasks could be picked up readily by other people when he disappeared on a drinking bout of a fortnight or so, as happened several times a year. He was the kind of alcoholic who, between bouts, maintained sobriety.

Bill had brown skin, hair and eyes and wore brown suits and shoes. He was of short stature, and both dignified and diffident. He wrote his copy by hand in distinctive, absolutely legible script. He had a pleasant voice and spoke in a deliberate way, enunciating carefully. He remembered most of the great early editors—Archibald, Edmond and Stephens—as well as most of the great early contributors and artists. However, unlike some office 'memories' he was interested in the present as well as the past.

Bill several times took me to evening gatherings at the Fellowship of Australian Writers which then had upstairs rooms in Clarence Street— and very bare rooms too, except for chairs. I was too polite to tell him I loathed the place, habituated as it seemed to me, by dreary has-beens or never-was-ers, swigging horrible sweet muscat from sticky, none-too-clean glasses. Every so often some ancient relic (like Will Lawson) would breeze in and most of the members would metaphorically go down on their knees and grovel.

I did not get to know my friend Walter Stone at Clarence Street. Walter later became President of the Fellowship, reformed it, and made it a much livelier organisation during the sixties. Until then some interesting people did belong to the Fellowship, I know, but I do not recall meeting many of them. I cannot remember what happened on those dreary evenings except that one was enlivened by a thief rushing up the stairs from the street, and grabbing the pitiful saucer of takings from the woman who always sat by the entrance. She wore her very thick brown hair in a splendid pair of plaits completely framing her head.

For Bill's sake I tried my best to exhibit the requisite fellowship, but I never officially joined the FAW. Years later I discovered that in Perth, Adelaide and Melbourne the Fellowship was, and had been during the forties and fifties, a quite different sort of organisation whose activities I would have enjoyed taking part in.

Bill was popular at Pennant Hills. My parents knew all about his 'failing' but he was careful never to fail in their presence, though once it was touch and go, for he was plainly set for a drinking bout and very nervous and unsettled. He held off the bottle in his overcoat pocket until he was safely, as it were, on the train back to Sydney; joining the train was the last he could remember of a lost fortnight.

One year he asked me to a New Year's Eve party. The evening began with a jollification at the Esperanto Society, somewhere in Milson's Point. It was a mere degree or so livelier than the Fellowship and I began to despair. My great uncle Maurice had been a pioneer of Esperanto. He also, in New Zealand, published some of the worst poetry the world has ever seen. I began to comprehend why Maurice Keesing was not much of a favourite with his generation of the family. However, before boredom became extreme we went on to a party given by the Halvorsen family who made me very welcome though I'm certain my arrival was not expected, and there I met Hilda Lane, niece of the Paraguayan settler William Lane, and daughter of his brother John, an early Labor activist. Bill often went to Hilda for a few days when he was convalescent from a drinking spell. Hilda was a splendid woman, handsome then, but in her youth she must have looked like a Valkyrie. Eventually she went to live in Toowoomba. She had a fund of fascinating recollections of the settlement at Paraguay, and of many Australian writers.

At the Halvorsen party I learned a facet of Norwegian/Australian history that fascinated me. The original man of the family who established the Sydney boat-building business was a Lars Halvorsen, or Lars son of Halvors. The firm took his name. His son was Halvors Larsen, Halvors son of Lars, and his son Lars Halvorsen again, at which point Norway for the first time decided that modern surnames would prevail, and everyone would keep the surname they bore when the decision was made. So the family remained 'Halvorsen' thereafter. I was too inhibited to ask these obvious proud Australians how or why they had kept the linguistic customs of Norway. I now realise they were an early model for a multi-lingual and multi-cultural society.

Bill put a few small writing jobs my way. Then he offered a large carrot to a willing but wholly ingenuous donkey. I was in the *Bulletin* office— or Doug Stewart's office more precisely—with an offering of poems. I noticed Bill lurking outside and when I emerged he invited me to the library. He was shakily recovering from a bout—thin, red-eyed, unhappy. He told me he realised he would never now complete, as he had hoped and expected, a history of the *Bulletin*. A major, sustained project was beyond him. He asked if I would take on the task, with every kind of help he could give. At the end of the building was a small, unused room that he was sure I could use, so as to be near the library.

Bill's suggestion was flattering and very tempting. It also forced me to try and sort out, in my own mind, what I really wanted to do with my life.

I was by now virtually second in command to Stella Davies, and the department was growing. Other fully qualified Medical Social Workers had joined it; and they, too, were finding it possible to cope with Stella. I could not expect formal promotion for which other people were qualified. I had been offered a job in Psychiatric Social Work, but that would entail an extra year's study. Another possibility was that with my basic Diploma I could take any one of a number of places available—and offers had been made.

But I also wanted to be a writer.

I confided my dilemma to Stella who still half-hoped I would qualify to succeed her; but she was immensely interested in my writing too. I also sought counsel from Diana Dupain, a Medical Social Worker in the department. She was the daughter of artists, her husband was Max Dupain the photographer and she understood the creative impulse. I spoke, also, to Una Gault, the psychologist at the hospital, and a good friend. Now at the hospital the 'in' method and word, as I have said, was 'non directive'. You never said directly (unless you were Stella who scorned theories): 'Mrs Smith, if you do not get away from that brothel and change your way of life, you'll be a syphilitic wreck in two years, and despite all our best efforts to help you keep the children, they will certainly be made wards of the state.' Instead you interviewed Mrs Smith for long periods and tried to find and describe to her 'respectable' work she might do—at the end of which process, according to received wisdom, she would see a way to her own rehabilitation, and suppose that it was all her own idea. In fact the system worked fairly well—at least as well as Stella's old-fashioned and bossy scaring of hell out of the Mrs Smiths who processed through our office.

So neither Diana nor Una would offer firm advice though they indicated I'd probably be wise to at least try a new direction. No one asked the obvious question that might have thrown me completely. 'What makes you think you're in any way equipped to tackle a history?'

Meanwhile Stella was characteristically direct. She talked over my problem with Dr Ratcliff, the Medical Superintendent, who sensibly suggested that if Miss Keesing cared to sacrifice one day's pay per week, and spent that day at the *Bulletin* office, he would wish her well and be interested to hear how she got on. I accepted his generous offer.

I spent each Monday in heaven, breathing the smell of the huge rolls of newsprint that took up every available foot of floor space in the *Bulletin*'s cavernous building, and listening to clattering typewriters from rooms nearby. From the ground floor the muted clatter of printing machines permeated when, rarely, the editorial floor was quiet. Doggedly I read old volumes of *Bulletin*s from 1880 on. I made copious notes. I gradually got to know some of the journalists who were mystified by my weekly appearance among them, and sceptical when they learned what my project was.

One Monday Douglas Stewart came into my room and perched on the table—its furniture was only that table and the ancient chair I used—and asked whether I'd agree to help him as I was, in any case, reading through early issues of the *Bulletin*. He explained that he had for a long time been saying, in print on the Red Page as well as in conversation, that an anthology of Bush Ballads should be compiled and published. His interest in the ballads had been aroused through the *Bulletin*'s association with this form of verse and the people who wrote it, and also because of his admiration for Banjo Paterson. Stewart had suggested to H. M. Green that he might take on the project; Green declined and Stewart then decided to do the job himself. He talked over the idea with Angus and Robertson and with their blessing, started on it.

Stewart's problem just then was that he had very little time for wide reading. Would I look out for suitable ballads? He did not think the project should too much interrupt my history research. If I could agree he would regard me as a collaborator and we could discuss formal arrangements, provided the scheme seemed worthwhile after a preliminary trial. Oh yes, yes and yes! This was the beginning of a friendship too, with Doug, Margaret and their daughter Meg.

So now, on Monday mornings after a weekend at Pennant Hills, my first port of call was 12 Bridge Street. Margaret Stewart, (the water colour painter Margaret Coen) was painting a series of flower arrangements and I brought into town huge bunches of flowers in season, and leaves and seeds, from Dad's wonderful garden. Often, when I arrived, Meg was listening to Kindergarten of the Air. One morning she was in floods of inconsolable tears—something she'd heard on that well-devised programme had seemed to her unspeakably sad. But what had she heard? She was not able to explain very well. Meg was, and is, the beautiful child of a beautiful mother. They are not alike except for their quality of serenity of expression: Margaret is a dark, Irish beauty with long, dark, straight hair drawn back to frame her oval face; Meg is tawny, her features mobile when she speaks.

In a very short time it was evident that the old *Bulletin* contained ballad and bush song riches and even convict verse. People who had long been forgotten had contributed excellent ballads. I soon began working two days a week at the ballad research, and three at the hospital, and two days were not time enough because Doug and I realised that the *Bulletin* was only one source among many potential ones, and that to do the job properly a great deal of reading in the Mitchell Library would be needed. Bill's history was virtually abandoned, but he was now so enthusiastic about the ballad project that he seemed not too disappointed.

The conflicting claims of my two working worlds were at a point where some resolution must be made. Though I seemed able to exist in a laissez-faire way, my conscience was vaguely troubled.

A baby, and its parents, whose names I scarcely knew, found the flaws in my comfortable failures of decision. Hospital departments then worked from nine to twelve-thirty on Saturday mornings on a roster system, with reduced staffing. That Saturday was quiet. At twelve-fifteen I told the clerk to go off and get smartened up for her Saturday afternoon with her fiance. I took off my uniform and waited impatiently for the clock. Near-ly at twelve-thirty a young couple arrived at the door with a note from Casualty. The woman carried a sleeping baby wrapped in a large woollen shawl. The note asked me to find cheap accommodation for them until Monday, when the baby had an appointment with a specialist.

Normally the clerk would have filled in the detailed form needed to open a file. Grumpily I found one on her desk and, with none too good a grace began to complete it while the mother, tiredly, explained that they had arrived from a distant country town this morning by train, that they had not understood hospital procedures or the delay involved, that they had never been in a city before and were bewildered, that they had very little cash but Casualty had said the Almoner's Department could provide money for emergencies, and...and...a sad tale I'd heard countless times before, from countless weary mothers and worried fathers.

'Yes, yes, but first I must register the baby on this form.' Name? Date of birth? (it was a first child), parents' names, father's job and income? etc. etc. I glanced at the referral form again. Casualty had not specified the child's illness. Strange. No doubt late Saturday morning-itis pre-vailed there, too.

Through all this the beautiful baby slept peacefully in its mother's arms. The father shifted restlessly in his chair and looked increasingly distressed.

'Now, what is the matter with the baby?' The father gave a cry. I looked up. Never had I seen such agonised expressions on two faces. The woman stood, put the baby on my table, and without a single word unwrapped the shawl. A lovely face; a perfect body; no legs or arms.

People in professions like social work, the law, medicine, must be able to put out of mind, out of working hours, or at least as much as possible, the terrible tragedies and problems of their jobs. Perhaps saints can carry intolerable cares and not falter, but saints are rare. More common are those who become callous and cynical, or take to the bottle or drugs. That baby (perhaps an early victim of thalidomide whose dire effects were not yet recognised) scars my mind for ever. I could combine the *Bulletin* and ballad collecting with the problems of ordinarily ill children, with bashed and abused children, with even the Polio Ward, but I could not share that limbless baby with any other career.

It was, and remains, my most appalling memory. I spent a good part of the afternoon arranging for cash vouchers, and all the routine involved. The People's Palace had a room, and would, bless the Salvos, be under-standing and helpful in many ways. Then I wrote up the case for whom-ever would tackle it on Monday, when I, of course, would not be there. I never saw the baby or its parents again. I could not continue to shilly-shally. I resigned from the hospital a few days later. I at least knew that, with the generous reference I was given, I could return to Social Work if I failed as a writer.

In the fifties Sydney was a brown city of gracious but grimy sandstone and Bill FitzHenry, brown of eyes, hair and clothes, seemed so much an emanation of the city itself that it surprises me how often I think of him in country scenes that I did not witness and during an episode with which I was not directly involved. I know well the background of people and place and heard about the event from Bill and another. Perhaps it is because it was at once so likely and unlikely that sometimes I *do* see it—not as an imagined thing or like a dream, but from the vantage of, if not the illusory fly on the wall, a fly on Bill's brown serge shoulder.

My picture is of Mittagong and, more precisely, of the older buildings and gardens of Frensham, and the tracks and roads between the school gates and the Hume Highway which bisects the town across the railway line (by overhead bridge) from the school. The time perhaps is 1954, give or take a year.

Bill was invited to address the senior girls. Had I suggested him? I hardly think so. Or Rosemary Dobson? Also unlikely. I would certainly have told Esther Tuckey, the English Mistress, of Bill's generosity to me, but that is not the same thing as a recommendation to speak. After my schooldays at Frensham and until her death Esther was a friend. It is more likely that she, or someone else, reading Bill's historical accounts of the *Bulletin*'s early days, and his reminiscences of some of its writers and artists, independently decided that he would be an interesting visiting speaker. No matter whose idea it was his hostess on that occasion was Winifred West.

Miss West, with her friend Miss Clubbe, had founded Frensham, a country boarding school for girls, in 1913. Miss West was long retired as headmistress, but she and Miss Clubbe lived at Sturt cottage and were still extremely active and creative women. Winifred West was English. A great educationalist. Beautiful, and commanding with a splendid voice and a marvellous, encouraging smile. She was a legendary woman too, and far beyond the boundaries of Frensham and of Sturt, the craft workshop she founded as well.

Bill was to arrive by a day train, dine at the school, give his talk and sleep in one of Frensham's lofty, country-smelling guest rooms, overnight.

Some epileptics have several minutes' or seconds' warning of an impending fit although few of them can give a precise description of this intimation. I have lived close to two people who endure severe migraine and I can often, a day or two ahead, predict that a bad attack is imminent;

but I cannot really codify or explain the signs I notice. Bill often—not always—did have some mysterious interior warning of an impending drinking bout. When that warning struck he was impotent to fend off the bender. Perhaps an element of auto-suggestion compounded its inevitability; perhaps, confronted with situations when to be drunk would be more than usually unfortunate, he pointed his own bone at his own deepest self.

An intimation of this kind sent its signals soon after his train left Sydney. He was aghast. He tried to put alcohol out of his mind and partly succeeded by watching the countryside from his window; he had not ventured beyond the metropolitan area for a very long time. It was some reassurance that the old-fashioned train carried neither buffet nor bar and stopped nowhere for more than a couple of minutes during the eighty-mile pull into the Southern Highlands.

I see Bill's brown small self almost disappearing against an umber leather seat. Behind him is a large framed photograph of stalactites and stalagmites labelled 'The Wonders of Jenolan' and opposite him is one of equal size and detail of orange orchards and dinosaur hills beside the Hawkesbury, labelled 'A peaceful river reach'. Bill's amiable face discloses no inward struggle.

Winifred West with her friend and colleague Miss Clubbe, and a cohort of dogs ranging from Great Dane enormous to Manchester Terrier minute, met Bill on Mittagong's gravelled railway platform. Bill noticed only Miss West and immediately, mystically, loved her. Her tremendous force, her handsomeness, her booming English voice, her bright, urgent gaze neither intimidated nor swallowed him. He perceived all her qualities in an instant and knew beyond doubt that she was a saint, a true saint marked by God and his angels. With gratitude and relief that dapper, slightly paunchy man of late middle age abandoned himself to a condition of rapture. In that exalted state, be carried his scuffed gladstone bag, strode from the station to the school between the two ladies and was shown to a bedroom where he left his luggage. And then, without encumbrance, he tramped the gardens, the playing fields and the bush areas of the Holt with Miss West.

Some time later when Bill told me about that day he recollected no companion but Miss West, but I see Miss Clubbe there too and also the dogs rushing through trees and bounding along tracks. Of the ordeal of dinner at the High Table raised above a couple of hundred girls, and followed by prayers, Bill remembered little. Yes it was noisy. No it was not alarming. Thank goodness there was only water to drink. Then came his talk which went well in a resonant hall; it was also a gymnasium. I see Bill under the gym's harsh lights like one brown pebble on the sandy bed of a still rock-pool. The senior girls were a lively audience and asked sensible questions. No, he could not particularly recall the headmistress Phyl Bryant, or Esther Tuckey, among a host of friendly and interesting women. He was gratified by their attention to his every word. He couldn't resist teasing them a little with some outrageous but carefully chosen stories of Bohemian events and affairs—that was later when they drank tea (or cocoa for those who preferred it) in the North Room. His anecdotes were received without blush or bridle and prompted hilarity and searching questions too.

Miss West guided him to his room. She made sure there was water and a glass, a bed-lamp, an eiderdown; and that he knew the bathroom's location. Then taking with her presence that metaphorical rod and staff which had been Bill's salvation all day, Miss West said goodnight and left. Alone he listened to the branches of a deodar fanning the night air outside. He visited the enormous tiled bathroom. He undressed and folded his clothes neatly and hung his suit. He went to bed. He craved a drink. Craved and craved.

When Bill told me the story that followed it was doomed and sad and he made no inappropriate attempt to turn it into jest. It was still quite early. Frensham's hours were so wholesome that younger staff, who occasionally made a night of it in one of the cottages, felt deliciously adventurous if their innocuous roisterings lasted until midnight. Somewhere in Mittagong Bill was sure that, despite six o'clock closing, at least one pub's back or side door was closed above a tell-tale pencil of light at its base. Somewhere in Mittagong a Sergeant and Constable would patrol far from that pencil seeing only what it was necessary they should see, and not a yard or figure further.

So Bill dressed again, very quietly opened the outside door near the bathroom, and walked out into the shadows of pine, lilac and gum trees, and through them to a deserted road, and down it to the railway. He crossed the bridge to the town, and walked directly to the Railway Hotel. Its thin ray of hope and despair was all the brighter because its side door was shaded from the street light by a huge elm tree.

Bill drank three brandies quickly and at the bottom of each polished glass he met Winifred West's intent eyes. They helped him to stop there, while he was sober yet. He did not even buy a bottle to take with him, but walked out and back the way he had come. Near one of Frensham's open gates the boots of Sergeant and Constable trod loud and firm. Bill gave them a civil good night and they responded affably but took a close look at him under a street-light.

Not wishing to be mistaken for a prowler, and aware that those who could attest to his legitimate presence in the grounds of a girls' school were probably all asleep, Bill thought it prudent to walk around the perimeter of the very large main school block. He entered the grounds at last by the main gate, and couldn't for the life of him recall which of the many shut doors led to the hallway near his room.

Highland nights are cold, even in summer. Bill shivered all through that one on a bench in the sunken garden which is surrounded by a hedge. First dawn came at five-thirty. At last he ventured back to the buildings across a frosty lawn, and had just recognised the door he sought when Miss Clubbe, with attendant canines, strolled round a corner. Breezily and with surprised approval, she invited him to share her early morning exercise.

Bill was sure though that Miss Clubbe soon noticed the marks of his footsteps across the lawn. He feared that three brandies might linger on his breath. He suspected that Miss Clubbe's hearty conversation was a deliberate tease. As to that my vision assures me that Bill was wrong, although his suspicion that she discerned his dark night of the soul was possibly correct. Miss Clubbe, too, was a remarkable woman, and a realist.

When he got back to his room a tray of breakfast waited for him. He ate it; then shaved, showered and dressed ready for the train. Miss West and other women staff appeared to farewell him and Miss West walked with him to the station. Again he felt enfolded by goodness and mercy. Almost he appealed to her for salvation, but did not.

At Picton he disembarked. That time he was away from his desk for more than two weeks.

VII

Ballads and Bush Songs

I WORKED fairly regularly at the *Bulletin* from about 1952. This was my first experience of a newspaper office, and I did not, at first, realise quite how unusual a place the *Bulletin* was. I had heard accounts of early Sydney journalism and was surprised, and a little disappointed, to discover no wild, hard drinking Bohemians. The men wore conservative suits, shirts and ties though at work they often discarded coats in favour of comfortable ancient cardigans. They donned hats whenever they left the building, had short back and sides and not a beard among them—the two beards were upstairs in the *Woman's Mirror* office! The women at the *Bulletin* were Pauline Dempsey who wrote a social jottings page and was more often out at social functions than in the office; and Sheila MacDermott, the receptionist, who had a desk in a glass-windowed office at the entrance to the editorial section. There was also a pretty blonde girl who did the small amount of necessary art work including lettering each week's crossword solution. Otherwise the editorial section was masculine.

The most raffish phenomenon consisted of the revolting mugs from which the men drank endless tea and coffee. They brewed their brews and kept their mugs in a dank, cold-water scullery near my cubbyhole; and they apparently recognised their own vessels whose pitch-black, seldom rinsed and never washed interiors seemed to cause them no harm. I never saw anything stronger consumed in the office.

Some journalists sallied forth to one of several favoured nearby hotels, often with long-standing contributors who had memories of the vanished boozy past. They always appeared reasonably sober at their desks. Douglas Stewart has written of his sessions at Mockbell's coffee shop with R. D. FitzGerald, David Campbell and others. But women did not venture into Mockbells by some curious tradition that I never quite understood, nor into Aarons Exchange Hotel dining room at lunch time. Nor did they have a drink in a public bar, except in Jim Buckley's Newcastle Hotel in Lower George Street where Nancye White, wife of *Bulletin* artist Unk (Cecil) White, was a part-time barmaid. Buckley had pioneered the opening of his public bar to women as well as the display, for sale, of pictures on its wall.

I went quite often to the Newcastle with several friends; one was Bill Howard who would descend upon Sydney annually. Bill was a wool-classer and for most of the year he worked on sheep properties. He con-

1 Margery Keesing, nee Hart, as a
young woman.

2 Gordon Keesing aged about
twenty.

3 Gordon Keesing with his daughters, Margaret and Nancy,
about 1938.

4   Nancy, in her mid-twenties.

5   Mark Hertzberg.

6   Margery and Gordon Keesing with daughters
       and grandchildren.

7 *Margery Sproule,* nee *Hertzberg.*

8 *John Hertzberg.*

9 *The Bulletin office at 252 George Street, Sydney.*

10   *Douglas Stewart.*

11   *Douglas and Margaret Stewart*
      with Fang.

12   *Meg Stewart.*

13   *David Martin.*

14   *Sydney Tomholt and
Maxine Murray-Jones.*

15   John Meredith.

16   Bill (W.N.) Scott.

17   *Russel Ward.*

18   *Robert D. FitzGerald.*

19 *Walter Stone.*

20 *Dame Mary Durack Miller.*

21 A scribble of authors, *1941*.
Standing, left to right, *Leslie Clarke Rees, Sydney Tomholt, J. J. Hardie.*
Seated, left to right, *Frank Dalby Davison, T. Inglis Moore, Peter Hopegood*

22 Peter Hopegood.

The
Miles Franklin
Award
1984

23   *Invitation to*
the Miles
Franklin Award,
1984. '. . .for the
novel of the year
which is of the
highest literary
merit and which
must present
Australian life in
any of its phases.'

Invitation

24   *Rosemary Dobson.*

25   *Beatrice Davis, Nancy and Sir Grenfell Price.*

26 *Michael Costigan.*

27　At a Ku-ring-gai College of Advanced Education graudation ceremony.

28 A corner of the
    Paris studio.

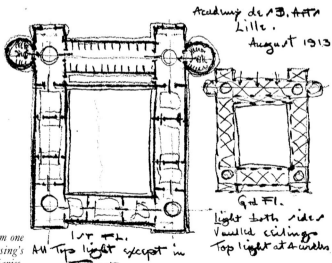

29 A page from one
of Gordon Keesing's
        diaries.

Academy de ^ B. Arts
Lille.
            August 1913

Gd Fl.
light both sides
Vaulted ceilings
Top light at 4 circles

1st Fl.
All Top light except in
Front

tributed excellent freelance articles on various topics to the *Bulletin*. (I introduced Bill to Betty Wilkinson, widow of Kenneth Wilkinson who had been a notable theatre and music critic for the *Sydney Morning Herald* and the *Age*; and later they married.)

Once, as we walked down George Street, Bill said to me: 'You know, Nan, I find it hard to believe you're a poet.' 'Why?' I asked. 'Your clothes are always so clean,' he replied. I can't think of anyone I knew whom Bill might have used for this curious comparison. It was more usual for artists young and old to look 'arty' than for poets to look 'poetical', perhaps because most of the poets I knew held daytime jobs as teachers in schools and universities, or else worked in publishing houses or libraries. Rosemary Dobson and Nan McDonald worked in Angus and Robertson's editorial department and apart from being beautiful women, each was smartly dressed. The closest approach to a 'poetical-looking' person was elderly Imogen Whyse who had founded the poetry journal *Prism* and who lived in rooms in an old building in Lower George Street, where one of the walls was painted as a mural depicting the Buddhist way to enlightenment. Imogen did rather trail clouds—if not of glory then of light chiffon scarves and stoles—and she had a somewhat lofty, wafty, facial expression. Roland Robinson was flamboyant, but, as to dress, only mildly unconventional in cord trousers and cord or leather jackets. David Campbell, in the city, looked like a high Monaro countryman; but that appearance probably derived from his mighty stride and broad-brimmed hat. Kenneth Slessor was so dapper and well-turned-out that people meeting him for the first time were frequently surprised; his one unconventional touch was an invariable bow tie.

With a very few exceptions poets in the forties and fifties published chiefly in the *Bulletin*. The quarterlies *Southerly* and *Meanjin* and a number of newspapers also published poetry but the *Bulletin*'s weekly pages surpassed other venues both for quantity of poetry presented and relative speed of publication. Another desirable feature was that, unlike most other venues of those days, the *Bulletin* paid contributors.

From 1941 to 1973 Angus and Robertson published an annual poetry anthology called *Australian Poetry* which had a different editor each year. I took down from my shelves the volume for 1949–50 because it marks the turn of a decade. The poems were selected by Rosemary Dobson. Acknowledgements are made to the *Bulletin*, *Southerly*, *Meanjin* and the *Sydney Morning Herald*. A comparison of that short list with the acknowledgements in any comparable publication today would say much about changes over forty years. Among the twenty-nine poets included nearly all are important. I notice only three poets who *perhaps* never contributed to the *Bulletin* (for which unfortunately no reliable index exists) and I can only think of two or three substantial poets of the day who are not included in the 1949–50 anthology. (Works by them however, do appear in the *Australian Poetry* series in other years.)

Of the twenty-six poets who were *Bulletin* contributors the ages (in 1950) range from Mary Gilmore, 85 and Ethel Anderson, 67, to Francis Webb, 24. Most were in their twenties and thirties, a few were of middle age. Twelve women and seventeen men are represented. In my copy I found a letter from Rosemary Dobson dated 17 October 1950 which replied to my note congratulating her on the book. Rosemary wrote: 'I believe the *Bulletin* review will be out tomorrow. That's the only one I really care about. The old SMH will probably merely list it in the "Books Received".' Rosemary wrote one sentence that speaks for countless anthologists in every era: 'I'm glad you commented on the arrangement [of the poems]. I thought it most cunning myself, but I imagine lots of people will imagine that one just throws them all in anyhow.'

Today many journals and newspapers publish poetry and that is a good and healthy development. But *Bulletin* poets in earlier generations had one advantage that poets today do not have: a weekly display centre with a large, nationwide circulation at a price (9d) that everyone could afford and where any poet of talent, established or emergent, could be sure of the company of peers. This tradition began with A. G. Stephens and continued with notable Red Page editors like Cecil Mann. For my generation the constant editor was Doug Stewart who was eclectic, sympathetic and fair-minded. Doug's art criticism is increasingly deplored and often rightly so. Some of his criticism of prose works is, especially with the benefit of hindsight, debatable, though considering the relative speed with which book reviews appeared on the Red Page that is inevitable. But as poetry editor he would, over months and years, become familiar with the work of many poets and have time to deliberate his assessments. Doug made no alterations to poems without consultation (unlike A. G. Stephens). One benefit of his long-continued editorial presence was that poets *knew* who was assessing their work and respected and valued his judgement. If they did not have that respect, or if they wrote a work that seemed unsuited for the *Bulletin* they sent poems elsewhere. Some of the *Bulletin* poets, most notably R. D. FitzGerald and David Campbell were Stewart's friends; several he did not care for as people; but as to the poetry itself, personalities had no place in his judgements. There were no cliques. So far as I know his greatest personal regret and uncertainty was Francis Webb. He had praised Webb highly and unreservedly when his work first appeared and later he feared (I would think quite wrongly) that in some way this early notoriety had contributed to Webb's appalling schizophrenic breakdowns.

To return to the *Bulletin* office. It was described by Doug in his ABC 1977 Boyer Lectures which were published as *Writers of the Bulletin*.

The Building itself was dark and huge and cavernous and gloomy enough
to have been positively mouldering with tradition. The floor we inhabited
ran or rather crept in one long tunnel from George Street right through to
Hamilton Street at the back. Its ceiling was supported by pillars, and it
looked rather like one of the more prolonged of the Jenolan Caves, propped
up by stalagmites. . . We were all practically invisible in its Stygian
recesses. People used to fall over each other in the corridor.

That corridor was even more hazardous because huge rolls of newsprint—
then a scarce commodity to be purchased as and when possible—were
stored along its length. It swirled with tobacco smoke and steam from
cups of tea, but there was little gloom among its journalists. As I understood it they were paid at less than the senior grade rates they might have
earned elsewhere, which suited them because they all worked at projects
of their own as well as writing their regular columns and pages and
commissioning and assessing *Bulletin* material. Doug wrote some of his
drama and radio scripts at his *Bulletin* desk. At least three others edited
smallish special-interest magazines; and one mass produced pulp novels.
Most of them could, and did, turn their pens to almost anything from
well-researched articles to short, humorous paragraphs and verse.

Stan Keogh wrote a weekly humorous verse signed 'Bo'; Phil Dorter
was the regular drama critic; Jim Blair wrote occasional, accomplished
and very amusing short stories; John Fountain wrote short stories of great
power and insight; Charles Shaw, late in his too short life, wrote a novel,
Heaven Knows, Mr Allison which was produced as a successful American
film; and, under the pseudonym 'Bant Singer' he also wrote three very
popular novels centering on a detective called Delaney (earlier in his
career he had published books of ballad verse). It was due to David
Adams, the editor from 1948 to 1961, that Rachel Henning's letters saw
publication. J. E. Macdonnell ('Macnell') wrote non-fiction books and
novels with naval backgrounds; and in 1956 he left the *Bulletin* to write
some twelve paperback novels for Horwitz each year.

Ronald McCuaig was, to *Bulletin* stories, what Doug Stewart was to its
poetry. Doug believed McCuaig was insufficiently celebrated as a poet,
and that his very important editorial contribution to Australian fiction
was not recognised, so he devoted one of his ABC Boyer Lectures to the
poetry and other work of Ronald McCuaig:

> It is in the nature of things that, until the literary histories are written
> editors must do their good deeds in secret. But besides [McCuaig's]
> publication of the later stories of Brian James and E. O. Schlunke, and a lot
> of first-class work by other writers, including Mena Kashmiri Abdullah,
> two of McCuaig's good deeds should certainly be known. It was he who
> encouraged, fostered, and published in the *Bulletin* the short stories of
> Ethel Anderson and Hal Porter. . . and he was undoubtedly the editor who

brought them forward and, riding high above some occasional murmurings from within and without the paper, steadfastly supported them. . . . Since Ethel Anderson, that grand, wise, witty old duchess, and Hal Porter, whose frosty blue eye has never missed a trick in human behaviour, are beyond question two of the finest writers in the whole history of the Australian short story, it was no mean achievement to have published them.

Malcolm (M. H.) Ellis, the historian and biographer, wrote feature articles, usually on historical or political affairs, which were often signed 'Ek Dum'. He was perhaps the deepest dyed conservative among the journalists. He was immensely generous to me in many ways. All these men I mention were friends and the *Bulletin* itself was, as it were, my host. It would not have occurred to me to discuss with them the paper's policies and politics, the racist traditions and prejudices that permeated all but the Red Page, the short stories and the poetry. However, even to my inexperienced view the slow decline of the journal during the fifties was evident—as was the increasing irrelevance of much of its content to even that stultifying era of Menzies in Australia and McCarthy in America. It lost circulation and money and in 1960 the Prior family sold it to Australian Consolidated Press; Donald Horne became editor, and fairly swiftly it changed its nature and direction. I rather sadly farewelled my cubbyhole in 1956.

Since those days I have several times been asked whether, as a Jew, I questioned the journal's continuing, old fashioned brand of anti-Semitism, especially in joke blocks. I did not. Nor did I ever hear anti-Semitic talk. Similarly the journal's antiquated racism, again very evident in some of its black-and-white art, infuriated me, as did its extreme anti-ALP bias. But I did not think it my place or business to protest. Perhaps I was wrong. In self-defence I can only say that, in this country at least, writers have almost always (as they still do) submitted poetry and stories to any journals that would accept their kind of material, and whose literary standards they could respect. Today, for instance, certain poets and other writers who are politically far distant from the New Right seem content to publish in *Quadrant*. I am not.

The ballad project gathered momentum and made demands of its own beyond anything Doug and I had foreseen. We soon realised we were working not on one book but two. The ballad of the nineties was a development from the old bush song, and the two genres had continued concurrently; but the ballad, usually written by a skilled versifier and intended for publication, was essentially different from the old bush song, often an anonymous folk invention. At first we considered one book with two clear sections, Bush Ballads in one, Old Bush Songs in the other. However quite early we had collected too much material for that to be appropriate. Doug discussed the problem with George Ferguson who agreed to two large separate volumes—then we could see our way more clearly.

We did not realise as we worked that a folklore revival was stirring worldwide. Not long before Burl Ives, the American folk singer, had visited Australia. He had sought to add early Australian songs to his repertoire but was assured that, although some folksongs once existed, most had been lost except for a few collected by Vance Palmer and set to music by Margaret Sutherland. Dr Percy Jones, the Vice Director of the Melbourne Conservatorium of Music, heard of this misinformation and made available to Burl Ives a quite extensive collection he had assembled, as a hobby, over many years. Later he allowed Doug and me to use the words of songs in his collection. We decided against including music in our book, chiefly because neither of us was qualified to collect or write music, also because of the huge extra cost, and not least because many people were beginning to collect and publish tunes. Tape recorders were soon to revolutionise collecting of every kind, especially from old people who tended to transpose lines of songs, or forget lines and remember them later, or include a missing line in a verse of something quite different.

John Meredith, Alec Hood and others formed the Bushwhackers Band and fashioned old bush instruments for it—like the lagerphone, a broomstick rattling with attached beer bottle tops. They collected; they sang at concerts and on radio. The Bush Music Club was established, and folklore societies followed in other states.

Everyone in the collecting field became friendly. Hugh Anderson and Ron Edwards in Victoria, who were collecting words and music and publishing at Edwards' Rams Skull Press, kept in touch with us and we shared discoveries and information. Russel Ward's collection and selection had a different slant and purpose for, with a trained historian's skill and interest, he was collecting songs for use in his PhD thesis. This work later emerged as his classic *The Australian Legend*.

Publicity and ferment led to increasing community awareness. People who still sang the old songs or danced traditional bush dances were much less hard to discover, and many joyfully got in touch with collectors. On a Melbourne Cup Day—perhaps in 1953—I was working in my *Bulletin* room keeping one ear on someone's nearby radio, plugged in for the occasion. I had several sweep tickets in the only race of the year that exists as far as I'm aware, and intended to invite myself to hear the event as soon as it began in half an hour or so. Sheila MacDermott, the office receptionist/typist/sorter-out-of-problems came to my room and explained that an elderly man had called to give some information about ballads in response to an article Doug had written that mentioned 'missing' verses and songs. Doug was too busy to see the man. Could I?

In strode 'Duke' Tritton—all handsome, white-haired, sunbaked, six feet, sixty-seven years of him. His nickname was not for nothing. He took my hand in one of his enormous shearer's 'dukes' and seemed to crush every bone while he summed me up with a very direct blue gaze. We talked. He had copied out some words we sought in his huge, carefully formed handwriting. He spoke of the station Goorianawa, subject of one of the songs we most needed. He sang Goorianawa and went on to song after song. A fascinated audience gathered in my room and in the lobby outside. Then the Cup began and most of the audience sloped away. 'Would you care to hear the Cup?' I asked. No, he said, no interest in it at all. Duke must be the only real Australian who ever lived who did not wish to hear the Melbourne Cup, and I missed learning about my customary losses till later.

I introduced Duke to John Meredith and through the Bushwhackers and the Bush Music Club he had a great second career, on radio and in public. Sometimes he went off to a place he knew near Mudgee and did a bit of prospecting for gold. He always arrived back with a few specks and some gold dust. He presented me with a couple of peculiar stones he found, and a curiosity that looks like a piece of carved and polished wood. For years, sniffing it, one could get a clue to its origin, but now it has long lost the faint scent of beeswax. In fact, it is the platform of a wild bees' hive, polished by generations of tiny insect feet.

One day I said to Duke, 'You really ought to make a book of all your experiences and yarns.' 'Well,' he said, 'how would I do that?' 'A start would be to go down the road to Coles and buy a few sixpenny exercise books and just write down your stories exactly as you tell them to me.' Duke took me up on the suggestion. Not long afterwards he came into the office with a bundle of ruled, school exercise books—sixpenny ones were the largest available in those days, filled with his big clear writing. 'Here's the book. You read it and see what you think.'

I read it and thought it was splendid. Duke's own drawling voice could be heard behind his well-told tale. So far as I could judge it was publishable just as it was, and ideal for a *Bulletin* serial. I asked Doug to read it. Read a handwritten manuscript! Not on your life! I pleaded that this was no ordinary handwriting—much easier to read than many people's typing with faint ribbon on bad paper. No.

So I took Duke's book a step down the road to Doug's wife Margaret at 12 Bridge Street, which had once been Norman Lindsay's Sydney dwelling. Margaret, a fine water-colour painter, is also a perceptive critic of literature, and her country background had added an invaluable dimension to our thinking about ballad collection. I hoped Margaret would tackle handwriting. I thought she would warm to Duke. She did, and persuaded Doug that this was a manuscript he must not miss. *Time Means Tucker* was published first as a *Bulletin* serial, and later as a book (Shakespeare Head Press, 1964). As far as I know the serial version was set directly from Duke's clear handwriting.

I worked several days each week at the Mitchell Library reading for the ballad collection. People doing research regularly got to know each other, were aware of each other's interests, and would keep their eyes open for items likely to interest someone else. One student of trades union history directed me to 'Queensland Ladies' in a learned article about the Queensland meat industry. But there is usually one snake in the nicest looking grass.

A man who later became a well-known academic was a senior editor in a publishing company. In the early fifties his reading was directed to earlier Australian history because he was editing two novels by convict authors. This man knew and respected Doug and was very helpful to me—until I became friendly with Russel Ward, whom he most actively did not like. Ward's socialist beliefs had already cost him academic jobs and loss of seniority and approval. (How the McCarthyist fifties affected the whole world!) For my part the loss of this man's cooperation was no great disaster but he could sometimes have saved Russel a great deal of searching, for they were reading in related or overlapping fields. 'Ah Mr Ward' (Russel was not a professor in those days) the man would smirk, 'I believe you are looking for an instance of the "Cat and Mouse Act" actually being invoked?' 'Yes.' 'Well, I've found a splendid newspaper report of a trial from 1837 that shows it certainly *was* more than a bit of paper.' 'That is interesting. Thanks. What newspaper?' 'Aha. *I* found it. And so can *you*!'

He remains the meanest spirited man of my experience. His behaviour to other writers and to his fellow academics was notorious and atrocious. But he wrote some valuable books.

In the early fifties it was possible to obtain photographic copies of certain items in the Mitchell Library collection, but the procedure was slow and expensive and mostly used for illustrations. Convenient cheap photocopying did not exist. Anything to be quoted was laboriously copied by hand or on typewriter. Duncan MacCallum, a distinguished historian on the staff of Sydney University, was often in the reading room, shortsightedly perusing long, closely printed, nineteenth-century reports as well as the tiny print of early newspaper reports of parliamentary proceedings and political meetings. Duncan, or the University, employed a typist. Once a week, rattling away enviably, she typed excerpts according to the instructions he pencilled on pages as he read. Maybe he was so learned he had special permission, for no librarian complained about his open defacement of irreplaceable print.

I first met Duncan and his brother George at dancing classes when we were in our teens. George died when a yacht called 'The Robin May' foundered tragically, drowning several young men who, like him, had just completed their medical degrees. I recall Duncan, ever serious, enquiring in the middle of a lively foxtrot, 'Nancy, what do you think of Kipling's imperialistic policies?' and spraying my face as he uttered every 'p'. He was scornful, though in a kindly way, about my present pursuits. A collection of ballads would, he considered, trivialise history. He lectured me severely about my lack of a degree and urged me to complete my education. I have met uncountable people since then who either cannot believe that many writers are not university graduates, or firmly think we should be.

Copying the ballad discoveries improved my self-taught typing enormously. As a privilege, not a right, the Library made limited space available to a few users of typewriters but would not allow one to leave the machine, or anything else, on the premises. Consequently over months I trudged uphill to the Library from 252 George Street carrying a portable machine and a case containing copy paper.

Doug worked with me at the Library as often as he could during our nearly three years of research. We ploughed through early newspapers, magazines, and every book and pamphlet of verse in the catalogue with key words like 'ballad', 'song', 'bush', 'old' or 'verses' in its title. We read vast amounts of awful and amateurish nineteenth-century verse, much of it self published. 'It was not the crudity of the verse that fascinated Miss Keesing and myself, but its appalling elegance,' Doug so rightly wrote. But such outpourings in their time followed a fashion—as a great deal of worthless poetic effort does in every era, not least our own.

Towards the end of our collecting we knew the Public Library of Victoria had certain holdings not available in the Mitchell, and decided we should look at these items. They were part of the Latrobe Collection, which was later housed in a magnificent new building, opened in 1965. So I went to Melbourne for a few days. The Library amazed me. I had long been familiar with its round, domed exterior, but I was unprepared for its antique interior appearance and seating plan and even less for its method. For a start very few of the items I ordered could be found. The staff were charmingly apologetic, but with the short time I had available delays were blows. Do not despair, they said. Here is a dust-coat to protect your clothes; there up near the roof, are the stacks. Just make yourself at home.

I did, as best I could, under the dome and high above the hushed reading room, embarrassed when the clatter of my shoes on perforated steel flooring sounded like explosions. I found most of the books I sought, usually four or five places to the left or right of where they should have been, or on a shelf directly above or below the correct one. But I also found treasures in the stacks that I would never have fluked from consulting a catalogue. Whenever they simply looked as if they might be possible sources, I took them down. I was covered in dust but it was worth it. I appreciate that major libraries cannot admit readers to their stacks, but I do wonder what we miss by being unable to browse. However, back at the Mitchell I never again muttered when the staff seemed slow but were utterly reliable in producing nice clean volumes.

The Commonwealth Literary Fund in the fifties had a low budget and chiefly supported 'creative' writers who were well known. For a project like ballad collection there was no public funding. I was fortunate in having a small regular income from a family fund, and the reassurance of knowing that if I struck disaster my parents would come to the rescue. However, since I had first gone to work on Garden Island some ten years before, I had been financially independent and wished to remain so. I had saved enough, during that first job, to pay my university fees; but while I worked at the hospital I also paid rent for the Bond Street studio and for the living quarters I rented and so I had few savings.

Doug, Bill FitzHenry, Ronald McCuaig and other *Bulletin* people put all kinds of freelance work my way. I did not have to slog as hard as had Gertrude Scarlett in her time, and some of the work I undertook was comparatively well paid—but paragraphs were still 2d. a line. *Bulletin* book reviews, usually farmed out by Doug or, in his absence, Ronald McCuaig were my staple. Very rarely I was asked to write a signed article, but most of the reviews were unsigned paragraphs of 150–300 words. Doug wrote the lead Red Page review article (many are collected in *The Flesh and the Spirit*). Ron McCuaig and Cecil Mann were other regular Red Page reviewers. My paragraphs were a fine training in brevity—I used to compare my carbons with the printed versions and learned greatly. Fortunately I am a fast reader because I often contributed three or four reviews a week and made a rule for myself then, that I still keep, to read the whole of any review book no matter how short the piece I have to write. An obliging secondhand bookseller in Crane Place would buy review copies for a fraction of their value. He was Stan Nicholls who, Doug told me, 'was a master collector of cigarette cards and official supplier of books, mainly biographies, to Norman Lindsay. He would send cartons of them by train to Springwood and N. L. would buy the lot.' Fairly soon I realised that greed was costing me a library and began to keep all worthwhile books.

I read and reviewed a lot of terrible tripe. But occasionally splendour came my way, because, I suspected no one eminent realised what was being handed out. If Ron McCuaig had glanced at Eric Ambler's first novel I'm sure it would not have got to me; nor would Barbara Jefferis' *Contango Day*; but, I imagine, I was given Roy Campbell's translations of the poetry of St John of the Cross because my enthusiasm for Campbell's poetry was well-known—to the point of boredom for my friends.

Ron McCuaig reviewed novels and often outlined most of the plot—a system I did not agree with, argued against, and have always avoided. He coined the phrase 'hovel novel' for one kind of fiction prevalent in the fifties. He will be remembered for his wise and witty poetry but he also wrote, as 'Swilliam,' a weekly topical verse. Ron's enjoyment of his weekly stint was joyful to overhear. 'Swilliam' often based his verse on some popular song or tune of the day, and hummed it as he prowled his office, or a corridor, finding words. When the words that came were right, and amused him, he'd stand still, stretch mightily—he is a tall man—and shout with laughter.

I was invited to climb to a higher floor where the *Woman's Mirror* editorial offices were tucked away. I must have known the editor was a man, but was unprepared for Llewellyn Griffiths and his assistant, John Brennan (nephew of Chris). Griff was short and grizzled, Brennan tall and brown haired. Both were bearded heavily, which was not fashionable, and their ziffs struck me as weird for editors of a woman's magazine. The *Woman's Mirror* always had a male editor. For some years, in the late twenties or early thirties, it was Cecil Mann—a strange fate for a Gallipoli veteran.

The *Woman's Mirror* offered me occasional, amazing jobs. Their weekly page 'Women's Health and Beauty' was signed 'Adrienne' but 'she' turned out to be a man who lived out of town somewhere. I never met him or knew whether he, too, wore a huge beard, but I did learn that 'Adrienne' sometimes went on a bender because at very short notice I was several times asked to supply his page. I used cosmetics as much as any girl, but without thinking about them; and the reading of beauty pages was not a pursuit of mine. I recall that one page I concocted extolled witch hazel as a cheap marvel that should be in every woman's handbag and desk—good as a cleanser, astringent, disinfectant—but how I padded out that notion to fill a page I cannot now imagine. Then there was 'Beauty on the Bus' where you could file your nails, do gentle exercises and goodness knows what else, while travelling to work. The pages of recipes I was sometimes asked to contribute were a good deal more reliable because I frantically enlisted Mum as a consultant.

I used an array of pseudonyms for hack work. I occasionally resurrect two of them but have discarded the others. The pseudonym I have most used appears on the very rare occasion when I do not wish to sign a review with my own name. Since I disapprove of unsigned reviews, whether in *The Times Literary Supplement* or less eminent pages, I never feel comfortable when I employ this stratagem; but it is, sometimes, justified. There was, for instance, a woman novelist of true worth and power who could not agree with any review of her books that said less than 'Miss Q is the greatest'. At the most minor criticism, or qualification of her new novel, she would telephone the literary editor of the newspaper or magazine in which the offending article appeared, and raise Cain. Next, peculiar letters of complaint would arrive at the offending journal or paper, arousing strong suspicion that Miss Q herself or her friends were their authors. Reviewers who discussed Miss Q's novels were similarly pestered.

Came the day when Miss Q brought out a fine novel that would plainly be in the running for major prizes, and which in fact did win her her third Miles Franklin Award. And the literary editor of Sydney's leading reviewing paper could not find a single reviewer willing to write about the new work. I flatly refused. The literary editor tried to persuade. Finally I said that if the literary editor would agree to a pseudonym instead of my own signature, I'd do it as favour. In my article I did question the treatment of one character, but otherwise high praise was not difficult. Nevertheless, Miss Q and her friends rallied as usual with letters of complaint and abuse.

One signed review I wrote for the *Bulletin* so infuriated the book's male author that he bombarded me with short, angry, signed notes that I first disregarded. The notes continued, but unsigned and increasingly obscene. I showed that correspondence to the *Bulletin* editor, David Adams, who guaranteed to stop the nuisance and did. He did not tell me how.

Doug Stewart would seldom review a book that was sent to him by an author rather than a publisher, and never if it contained effusive flattering remarks about Doug's own work. I've found that a good rule too. Another rule took me years to learn: never be unnecessarily facetious. It can be a great temptation to guy a bad book, or the bad parts of a fair sort of book, often by quoting awful passages from it. I used quite often to enliven my efforts in that way. Then, as my writing acquaintance grew, I met the authors I had 'sent up', and they remembered. Oh how they remembered. And what likeable people most of them were. There is no need to hurt people; there are many dignified means, compatible with honesty, to describe, or denigrate, a work, and there are acceptable ways of being funny if that is appropriate.

Although I do not type well or professionally, if I go slowly and take care I can produce a reasonable looking page. My typewriter was a good deal less ancient than most of the museum pieces used by *Bulletin* journalists, and so some of them gave me typing jobs for which I charged less per page than professional rates. I typed Charles Shaw's novel about his detective, Delaney, and became so engrossed in its exciting plot that it was not easy to plod along at my slow optimum speed.

Bulletin journalists had low rates of pay, but less pressure of work, than those in daily journalism. They were their own bosses and could apportion their time to suit their own pace of writing and interest. Whether or not Charles Shaw wrote his novels in the office, I do not know. When first his Delaney detective novel was a success and then *Heaven Knows, Mr Allison* became an international best-seller and an American film, everyone was delighted because it seemed as if he, his wife, and his son Lachlan (who is now a well-known journalist) were about to enjoy success. Long before his projected Delaney series was completed, Shaw died, in 1955. He was a writer of good ballads, very knowledgeable and helpful to me and I remember him with admiration and gratitude.

Cecil Mann was a fine writer who every year read the complete Old Testament and Shakespeare's historical plays. That was remarkable, but not mysterious. Cecil did begin to mystify me, however, because as I came up Wynyard ramp of a morning I often noticed him, emerging from a florist or fruiterer's shop, his gladstone bag bulging and a green leaf or two escaping from its clasp. To satisfy my curiosity he and his wife Duggie invited me to dinner at their Neutral Bay home. The hour suggested seemed early for a meal and I arrived in late daylight. At the back of the house, which was built on a slope, there was a large balcony dominated by a big deal table on which Cecil set out what proved to be a banquet for possums. A heap of rose petals at one corner; apple pieces in another place; chopped potatoes; outside leaves of vegetables and wilted silver beet; a pile of stale bread. At dusk, climbing up a ladder from below, or dropping from an overhanging branch above, his friends arrived. Each went directly to the fare it favoured. Cecil said none of them ever deviated from their preferred food. Several females had babies on their backs and these clambered off when mother reached the table, and nibbled at her choice. It was charming and civilised and a fine demonstration that there need be no arguments and fighting—provided each animal, or human, can have exactly what it wants.

For more enigmatic reasons Malcolm Ellis mystified me too. He was tall, chubby-faced and always more formally dressed and barbered than most of his colleagues though he was said, on excellent authority, to have been in his youth one of the wilder guests at Norman Lindsay's Springwood house. Malcolm acquired his passion for Australian history when he was a boy at Brisbane Grammar School. On holidays at Oxenford (near Beenleigh south of Brisbane) he got into conversation with an elderly bullock driver who, as a lad, had arrived in Australia as a transported convict. The man told his tales to the fascinated boy and the boy became a pioneer of readable, well-researched Australian biography.

Ellis' books and opinions are in eclipse at the moment, no doubt because later discoveries and assessments have been made since his time, but also, I would suspect, because he seemed to go out of his way to quarrel with, offend and speak against the generation of young historians who were emerging in the fifties and destined to be distinguished. I once typed a running series of furious letters for Ellis, concerning one of his quarrels and arguments. Much as I liked and admired him, and little as I understood about the issues and people involved, I could not but think he was intemperate, and strongly suspected he was unfair.

Ellis wrote articles about defence and related matters using the pen name 'Ek Dum'. He was an arch conservative politically and a chief moulder of the *Bulletin's* political attitudes. He knew the Mitchell Library's holdings better than most librarians and directed Doug and me to invaluable books and papers, including the fairly obscure ballads of F. C. Urquhart which are based on his experiences as an early police officer in Queensland. Ellis averred that the German settlers in South Australia and elsewhere had a German language range of bush songs akin to those in English, but we were never able to find any of these. Eventually he was one of the people who spent hours checking the proofs of the ballad and bush song books. During the sixties I phoned Ellis for advice about historical research. His slightly stuttery voice never failed in help and friendship.

In the fifties after evening meetings, groups of my friends patronised a large coffee shop near the Queens Square end of King Street. With the proprietor's blessing we moved tables together, linen cloths and all, so everyone could sit and talk; but first he removed the slender silver vases each crowned with a wilting flower or two and put them on the counter near the cash register.

Often an ancient, twisted woman came in the doorway. She wore layers of grimy rags topped by a shawl whose floral pattern was nearly obliterated by age and fading. From the vases she added falling poppies or withering carnations to a bunch of flowers in her old wicker basket. Everyone familiar with night-time Sydney knew her by sight. A little later, when the show at the Theatre Royal ended, she would stand near the main doors holding out her dying flowers. A few people from the emerging audience would buy a couple for a penny or so and toss them into the gutter on their way to the tram.

Unlike some other Sydney eccentrics—Bea Miles, The Bengal Tiger,

Rose of Martin Place—I never heard the old crone referred to either by name or nickname, but stories were told about her. One had it that she was the procuress of a brothel but that seemed unlikely; she never spoke and her old, reptilian face and weird rags would surely deter the most necessitous of customers, let alone those with the price of a theatre ticket. Another account said she had been a most beautiful girl, the toast of Bohemia in the days when Sydney really *had* a Bohemia. No, she was a famous actress who twisted her spine and lost her voice after falling from her steed during a mad midnight ride along Bondi Beach with an illicit lover.

One of my Social Worker friends in the welfare department of the Red Cross Society rang up. She knew Doug and I were collecting bush songs and ballads and thought we might like to know of a client, a destitute old woman who had come to her office the week before and for over an hour had sung songs and told stories of her youth in the Monaro district. My friend could speak to the old lady and get her permission for a visit. Her name was Mrs Ivy Popplewell. She lived at Darlington.

A few mornings later I set out for Darlington with instructions from my Red Cross friend. Mrs Popplewell's house was in an un-named lane behind a factory with a frontage to a back street whose name I can't remember; I'll call it Back Street. Anyone at the facotry would direct me to Mrs Popplewell; she would be delighted to meet a ballad collector.

Darlington was the smallest Sydney district. Sandwiched between Newtown, Chippendale and City Road most of its few acres have long been razed and re-built by Sydney University and other landowners. The population was so miniscule that even in my Social Worker days I'd seldom had need to explore its narrow streets. Back Street was itself a lane even by the standards of most broken down areas. The 'factory' was a rotting tin shed in which three or four sinister-looking elderly men perpetually stirred something vile smelling in rusting forty-four gallon drums. One of them directed me to a slimy dirt pathway between the factory and a leprous brick wall; this led to a tiny court, rather than a lane, in which, side by side, stood the two smallest stone houses I've ever seen; cabins really. History had not so much passed them by as forgotten them utterly. They still had shingle roofs, one door and one window apiece. The second looked abandoned. Mrs Popplewell lived in the nearest. A gap-toothed fence barely supported a ricketty gate securely tied with an old lisle stocking, to 'keep out the bandits' as Mrs Popplewell later explained. I knocked at the half-open door; there was a shuffling sound; she opened it.

I hope I hid my surprise. She was the old dead-flower seller, now dressed in some decaying brown covering that jolted me even more off balance because I realised, with terrible sadness: 'My God. The rags I know are her *evening* dress. She dresses *up* in that dreadful floral shawl.'

Mrs Popplewell did have a voice of course and asked me into her house. A nice, slow, country, educated voice. And a sly, but sweet smile. We sat, each on a wooden chair, near the door. The whole house, all one room of it, was crammed with the dirtiest furniture I'd ever seen, and it was beautiful. Cedar I thought. Two immense, elegant sideboards. A dresser, empty. Some small tables.

Mrs Popplewell began to sing directly. Song after song. Sentimental drawing-room ballads of a hundred years ago; some rollicking ballads that sounded as if they might refer to places and events of Wellington's wars; the ubiquitous dying stockman; and one, thoroughly jumbled, about the bushranger Frank Gardiner. Not only were the lines of the song all over the place but she kept interrupting to say she knew Gardiner—or perhaps not the Darkie himself, but old Mother Brown who betrayed him. It was further confused because when she spoke Mrs Brown's name she also spat.

My pencil flew over notebook. Her voice grew tired. The smell of dirt, grease, age and rags became nearly intolerable. I gathered from all she told me that her father was a travelling man, a solicitor 'who went as Collins'. She was born at Queanbeyan. Her mother lived in a beautiful house. The furniture came from there. Mrs Popplewell grew up in it. As a girl she knew and visited many Monaro stations and station families. (So was her father an itinerant lawyer, or station book-keeper perhaps? And was she born to some squatter's daughter on the wrong side of the blanket?)

In her teens she went to the city to work, and there she married the man who built St Mary's Cathedral—yes, she said, time and again, Popplewell built the Cathedral. But he was much older than she; the cathedral was built before her marriage. My guess is that Popplewell was a small quarry-contractor who carted stone for the Cathedral from Pyrmont. How did they meet? Was she working as a maid in someone's house? They had no children. He died long ago.

It was, I think, through Russel Ward that I had met John Meredith, a collector and performer of bush songs and lore, and one of the founders of The Bushwhackers. I told John about Mrs Popplewell and showed him her Frank Gardiner song which Doug and I had reconstructed, putting its scrambled lines into sequence. Could he, I asked, try to get down some of her tunes? He could, he said, do better.

John had a marvellous new contraption that would record her actual voice on magnetic tape. One morning he took a 'sickie' from the pharmaceutical warehouse where he worked by day and, with Peter Hellier from the Australian Folklore Society we went to see Mrs Popplewell. That early 'Pecotape' machine weighed forty-five pounds. John lugged its cumbersome bulk onto a tram, Peter carried a box of tapes. John has since given me the following information:

> My machine was the first to be designed and manufactured in Australia. 'Pecotape' used tape, reel to reel, at 7½″ per second and gave really superb reproduction. This was obtained by the use of a ¼ hp. motor, such as is used in electric lawn mowers today, and a massive 7″ bronze flywheel. It was a valve job and had a 5-watt amplifier. The whole machine was very advanced for the time.

Mrs Popplewell was delighted by John's quiet, Australian-Irish voice and his knowledge of country matters and bush lore. After a while he attached flex and spools to the recorder and said: 'Now, where is the power point?' There wasn't one. It had not occurred to either of us that in Sydney in February 1954 there would still be a cottage without electricity or, as Mrs Popplewell later told me, running water. A pump in the yard had long ago been dismantled. Mrs Popplewell got water from a tap at the back door of the factory and used its outside lavatory.

We debated whether some local pub might lend us a room for the recording, but Mrs Popplewell thought of a friend who lived close by, though she had no idea whether electricity was available there either. It was a terrace house. The good and generous friend was the elderly wife of a shearer; she welcomed us into her exquisitely scrubbed and polished front room complete with power points, and as John Meredith recalls:

> Mrs Popplewell became almost the first folk singer to be recorded on tape. She was preceded by about a week by Hoopiron Jack Lee with his brother, and his friend Joe Cashmere. They were on side 1 of my first tape, and Mrs Popplewell was on side 2.

The tapes are now in the Australian National Library. The material recorded that morning was: *(1) Frank Gardiner, (2) As I Was A-walking, (3) I'm Carrying Bricks and Mortar, (4) When First I Saw Monaro Plains, (5) I'll be Your Butterfly, (6) Stick to Your Mother Tom, (7) Swagman's Joke, (8) Recitation about Monaro, (9) Last of His Tribe, (10) Finnegan's Wake, (11) Wearing of the Green, (12) Wild Colonial Boy, (13) Battle Cry for Freedom, (14) Girl I Left Behind Me, (15) Babies on the Block, (16) Darling Nellie Grey, (17) Take me Down the Harbour, (18) Sydney Cup Day, (19) Rise up now Willy Reilly, (20) Rattling Boys of County Down,* and *(21) Botany Bay. Monaro Plains* was a recitation which Mrs Popplewell said was written by her father, Collins:

> When first I saw Monaro Plains before that I could ride
> I scarce had sense to hold the reins when first I got astride.

The horses then were big and strong, when four and five year old
When broken in they tore along, some very hard to hold.

And men toiled hard day after day
In carting goods in bullock drays right up from Twofold Bay.
The teams that came from Cooma side were mostly fat and strong,
The greenhide whip was often applied when anything went wrong.

And men like Boyd, that grand old Scot that called his place Boydtown
Built whaling-boats, harpoons a lot and works for boiling down.
He toiled hard each day from dawn to dark when he was in his prime
And when he died he left his mark upon the sands of time.

And poor old John McLoughlin (now dead and gone) one of old Erin's sons
He sold the country out and on it named the different runs.
A familiar name 'Mahratta' where horses grew up grand
And sheep and cattle done the same, with the noted MJ brand.

And Bibbenluke in Bradley's time some fifty years ago,
Sent cattle that was very prime to every local show.
And from Cumbelong to Delegate and names that I've forgot
The Campbells owned a fine estate—they nearly owned the lot.

'Tobetangbanang' was Boyd's furthest station out when I was quite a boy,
I seen him mustering with his men when Ross lived at 'Glenroy'.
And further out at Currawong where others live today
The Stantons settled, not for long, sold out and went away.

Neil Gow of Wollondilly Plains the furthest then was out,
Tied watchdogs up at night when blacks were camped about.

And many changes we have seen, and stories often told;
The grass upon the graves is green and we are getting old.
So friends, you mustn't think this idle tale dates back to Captain Cook
Lines wrote in haste are sometimes stale, I'll stop and close me book.

And when Mrs Popplewell finished the last line of *Frank Gardiner he is
Caught at Last* she went on to say 'Mrs Brown shot herself when she found
she couldn't have Frank Gardiner, but Queen Victoria got him in the
end':

> Frank Gardiner he is caught at last
> And now in Sydney jail—
> For wounding Sergeant Middleton
> And robbing the Mudgee mail,
> For plundering of the escort
> And Cargo mail also
> It was for gold he made so bold
> And not so long ago.
>
> His daring deeds surprised them all
> Throughout our Sydney land;
> He gave a call unto his friends

And quickly raised a band.
Fortune always favoured him
Until the time of late;
There was Burke, the brave O'Meally too,
Met with a dreadful fate.

Young Johnny Vane surrendered,
Ben Hall received some wounds,
And as for Johnny Gilbert,
At Binalong he was found.
Alone he was, he lost his horse,
Three troopers hove in sight;
He fought the three most manfully,
Got slaughtered in the fight.

Farewell adieu to outlawed Frank
He was the poor man's friend;
The Government has secured him,
The laws he did offend.
He boldly stood his trial
And answered in a breath
'And do what you will, you can but kill,
I have no fear of death!'

Fresh charges brought against him
From neighbours near and far
Day after day they remanded him,
Escorted from the bar.
And now it is all over
The sentence it is passed
Reprieving from the gallows cursed
This highwayman at last.

When lives you take—a warning, boys—
A woman never trust;
She will turn round, I will be bound,
Queen's evidence the first.
Two and thirty years he's doomed
To slave all for the Crown;
And well may he say he cursed the day
He met old Mother Brown.

Frank Legge of ABC radio had a weekend programme in which he interviewed all sorts and kinds of interesting people. Either Doug or John
mentioned Mrs Popplewell to him and he invited her to record a few
songs for his session. One morning I met her in town and we walked to a
studio in William Street. Her good friend the shearer's wife had washed
her hair and skin; she wore a new skirt and twin-set from a Red Cross
clothing parcel. She was excited, rather bewildered, as we walked up

William Street, and suddenly subdued, and shy inside the studio, al-most hypnotised with staring at the turning disc. Frank Legge soon had her at ease, and laughing. Then she sang. And sang. And sang. After about ten minutes Legge said to me, 'I've got all I need, it'd be a shame to put an end to her enjoyment. Press that button when she runs down, and I'll come back and rescue you.' The disc was processed when he re-turned, and he asked Mrs Popplewell if she would like to hear the songs to be broadcast.

The record began with Legge's brief lead in to Mrs Popplewell's sweet, cracked voice singing a British Army song. She listened intently. The next song began. Suddenly she got up from her chair and twisted her bent back towards the machine. And she shrieked: 'Some bloody old totty's pinched me songs!' And she wailed: 'She can't sing! That's not how they ought to sound. Bloody old cunt. Pinched me songs. . .' In her distress the quiet voice I knew changed to the howl of an outraged virago.

At last we calmed her down. Legge very considerately had her cheque ready there and then and, though she was puzzled about a payment for singing, and rather tired, she was good-humoured again, though appre-hensive about the taxi which the ABC ordered for her return to the city where her friend waited. I suggested a cup of coffee before they caught their tram.

In a nearby Repins we sat on straight backed seats like church pews while a sniffy waitress, after one look at Mrs Popplewell, tried to pretend for as long as possible that we didn't exist. I said: 'We're thirsty and starving. The ABC have been recording our friend's songs all morning and we'll celebrate with some really gooey cake.'

Fortunately Mrs Popplewell was too weary to give a repeat perfor-mance. As we tucked into mocha slice she spoke softly: 'You know I come into town most evenings and I get into most of the cafes but this is the first time I ever sat down to eat in one of them.'

Early in our collecting Doug and I decided to exclude certain categories of ballad material. For one thing it was plainly absurd for me to type, at the Mitchell Library, masses of items that would probably not be used. Even so we did type just about twice as much as we eventually printed. It was from this mass that we made a final selection. We gave the rejects, along with our notes, to the Library.

Our chosen term 'Bush Ballad', rather than, say, 'the ballad of the nineties' allowed us to decide against ballads of city life and of politics. Fortunately C. J. Dennis wrote a few bush ballads in his youth, and we found a beauty to include. We rejected a great deal of latter-day balladry, particularly that of the 'I remember when. . .' and 'Oh how much I miss . . .' variety. However in that category we made exceptions for really compelling items. One exception Doug refused to make was *Bannerman of the Dandenong* by Alice Werner. He scoffed at the notion of a tough bushman riding through a 'burning noon' with a 'blood-red rose on his breast'. I was meanly pleased when Russel Ward allowed Bannerman, blood-red rose and all, into his *Penguin Book of Australian Ballads*, for Bannerman was one of the first Australian poems I knew in childhood, and precious. I have forgotten why Doug would not allow *Clancy of the Overflow* a place. Community outrage ensured Clancy's entrance to the *Pacific Book of Bush Ballads*, a paperback we compiled from the best of the bush songs and bush ballads.

One of Doug's criteria was that in many of the best ballads you can hear the metre of a rider on horseback—or the weary trudge of walking.

Several times we were so touched, or amused, by a piece which did not come anywhere within cooee of our rules that we cheerfully broke them. *The Bullocky's Love Episode* by A. F. York is scarcely a ballad and nor is the delicious Tennyson parody *The Shearer's Serenade*.

It was fairly simple, towards the end, to finalise headings and categories. At last, one morning, Doug, Margaret and I sat on chairs at the edge of a large cleared carpet in the Bridge Street studio and considered at our feet the neat piles of paper that were our book. Before long they were no longer neat. Margaret has an oval, beautiful Irish face that is marvellous to watch when she is amused, and that morning we were often amused, or moved, as we re-discovered treasures that we had not really looked at for several years. We read snatches of favourites; reluctantly tossed ballads that seemed too thin or that failed to measure up to a final standard. Doug would exclaim 'By Jove, that *is* good!' and Margaret would discover something new to make her laugh or nearly weep. She was a magnificent first audience.

Beatrice Davis, Angus and Robertson's editor, consulted with Doug and it was decided to preserve each item as it had appeared. As consequence the proof-reading of the books was onerous. Many people gave generous time to reading the ballad proofs: Beatrice Davis and Kath George at Angus and Robertson; Doug and I; Malcolm Ellis; John Fountain; and Keith Ross, the head proof-reader of the *Bulletin* who spent a weekend of his spare time checking. Each successive reader found and corrected mistakes. One might have hoped for perfection, for once, but when I first opened the book, there on the contents page was an error looming as large as Ayers Rock.

I knew nothing whatever about formal arrangements with a publisher and left the doing of the deals to Doug. I've long had reason to be grateful for the contracts he drew up with George Ferguson, and for Angus and Robertson's handling of the books over nearly thirty years. They have never been out of print and successors like *The Pacific Book of Bush Ballads* sold steadily. We shared equal royalties and when letters or questions arrived about the books, we consulted. My collaboration with Doug Stewart was a truly fortunate thing for me, and I trace my luck back to Bill FitzHenry too.

This chapter was completed before Doug's death. He read my first draft, suggested a few corrections and additions and in a true sense therefore our collaboration ends only now. Thank you Doug.

VIII

Rooms of Their Own

I N 1953 and 1954 my friend Mary McLelland and I had rooms in a building that faced the charming, small park-like square at the end of Elizabeth Bay Road. We each had a self-contained bed-sitting room and shared a kitchenette converted from a balcony. The large old house belonged to John Mansfield, a leading architect, who lived in half of it and had his office and studio on the ground floor of his section. Mary's rooms, and mine, were on the entrance floor which was at the Elizabeth Bay Road level but below that was ground floor room that was let to a young man. There was a large ground floor flat at garden level where Lily Bruce, who managed the tenants' building for John Mansfield, lived. In the large top-floor rooms above Mary's and mine, and similar in design to ours, were Maslyn Williams, now a distinguished author but then a film-maker, and a colleague. In a small top-floor room lived Scottie Bear whose chief claim to my memory is that he was somehow descended from the family of Governor Macquarie, and once showed me a handsome pair of silver shoe buckles said to have belonged to the Old Viceroy. I often wonder what happened to them. Bathrooms on each floor, and a telephone in the entrance hall, were communal.

At about the time I moved to Elizabeth Bay the lease of the studio terminated. The old stone building was then demolished and on its site arose the Hospitals Contribution Fund building. However, since the Elizabeth Bay room was adequate for modest entertaining, the loss of the studio was not a disaster. It was nicely furnished and contained a handsome carved oak sideboard that Lily Bruce had purchased and had lovingly rubbed free of varnish and 'pickled' with lime. From the studio furniture I kept a glass-fronted set of book shelves and my wooden work table and chair. I bought a very sharp carving knife and a two-pronged fork from Nock and Kirbys (I still use them) and a few other basic needs, not least a mouse trap because the kitchen cupboard was infested with mice. Each shared kitchen had a penny in the slot gas cooker. These antique contraptions were rather larger than most micro-wave ovens and consisted of a small oven with two burners on top. Where Lily had discovered them I've no idea but even at the nineteen-fifties price of gas, they devoured pennies and their coin containers had to be frequently emptied. They provided *one* of Lily's good excuses for often entering our rooms.

It was in the Elizabeth Bay room that I first met Hal Porter who called in one evening with Beatrice Davis—they were on their way to dinner somewhere. I had admired his stories for a long time, chiefly in the

Bulletin. I knew Doug did not care for Hal much, and could see why. His 'dear boy', high camp affectedness would not appeal to Doug. I found him...enigmatic, then and later. The puzzle of Hal, the person, is one I never solved. Hal the writer, except for reservations about *The Actors*, I admire tremendously.

As soon as I set eyes on Lily Bruce I recognised her as a figure from my childhood. For years she had worked in Angus and Robertson's lending library which my father visited regularly to return and borrow books. When I sometimes accompanied him she'd caught my eye, darting like an energetic little bird from the book shelves to the polished wooden counter of the borrowing section. She was a tiny, eager woman who was now hell-bent on making a success of managing John Mansfield's 'boarders'. She tended the gardens, cleaned hallways and bathrooms and could be disconcertingly ubiquitous. For Lily the sun rose and set about Mansfield. In a vicarious way she was delighted with my arrival because I was the daughter of an architect who greatly respected him. She was immensely interested in his tenants—sometimes too much so. She wanted to construct her life around them, and their visitors. Often when we came in of an evening she lurked on the stairs clutching a book—usually a biography. 'I'm just off to bed with the Duke of Wellington.' But she obviously hoped for an invitation. Sometimes Mary and I were happy to ask her in for a drink, or to meet someone we thought she'd like, but her attentiveness and her curiosity could be intrusive.

One evening, not long before we left Elizabeth Bay, Lily was drinking coffee with me. She stayed and stayed. We had a glass of sherry. Quite suddenly, she became weepy. She said she had something to show me, went down to her own flat and returned with an exquisite collection of framed and unframed embroideries that her mother had sewn when she was a girl. Part of her account of her mother's background was to make the point that she came from a prosperous family whose daughters were instructed in so intricate and ladylike a pursuit as these fragile silk pieces exemplified. It was by now very late and I wished Lily and her voice, which as she went on became more and more refined, anywhere but in my room. Then she began to speak in a more natural tone. 'I shall tell you my story. I'd like you to know it.'

It was an almost unbelievable tale, but I had to believe it. Lily, an only child, described a happy Sydney childhood until her mother died. Her father re-married and the tale turned into a classic wicked stepmother account. Lily attended a famous private school. Early in the year during which she expected to study and sit for her Leaving Certificate, she went to school as usual one morning. Her father was away from Sydney at the time. When she came home in the afternoon she found the family house closed and locked. She had no key. While she puzzled as to what might have happened, and how she might get inside, a neighbour noticed her and called to her to come next door.

'Surely you knew,' said the neighbour 'that your stepmother moved out this morning. All the furniture has gone to her new address.' The neighbour did not know this address or how to contact Lily's family, but she offered the distraught girl a bed in her own house while enquiries were made. The rest of the affair was handled by her father's solicitor. Neither he nor his wife wished to see Lily again. She was about sixteen and virtually alone. Even her clothes had been packed and had vanished. She had a small living allowance from her father but no money for school fees. The worried solicitor found her a room in a boarding house and an unskilled job. Eventually her father returned to her some keepsakes of her own mother, the embroideries among them.

Soon after I moved to Elizabeth Bay I invited my mother to visit one afternoon. It was the first time I'd had a room that I thought she would approve of. She was delighted that I'd departed from the Kings Cross, Potts Point area, considering Elizabeth Bay a much better address. Lily knew of Mother's impending visit because I'd dashed home early from town. Lily changed from her usual blouse and skirt to a dress and lurked skittishly, as only Lily could, ready to appear and be introduced the moment Mum was inside the front door. To my utter fury they had a long conversation in the hallway, chiefly about me, in terms that suggested they'd quite forgotten my presence. I was determined that Lily would *not* join us for afternoon tea and at last, with great cordiality, the two ladies parted. 'Such a *charming* woman,' said Mum, admiring the sideboard. Indeed she seemed to approve my room and living arrangements and sent her warm greetings to absent Mary whom she liked. When she was ready to leave I offered to call a taxi to take her to Wynyard but she said she would prefer to walk up the quite steep hill of Elizabeth Bay Road and along to the tram stop at the Cross. I walked with her. Now in those days, before the Rex hotel at the top of Macleay Street and then the Chevron further down Potts Point were established, there were no public houses or bars in the whole area. The curious sights one might occasionally see seldom included drunks. If a person behaving eccentrically was high on drugs that explanation did not occur to us. We were never approached by sellers or pushers of drugs. Nor, as we walked those streets at all hours did we ever fear or expect muggers.

The afternoon with Mum had been successful; she was not censorious; I was feeling relieved and relaxed when, oh hell! some distance ahead of us on the pavement, a woman staggered into view who was so very drunk that it was pretty inevitable she should subside on the kerb, her feet in the gutter. As we approached her Mum gave her a sharp considering look.

'Oh come *on* Mum!'

'Are you all right?' asked my mother.

'Sh' OK,' said the disgrace.

So we walked on. 'Do you know who that was?' asked my mother. 'Good heavens,' I snapped, 'you hardly ever see an intoxicated person in this area and what is more, why would you suppose *I'd* know any of them?'

'Do you know who that *was?*' she repeated.

'No.'

'That,' said my innocent mama, 'was Miss Smith.'

'Miss who?'

'That charming receptionist at my hairdressers. I knew she drank a bit, but what a shame for her to get into that condition. When you walk back down the hill please try and make sure she's all right.'

But by the time I retraced my steps Miss Smith had vanished, leaving a puddle of vomit behind. Some weeks later I asked Mum whether Miss Smith was still employed by her hairdresser. 'Of course she is. She is a thoroughly competent girl. It is *most* unfortunate she has this failing. Otherwise she might have had a very good job indeed.'

I am glad that Providence ordained I should spend most of my childhood and youth in a Sydney that has vanished. I am equally thankful to have spent most of the rest of my life in what Sydney has become because of growth, technology and vision.

It used to be said that after twelve o'clock on a Saturday you could fire a rifle down many Sydney streets and not hit anyone, provided you avoided the queues outside movie theatres. On Sundays when theatres and corner hotels were closed city streets were even more deserted. Pleasant public places like the Queens Square and Martin Place mall of today did not exist. It was just as well that shops usually provided chairs for customers because there were no seats in arcades or at tram stops. Few buildings were taller than six storeys. Those in the centre of the city chiefly dated from the late nineteenth century and later. They were built of warm brown sandstone and of brick.

Some banks and major commercial buildings of the twenties and thirties were grand and decorative outside and indoors but many of the older structures that appeared pleasant and gracious from outside were often cold, badly lit, musty smelling and inconvenient inside. If they boasted a lift it was an ancient wrought iron cage driven by an attendant who was frequently an incapacitated returned serviceman from World War I. In many of them every floor was a rabbit warren of small businesses— hairdressers; agencies; tailors; music teachers; printers; stock brokers; merchants; and often they also housed small factories—book-binders; cabinet makers; picture framers; jewellers' workshops. Many of these must have been appalling fire hazards.

Dead as Sydney might look at weekends during the forties and fifties behind its sooty facades there was a lot of life because surprising numbers of people lived in its centre. One afternoon in George Street I met a young mother I knew who, with another young woman, was shepherding a chain of about twelve small children all holding hands. It was their turn to pick up children from St Patrick's school in Grosvenor Street and deliver them safely to their parents, most of whom were caretakers. I walked along with them. The party would pause at the front doors of buildings. An inconspicuous bell in the door embrasure alerted the caretaker or his wife who dashed downstairs to collect their child.

In George Street, near Bond Street a couple I knew lived with their small daughter in a penthouse surrounded by a garden planted between ventilators and chimney pots. Doug and Margaret Stewart, with Meg, lived at 12 Bridge Street. The Botanical Gardens were Meg's afternoon playground. Near Bathurst Street a conspicuously unreligious musician lived in a building that had no hot water or bathrooms—so he joined the YMCA to use their showers. There were a few elegant expensive apartment buildings like the Astor which is still in Macquarie Street, and several private houses remained, but most city-dwellers inhabited space in commercial buildings. Among those I knew the doyen was the playwright Sydney Tomholt. Maxine Poynton-Baker, nee Murray-Jones, was Tomholt's dear friend and I asked her to write a piece I could use here, because he, his circle of friends and The Room she describes are a part of Sydney life that should be recorded.

I did not know all of the people of whom Maxine writes but many of them have their place in this book. Together they are a roll-call of much of Sydney's creative life. Sydney Tomholt was born in Melbourne. He fought in France in World War I and thereafter travelled widely in China, Mongolia and the Philippines. He chiefly worked as a journalist.

I add to this account its missing person—Maxine herself. She has a wide knowledge of literature and the theatre and continues these interests in her retirement—before that she conducted a specialised employment agency for senior office and business personnel. Her warmth and charm, her eager beautiful speaking voice, her skill in catering at The Room in Granville Buildings made her a central half of the duo usually known as Tommy 'n' Maxine.

After the front door of Granville Buildings was closed at night unexpected friends would call loudly, from the corner of Hamilton Street 'To-o-o-m-e-e' until he responded; practised vocalists could shout his name in a most penetrating 'coo-ee'. A different world without even doorbells let alone security and intercom systems to announce and screen visitors.

Tommy thought and spoke so rapidly that he often uttered delicious malapropisms. Each of his friends could recall a favourite. I heard mine one very hot day when Mark was painting the ceiling of the flat Tommy rented after he left The Room. Tommy fussed and worried about Mark aloft on a ladder, and produced a jug of iced fruit juice, calling upwards: 'Do give yourself a break. Come down and take your feet off your body.'

Back to Maxine, however. Maxine remembers The Room:

Sydney Tomholt moved into Granville Buildings, Number 17 Bond Street, Sydney in January 1937 and lived there for more than twenty-seven years. He moved only when the building was pulled down to make room for Australia Square and he and his friends regretted the loss always. 17 Bond Street was a partly residential building that had originally been built and owned by Freddy Lane, the Australian Olympic swimmer and partner in Smith & Lane, printers. Much later it was owned by the AMP Society. Tomholt moved to the city because he had just joined the *Sydney Morning Herald* as freelance film critic to assist Kenneth Wilkinson who was Theatre, Opera, Film and Art critic on the *Herald* and the *Home* and also editor of *Art in Australia*, another *Herald* publication.

Among the people who lived in the building were Lute Drummond who had the penthouse on the roof and who taught and coached almost all the top, or coming, singers of the day in Sydney. Lute was an astonishing Australian of great simplicity who had lived in Europe and England for many years and had come back to Sydney to teach. Among her students were Kenneth Neate, a most successful singer for some years at La Scala, Milan, and Constance Pickworth and Robert Livingstone. Other tenants were Dulcie Wells who had divorced Ernest Wells, the novelist; Sampson, an accountant who had written a number of unpublished plays and stories; and Olga Gibson, a physiotherapist. There was not a great deal of fraternising among the tenants except for the occasional conversation in the lift.

Over the years Tomholt's friends included most of the literary figures who were his contemporaries and many who chiefly flourished in an earlier period. Tom Inglis Moore, poet, novelist, essayist and academic was among his oldest friends: they had met in the Philippines during the late twenties when Tom was Professor of English at the University of Santa Tomas and Tomholt was with the noted American Pacific Commercial Corporation. Tomholt returned to Australia in 1932; Inglis Moore in 1931 to find the Depression of that period well advanced. It was unnerving for both.

When Neville Cardus decided to settle in Sydney during World War II, and became Music critic of the *Sydney Morning Herald*, Kenneth Wilkinson left that paper and went to Melbourne where he worked in very much the same capacity for Sir Keith Murdoch. Tomholt then became Film and Theatre critic, and he also wrote the Music and Drama column each Saturday. Many theatre personalities who hoped for a line or two in his column called in to give Tomholt news of their current or forthcoming projects; others included Lew Parks who was J. C. Williamson's publicity officer, and various people who were from time to time public relations officers for the Tivoli Theatre. Doris Fitton, founder of the Independent Theatre and her husband 'Tug' Mason were frequent visitors and so were May Hollinworth, director of SUDS (Sydney University Dramatic Society) and, later of the Metropolitan Theatre; Beryl Bryant, founder with her father, Charles, of Bryant's Playhouse, called in often with news of their latest productions.

One colourful visitor of that period was Pierre Stuart-Layner who had been manager of the well-known Renaissance Theatre in Paris; he came to Sydney with his wife when the de Basil Ballet Company were here in 1940. Stuart-Layner brought many friends to visit Tomholt including, one night, the young cousin of King Farouk the ruler of Egypt at that time. On that occasion a very good friend, John Carrington, called in and was a trifle taken aback at being introduced to His Highness; but he took it in his stride, saying only afterwards that at first he had thought Tomholt was entertaining the local icecream men—both Stuart-Layner and the prince were wearing their tropical whites.

Tomholt's place was never called anything other than The Room (and he was always called Tommy). It was generally a casual 'See you down at The Room tomorrow night?' which decided who would be coming to have a sherry and a sandwich. A photograph taken in 1940 when Tom Inglis Moore joined the army—it appeared in *Southerly* at the request of the editor, Guy Howarth—shows Frank Dalby Davison, J. J. Hardie, Peter Hopegood, Inglis Moore and Tomholt; it should also have included Hugh McCrae but he had quickly made his getaway before the photographer and Tomholt could get hold of him. Hugh was a rare visitor because he was so shy, and would not even knock at the door if he heard voices inside The Room; but later he would send Tomholt a little note, with a pen-and-ink illustration, explaining why he had not joined the group—whereupon Tomholt would ring whichever of Hugh's daughters the poet was staying with while he was in Sydney, and call to see him instead.

Beatrice Davis and Hal Porter, Professor Henry Brose and his actress wife Jean Robertson who was Maurice Moscovitch's leading lady in America; Robert and Marjorie FitzGerald; Gwen Meredith of *Blue Hills* fame and her husband Ainsworth Harrison; J. J. Hardie, novelist and wool-classer and his French wife Margot; Tom Inglis Moore and his wife Peace; Nancy Keesing and her husband Mark Hertzberg; writers Max and Thelma Afford; artist Lindsay Parker and Joan; Kenneth and Betty

Wilkinson and later, after Ken's death, Betty with her second husband, journalist and wool-classer Bill Howard; solicitor Maurice Isaacs and his wife Eva who was an educationalist and writer; Tom Fitzgerald, the financial editor of *The Sydney Morning Herald* and his wife Margaret; James Meagher, the witty Irish solicitor and darling old Freddy Rayner, father of the Rayner sisters who began their Theatre of Youth and took it all over the world. Freddy also first taught David Low, the New Zealand cartoonist to draw; he had an immense fund of witty stories to tell. Walter Stone and his wife Jean were also among the groups of friends who collected at The Room to talk and laugh and argue.

Constance Robertson, a daughter of A. G. Stephens, and a colleague of Tomholt's at the *Sydney Morning Herald* where she was head of The Women Writers as the female journalists were known there, was a frequent visitor; and so were Guy and Lilian Howarth. There were Professor Robinson of the English department at the University of Brisbane, playwright Eunice Hanger, Cecil Hadgraft and David Rowbotham the poet, also of Brisbane and Miles Franklin, Frank Dalby Davison and his wife Marie; and so many others; Marc Greene, the roving correspondent of *The Christian Science Monitor* who had known Tomholt in Shanghai and encouraged him to apply for a job as journalist with the *Shanghai Times*, and called to see him whenever he was in Sydney; Tod Duncan, the original Porgy of *Porgy and Bess* in the New York production, and his accompanist on his Australian concert tours, William Allen; Dr Keith Macarthur Brown, president of the PEN Club in Sydney for a long period; Violet Roche who was public relations officer of the old Hotel Australia; Geoffrey C. Ingleton; George Ashton and his painter wife Dorothy; the writer—naturalist Archer Russell; Kenneth Slessor; Michael Noonan, a successful radio playwright in Sydney and Brisbane and later in Germany and the UK; Keith Planta Phillips and his wife Alice from Adelaide, whose excellent photographs of the Flinders Ranges and the Barossa Valley were printed by Rigby. Charles and Elsa Chauvel were also very good friends. Tomholt was called upon by Hoyts Theatres Ltd to 'vet' the scenario of *40,000 Horsemen* before they ultimately decided to part-finance the production. And another good friend in the Australian film world was Ken G. Hall.

During the war years John Carrington who at that time was the Registrar at Concord Military Hospital would sometimes bring a party of doctors to The Room for a night of talk; for Tommy was a raconteur with many stories of his life in Mongolia, Shanghai and the Philippines (he had lived in the East from 1922 to 1932) and it was a complete contrast for doctors, who were themselves recovering from the strains of operating on troops who had been brought by air from northern battlefields, to have some fun and laughter.

Although 17 Bond Street was residential and the bathrooms on each floor were more than adequate, cooking arrangements were fairly primitive; so guests generally had to be satisfied with limited salads and open sandwiches. However people visited for Tommy's company and not for gastronomic treats though, occasionally, if there were only two or three friends he would make a superb omelette which they enjoyed. During the war period it was practically impossible to buy toasters, electric kettles or stoves because all the materials used in their manufacture were used for the munitions industry. The tiny electric stove was little use for more than one but later an electric frypan made its appearance in The Room and very welcome it was.

Tomholt was an immaculate man, extremely systematic, so that The Room was always tidy, and though books and papers and magazines might have to be swiftly moved to make room for another body to seat itself, the situation was handled so lightly and with so many funny remarks that the unexpected or late guest was never made to feel anything but doubly welcome. His two big bookcases and his pictures, and the ornaments from China, Mongolia and the Philippines all added to the warm and personal atmosphere which was so particularly Tomholt.

I was constantly in or out of love, or half love, or imagined love, but never with a writer. Sometimes I would invite the man of the moment to a literary event and agonise because he seemed bored, or I worried that he might be bored, or boring to literary people, even when all evidence suggested that everyone was getting along perfectly well. If I record no romantic affairs with writing friends it is not that I have anything to hide on my account or theirs; there were none, or only the most occasional and impetuous expressions of affection. Once, for instance, after a fairly boozy English Association dinner, David Rowbotham and I realised that after midnight it would be *Bulletin* publication day. We both hoped poems of ours might appear, and devised an idea, most uncharacteristic for both of us (David was a quiet, rather shy young man), of visiting the loading dock behind 252 George Street in Harrington Street, and pleading for two copies hot off the press. Loading had not yet started but we decided to wait for doors to open, feeling increasingly cold and flat. A door did open. I turned and kissed a very startled David. The foreman in charge sent us packing without our hoped-for copies.

Ray Mathew began publishing his poems in the *Bulletin* in the late forties and poetry readers responded to his singing early poems immediately. No one had met the astonishing newcomer. He was a school teacher in a small western NSW town. He was just twenty-one when he came to Pennant Hills one weekend to talk about possible publication by

Lyre Bird Writers. He walked across the grass looking nothing like a rising star, but a nervous, plump boy dressed in shirt, slacks and sports coat. We sat in the garden and mother and I desperately tried to find topics that would rescue him from obvious sheer fright. Dad, so often impatiently discounted by me, took matters in hand and whisked Ray off to inspect his flock of Rhode Island Red poultry, his orange orchard and vegetable garden. Just as I worried about my non-writing friends in gatherings of writers, I worried about my writing friends in Dad's clutches despite clear evidence that most of them found him an enchanting eccentric and greatly enjoyed his booming observations. By the time the tour was complete the two men, talking eagerly together, and on very good terms, came in to lunch.

Lyre Bird Writers agreed to publish *With Cypress Pine*, which came out in 1951. Arrangements were made by letter. The book must have appeared during a school term for I remember posting copies to Ray and also to his parents who had a small shop in a beachside suburb. They replied with a letter that touched me immensely, because they were so very proud, and yet so obviously not aware of Ray's poetic gift, or what he was doing and hoped to do in life.

Within a year Ray left the country school to live and work, but not again as a school teacher, in Sydney. He was writing plays and poetry and meeting writers and actors, and had some paid work as a Sydney University extension lecturer and other jobs. He lived in a succession of grotty rooms around the Cross, and the Rocks. His friendship with the artist Pixie O'Harris (Mrs Bruce Pratt) began when she visited him in 'an awful little room in Victoria Street' and found him really ill. She bundled him into a taxi, took him home and nursed him—one of her daughters was ill too, so she had two patients on a verandah. I think the Pratt family truly were the fixed point of Ray's turning world at that time.

I have never met anyone who did not like Ray, but he seemed never to quite find his own spiritual place or, beyond a city full of friends, have a central one. Except, possibly, for Mena Abdullah. I never met her. At the time of their collaboration on the stories in that jewel of a book, *The Time of the Peacock*, I was housebound with young children, and also sometimes away from Sydney. Ray used to visit us at home, but always alone.

When I married he gave us a set of silver coffee spoons 'to measure out your lives by'. Then, at the height of the 'brain drain'—and the beginning one might have predicted, of a meteoric rise—he went to London. He has never returned. Unlike many expatriates of that time he did not win fame and fortune overseas. Mark went to see him a couple of times in London, but I had never met him again until we met twice, in New York in the late seventies.

Playing games with the 'ifs' of history is a pointless pursuit but when

the Literature Board was established in 1973, I used to think how different Ray's career might have been had adequate subsidies for great talent
been available fifteen years earlier; and ponder, too, as to what his place
might have been in the upsurge of local drama during and after the late
sixties. No country can afford to lose poets like Ray Mathew or they to
lose themselves. His poem 'Small Town' is from *With Cypress Pine*:

> It is a quiet place in the sun, tired
> and without apparent life, but warmed by a road
> fox-red and lolling on its way, and wired
> to the big towns for news—but weary. Time passes, slowed
> so that day dies without apparent effort, fired
> to colour like a parrot's wing, yet fitting in
> with the long yellow sweep of the plain, and the admired
> charm of our three-house town—respectable as sin.
> Our corrugated town with its peel-paint walls
> stares at the sunset, till stared-out the sun falls.
> Then it sinks into soft night as though it belonged,
> loses its shape to the dark like a fluid cat;
> an occasional glint of an eye, but still—though thronged
> with dream that gnaws the young heart like a quiet rat.

Yvonne Webb, a poet, took me to meet Dame Mary Gilmore in her flat
in Darlinghurst Road near the actual cross roads of Kings Cross. In a
dark, orderly room Dame Mary sat in a straight backed chair by her desk,
Australia's grandmother. Outlined against a window she looked formid-
able, but her warm manner and voice put one at ease, and so did her
unforgettable sweet smile. She wished to hear about Lyre Bird Writers
which she thought was a splendid project. She spoke of Roland Robinson's poetry which she admired but she was cross with him about some
matter in his personal life and tart, and direct in her strictures. As was her
way, and privilege, she claimed to have inspired Roland to found the
group. Perhaps she did.

Yvonne was one of several girls whom Dame Mary had encouraged to
write when they were children. The *Australian Author* of December 1985
includes a long article by Yvonne Webb about their friendship. From
that time I visited Dame Mary but only if I had reason—a book to show
or give, or news to interest her. She had many friends and I did not want
to intrude on her old age. She spun a yarn or read poetry in her beautiful
resonant voice, or sometimes, for she was no effigy, gossiped enjoyably
not only about people from the past, but present happenings. Anyone
who acted in a way she thought hurtful to someone else made her truly
angry.

When I became engaged to Mark Hertzberg Dame Mary wrote me a
very excited letter. Henry Lawson sometimes signed himself 'Henry

Hertzberg Larsen' and she was sure of a link. I had to explain that Mark's German Jewish forebears could not be connected with Henry's Scandinavian antecedents.

Yvonne Webb had some talent in writing poetry, but her real genius was for living and enriching life for others. She was the most self-reliant person I knew. I think her sister was her only living relative; to me, who often felt constricted by a large, loving, extended family, Yvonne's absolute freedom seemed enviable.

For instance my mother took great exception to a sequence of poems called 'About Caroline' and was angry when I not only published them in the *Bulletin* but also, despite her wishes and quite rightly, in *Three Men and Sydney*. The sequence owed a good deal to a print of a painting by Doris Zinkeisen showing the traditional 'furry dance' performed annually somewhere in England, and much to ideas of myth absorbed from Peter Hopegood and my reading of Robert Graves. No part of it was intended to symbolise my mother though it did express some deeply unhappy feelings about myself. During my childhood my New Zealand cousin Charles Brasch, who was a fine poet, early imbued with a 'modern' approach to his art, would send copies of his works to my grandmother Hart, whose drawing room, full of aunts and other family, would make merry about Charles' incomprehensible 'rubbish'. I was too young to comprehend his talent or meaning, but I *knew* they were wrong, absolutely.

So Yvonne said she envied me my family, and enjoyed coming to barbecues at Pennant Hills, whereas I thought *her* state desirable indeed. She had a charming small flat in a then fairly new building in Stanley Street off William Street, at a time when it was difficult for young single women to rent flats. Her sadness was that animals were forbidden. She yearned for a dog; she rode well, too, and often spent weekends with friends who kept horses.

When Yvonne ate a carefully prepared evening meal by herself she set a table mat, with good cutlery and nice glass, and arranged food on her plate carefully, as I discovered once when I arrived unannounced as she was about to begin her dinner. A revelation not so much about living alone, as about being alone, and having standards.

She was a slender woman with hands like the wings of birds—long-fingered, expressive. In her warm caressing voice she could turn almost any incident into a good story. As well as a routine, regular clerical job she had several sidelines such as typing addresses on hundreds of envelopes for a mail-order business. Yvonne could find entertainment for her friends even in that boring task.

Yvonne answered an advertisement for a woman to demonstrate a new sort of fruit-bottling kit in department stores. She was interviewed, and got the job. High drama! She had never filled and processed a vacuum jar in her life, but a crash course from a domesticated friend over a weekend gave her confidence to sail into the work—which she did so well she was asked to judge the bottled fruit section at the Royal Easter Show. The usual judge who had performed the task for years beyond memory was not available.

Yvonne caused a sensation by asking for each bottle to be opened so she could not only admire their jewel-like appearance, but taste their contents. It turned out that the immemorial system had been for the entries to be judged on appearance, evenness, skill of arrangement, and so on. Knowledgeable Show entrants bottled their fruits and vegetables in brine, a method that gave them a lustrous look, but it was not intended for them to be actually eaten. Some competitors entered prize bottles at one show after another. Yvonne was adamant, the competitors dismayed and angry, but the prize was awarded to an amateurish entry whose maker, inexperienced in show competition, had bottled her fruit in sugar syrup.

In people's flats and houses, in coffee shops, at my studio, we read and gossiped. Our 'Balmain' was all over Sydney. Our groups overlapped. Donovan Clarke and his following might be at Yvonne's rather than at Roland Robinson's flat at Rose Bay where Barbara, Roland's wife (too seldom because we all talked too much) might play the piano. Joyce Shewcroft, poet and legal officer at the ABC, and her friends and David Rowbotham, who worked briefly as a salesman in a shop in Sydney before he embarked on a course at the University of Queensland, might be at Roland's, but not at Yvonne's. We reached high pitches of fun or fury on cups of tea, or perhaps a glass or two of cheap sherry or beer. No one served expensive food and there was no keeping up with the arty or poetic Joneses.

One day while Dorothy Fairbridge and I were at the studio, a diffident poet, newly arrived from New Zealand, came in and showed us a sheaf of handwritten poems. His name was Bruce Beaver. We thought his poetry very fine and Dorothy offered to type his manuscript so that he could submit his work to editors.

At Doug Stewart's flat conversation was considerably more authoritative and much less scatty. Poets like David Campbell and Doug were beyond exhausting endless chatter, and in time I, and most of the participants, tired of it too, or went elsewhere, or married and went home of an evening.

Wolfe Fairbridge, a distinguished marine biologist was a fine poet and the most handsome man imaginable. He and Dorothy had not been long married when they joined the English Association. Dorothy's first marriage had been disastrous; her life had been difficult; now she was happy; they were a couple from whom joy emanated. When their new house at

Cronulla was built Wolfe celebrated with his joyful, optimistic poem, *Consecration of the House*. Not long after they moved into their new home, Wolfe went to the Marine Biological Station at Perth for several weeks. While he was away Dorothy became suddenly ill. She was partly paralysed until her doctor found, and removed, a tick that was discharging its poison close to her spine. She recovered quickly. Wolfe returned home feeling ill; *he* became paralysed. It was no tick but a rare and almost invariably fatal form of polio. Victims who lived were doomed to be extensively crippled. Wolfe died, within days, in 1950.

In 1953 the CLF sponsored his book, *Poems*, which has a pastel portrait of him as a frontispiece, and an introductory account of his brief and distinguished career in science and poetry written by Tom Inglis Moore.

I found for Dorothy a room on the same floor as mine, in a block of flats called 'Carinthia' in Springfield Avenue at Potts Point. Her landlady was a sympathetic and understanding woman. Dorothy was a first-rate typist and secretary and took a congenial job. She tried to rally and to put on a brave face, but remained stricken and exhausted. In the face of appalling grief there is little anyone can do except be available.

It may have been my mother or perhaps it was Dorothy's landlady who suggested that a change of scene to a place without associations with Wolfe, or her past life, might improve matters, so we planned for a fortnight's holiday. But where? It must be a reasonably cheap place that we could get to without a car. We did not want to be among jolly young holiday makers and honeymoon couples but neither did we want to be bored, or entirely dependent on each other's company. My somewhat difficult list of requirements posed no problem to the understanding man I interviewed at the NSW Government Tourist Bureau. He told me of a farm house at Oberon which recently had been acquired by Mr Pitt, a retired officer of the Australian Red Cross Society, and his wife. From Oberon regular bus services ran to the Jenolan Caves which neither Dorothy nor I had seen. The Pitts usually had several guests, chiefly trout fishermen at weekends, so we should find company.

Our journey began with a train on the Bathurst line. At Tarana, a tiny junction, we waited to change to the small train, or it may have been a rail motor, that climbed up to Oberon. As we stood on the Tarana platform the only other passengers for Oberon were a pair of archetypal hayseed youths who spoke as one and seemed to share one not very powerful brain. They followed us into our locked, dog-box compartment where we faced each other on rigid benches. After the formalities of 'Where y' goin?' and 'Why?' the train climbed up steep grades and the boys looked out the windows to spot rabbits, a pastime of endless fascination for them.

'Look!' they kept calling to Dorothy by her window, 'There he goes.

Can't you see 'un? Y' can spot 'un by their liddle white tails.' After the umpteenth repetition of 'liddle white tails' our faces cracked into violent fits of giggles. Dorothy's eyes streamed with tears—of laughter. The boys looked hurt and puzzled and as soon as we recovered we invented some lying explanation for our mirth. For the rest of the holiday 'liddle white tails' became a talisman phrase. Those lads were better companions than they could ever know.

The Pitts were admirable people, their farmhouse large, sprawling and comfortable, set low to the ground on stone foundations. There were good walks nearby to the Fish River, or along back roads, but we spent the first few days at Jenolan and enjoyed ourselves.

In the large dining room we came to know people of the household. Elderly Miss Grimshaw, very stiff and haughty, was a permanent boarder. Dorothy discovered she was the legendary Beatrice Grimshaw, author of many novels of adventure and romance in New Guinea—a country where she had lived and which she had explored, in her youth.

Dorothy became a great favourite of the old lady's, but I blotted my copybook early in the acquaintance, and was not forgiven. Miss Grimshaw looked rather like Dame Mary Gilmore, and her voice bore some resemblance, though she lacked Dame Mary's warmth, vitality and charm. I addressed her as 'Miss Gilmore' by mistake. Green-eyed jealousy glared from her old eyes—a smart reprimand snapped from her mouth. However, she asked Dorothy, could she, a mature woman, choose to come away with that Nancy person? To Dorothy she confided the story of her great love. The man died of fever with his head resting in her lap, as they drifted by boat down a New Guinea river. Whether or not one liked Miss Grimshaw, her intrepid youth had to be wondered at, and her achievements in writing respected.

Perhaps we might have improved our feelings about each other, but I blotted my copybook again. In the dining room a man and his wife who had driven to Oberon by car asked Dorothy and me whether we would like to accompany them on a drive—the man was going to visit the local abattoir. I said yes. Miss Grimshaw turned round from her table and boomed: 'Reahhllay young woman, what will you agree to next? An abattoir is no place for young ladies.'

I have never seen an abattoir.

Two competent girls helped with the kitchen and housework and served in the dining room; their sisters and cousins lent extra hands at weekends when the house filled up with fishermen. Their willing meal-time service was seldom prompt enough for Miss Grimshaw who would clap her hands emphatically and call 'Gurrl, Gurrl,' as I suppose she once called 'Boy! Boy!' to native servants in the good old days. The Pitts were infinitely kind to their difficult guest.

At last she really did have legitimate cause for complaint when a gravid bitch belonging to the house crept under its foundations and whelped directly beneath the floorboards of her room. The pups squealed and disturbed her sleep. The place was built too close to the ground for anyone to move the pups, so Miss Grimshaw was given a temporary room elsewhere.

One day, dressed in her best clothes, hat and gloves she awaited Eris O'Brien, the historian, who was the Roman Catholic Bishop of Goulburn. Mr Pitt told us that the bishop called for Miss Grimshaw once a month and took her for a drive.

I later described to Dr George Mackaness our strange meeting with Beatrice Grimshaw in that cold mountain place, and spoke of Eris O'Brien's kindness. My story was no news to him.

'Did anyone tell you why she lives at Oberon? Or where he takes her on those outings?'

'No.'

'They go to visit her brother. He's a lifer in Goulburn Gaol...'

Dorothy and Yvonne found a run-down, dirty sandwich shop in a factory area, and took it on very cheaply. They cleaned and scrubbed fanatically, then painted and furbished. They cooked their own meats and other sandwich fillings instead of buying from suppliers, not so much to save money as because they had strong ideas about food and quality. They made no fortune but did rather well.

Dorothy met a journalist, James Holledge who wrote regular pages of history and biography for an evening newspaper. He had the most comprehensive and exquisitely ordered filing system of reference material I've ever seen. Dorothy and James moved to a cottage with a huge garden near Mittagong. Yvonne married, went to live in an outer suburb, and had not one but many dogs at last because she operated an excellent boarding kennel.

One morning in about 1950 I stood on the railway platform at Pennant Hills reading a book and waiting for a train to town. An elderly man whose slightly familiar face I could not place came up and reminded me that we'd met at the house of Clyde and Dorothy Moyes—Clyde was editor of the *Bulletin's* financial pages. He was F. M. (Fred) Cutlack, a retired senior journalist who now, he told me, lived at Castle Hill. Years ago he and Dad knew each other: 'I decided to interrupt your reading young Nancy because there is something important I want to say, especially to someone of your generation. The greatest writer this country has ever produced, maybe one of the greatest of our times in the world, has come home after years overseas. He's a neighbour of ours at Castle Hill. You probably haven't heard of him because his novels so far have scarcely been noticed in Australia and the great books that are in him haven't been written yet. But sometimes you can sense a climate changing—I want you to remember what I've told you. All the best to your Dad.'

The train pulled in, he turned away. 'What's the man's name?' I called after him.

'Patrick White.'

By 1956 Mark and I had painted the shabbiest rooms of our new house, and bought furniture, and unpacked wedding presents and settled down with our first baby. I was at least managing to write radio scripts and reviews. Then Mark announced that from August he would have to spend a few weeks in Perth installing a new process. Now I have never minded being alone in houses, and had, indeed several times been alone in ours, but for some reason I decided Margery and I must travel to Perth too. As matters turned out Mark struck problems there, and the few weeks became nearly five months. I was more than thankful for whatever premonition prompted my decision, especially as the Perth interlude was one of the great experiences of my life.

Confusion reigned, and in making arrangements, and finalising my own projects, the publication of *The Tree of Man* claimed little of my attention. It had to claim *some* attention, however, because of Kylie Tennant's warmly expressed feelings about the splendour of the novel and the wretched ineptitude and insensitivity of a couple of its reviews. She published a hot defence of *The Tree of Man* and, in consequence, she and Patrick became friends. Eventually, through her, we met him. But just then I had neither time nor inclination to begin reading a major new work.

Our ship stopped for a day in Adelaide where I rushed into the first bookshop I saw and bought a copy of *The Tree of Man* for 22/6d. I have never suffered from sea-sickness but reading was scarcely possible as our ancient P & O vessel pitched and tossed through the Bight. Indeed I spent much of my time sterilising the baby's utensils under a steam jet available for that purpose, and waiting for a comparatively calm moment before venturing my hands near its hissing vapour.

So I first read *The Tree of Man* in Perth and, without benefit of Fred Cutlack or Kylie or anyone else, I would have been bowled over. In the circumstances it acquired the added dimension of making me homesick, for its Sarsparilla landscape is my heart's country—the Hills district near Sydney that I'd explored in the forties on horseback, foot and bicycle. I knew its side streets and tracks into bush, its farms and hidden ways. I was not aware of an allegedly difficult style as I read. I found Patrick White's prose, and his way of conveying the accents and cadences of dialogue, glittering and exhilarating. I'm thankful I came to him without benefit of critics and commentators. Stan Parker's rows of dewy cabbages were our cabbages. His bushfire was the one in which Dad and one-armed Mr Morrison, our Scottish neighbour, dashed into the bush to carry forth the comatose Browns, two old pensioners who drank their cheque each weekend in a shack that burned to the ground. Mr Whye, down the road from us had axed and cleared his farm from virgin bush and built his own house of slabs, and, like Stan had raised a family that turned out puzzling and uncongenial to their parents.

Back in Sydney Mark and I met Patrick and Manoly, visited each other's houses, and ate each other's cooking experiments. I am puzzled by Patrick's frequent references in *Flaws in the Glass* to disasters with cooking, because I recall delicious meals of adventurous food and only one *contretemps*, when someone's hand slipped adding chilli in Chilli con Carne, which was most fearsomely hot. I must say, though, that at the time we wondered whether that dish was a test for guests—there were some exceedingly ingratiating and pretentious people at Castle Hill that night and long after most friends had given up on the chilli these people, with insincere protestations of enjoyment, continued to eat it. I would not have put it past Patrick to sort out sycophants in such a way.

Then we fell out of touch. One reason may have been a petition that Patrick circulated and that I would not sign, though I'd signed others he had sent me before. I support a similar progressive and compassionate brand of political thought and action as Patrick. I admire, very much indeed, his emergence into political action and public speaking, for he often said how little he cares for platforms and public appearances. I have forgotten the precise occasion for, and topic of, the ill-fated piece of paper but do recall that it contained a paragraph phrased in a way I could not accept, and would not, in honesty, put my name to. I telephoned him to explain—a distinct cool blast entered my ear through the receiver.

I am sorrier for the other reason, which I did not suspect until I read *Flaws in the Glass*.

The beginning of the incident was when I mentioned to Patrick, not when he was 'an old man' as he writes in his book, but in his middle age, that my babies were born in Lulworth, the maternity section of St Luke's Hospital, and once the house where the White family lived. We then swapped stories of infant walks in Rushcutters Bay Park, for I grew up at Darling Point. Patrick and I shared considerable early childhood territory. Patrick and Manoly kept pug dogs and I recalled how old Mr Edmund Resch, the brewer who lived on Darling Point Road in a huge stone house called 'Swifts', would in my day—which was a decade later than Patrick's—control his pug dog not with a lead but with a little leather whip. If he tapped the dog on its right flank it would turn left, and vice versa. Once the tiny local bus drove by and tooted Mr Resch, and whoever was conducting my walk that day said how rude the driver was to tease a lonely old man. Patrick capped that by telling me a story that conveyed, even after so many years, a residue of bewilderment, and a feeling of something horrible from his childhood. His much-loved Scottish nurse, during the excess of anti-German fever of World War I, took a very young Patrick (he was born in 1912 so he cannot have been more than four or five) and his sister on one of their daily walks to the massive iron gates of 'Swifts', and made them spit on the gates.

Years after Patrick told me this I wrote a verse sequence about my Darling Point childhood and some of the incidents and personalities of the peninsular which had several well-known promenading eccentrics; and the sequence included a poem that recounts Patrick's story. I sent him a copy of it in all good faith and trustfulness. In *Flaws in the Glass* Patrick imputed that I was after a cheap laugh, and gratuitously lectured me about what my feelings as a Jew would have been if...

If, in its entirety, the poem does seem cheaply funny, by intention or not, then I really am an atrocious poet:

> Mr Resch walks a pale sad pug
> Which snuffles. Aunt calls it 'Edmund's Bug.'
> It is not on a lead. With a plaited whip
> He taps its right shoulder
> Or its left hip;
> So the pug walks straight on the wide footpath
> Ahead of Mr Resch. We laugh.
>
> Mr Resch lives in a grey stone mansion;
> It has battlements and gates of iron
> The Darling Point bus like a red toy tub
> Drives past and toots
> Mr Resch's pug
> Which snuffles. Resch seems not to hear.
> Aunt says he's a brewer of excellent beer.
>
> But Patrick White has a tale that's worse.
> He was marched one day by his patriot nurse
> From Elizabeth Bay to that castle called Swifts.
> At the gates of iron
> Of the German's house
> His nurse said 'Now!' and she made him spit.
> Innocence falters because of it.

Here is what Patrick wrote in *Flaws in the Glass*:

> Lizzie's [his nurse] hatred of Germans set solid. When we were slightly
> older she once took us on a walk and had us spit on the gatepost of Resch
> the brewer's Gothic castle. As an old man I described this incident,

jokingly, to the poet Nancy Keesing, who wrote a poem referring to 'the righteous indignation of Patrick White's nurse'. She got her laugh, like some journalist, for telling only half the truth, though the fault was mine. If I had projected Lizzie's figure, crumpled on the bed, her grief, my childish impotence and misgivings, the poem might never have been written. What to tell and what to leave out while conveying the truth remains the great question. The actor in us cannot always resist the laugh, just as the journalist has to impress his personality, as I found out during Hitler's War when facts I had given correspondents were falsified in the writing up. I am pretty sure Nancy Keesing if led by a Jewish nurse past Resch's gatepost after Hitler's War would have found it perfectly natural to spit.

Well, as it happens, no. Apart from being adult by then, it would never have occurred to me during Hitler's War that Germans *long established* in Australia had anything to do with the carnage in Europe and the genocide of my people.

As footnote to this episode of misinterpretation, Christina Stead heard me read the sequence. She liked it very much and particularly the Resch/White poem, so I typed a copy of all the Darling Point poems for her, with a dedication.

It is sad to lose friends for whatever reasons. I do miss Manoly, but after *Flaws in the Glass* can't feel the same about Patrick. I think that *The Twyborn Affair* is one of the most imaginatively compelling novels of this era. Once I'd have written to say that to Patrick.

I *did* write to him in 1959 to say how much I liked *The Aunt's Story* which I had just reviewed for the *Bulletin*. Patrick wrote back: 'Thank you very much for your letter and the article... You have the distinction of being the first person to write an understanding review of one of my books for the *Bulletin*, although I think possibly Douglas Stewart understands them better than he would care to admit...'

In any event the truest way to 'know' artists is in and through their works. I've always been thankful that I could enjoy and admire Dylan Thomas without having to endure his difficult acquaintance.

IX

Hunters Hill, and Perth

FOR twenty years Kylie Tennant and I were neighbours in Hunters Hill. She and her husband Lewis Rodd and their children Benison and John (Bimbi) at number 5 Garrick Avenue; Mark and I and Margery and John at number 3. Kylie and I had never met until we lived in adjoining houses.

When Mark and I married we leased a house at Lane Cove but hoped to find a place to buy as soon as possible and before the birth of our first child. John Robertson, a CSR colleague of Mark's and his wife Rua lived at Hunters Hill and knew of our desire. They also knew, as a very slight acquaintance, a man whom I'll call Jones whose wife had recently left him. Mr Jones needed a quick sale for his house and would shortly be approaching an agent to put it on the market. The Robertsons said it looked quite nice from the outside; they arranged with Jones for us to inspect it. Rua in fact did know Kylie from their schooldays in Manly.

Our knowledge of Hunters Hill was slight. The poet R. D. FitzGerald lived there, as his family had done for generations. We sometimes met Fitz and his wife Marjorie at Doug Stewart's house and at Sydney Tomholt's Room. In my schooldays I'd journeyed by ferry up the Lane Cove River to play tennis on the court of St Malo, a famous early house owned by the uncle of my friend Suzanne du Boise. I also knew that one of the old mansions was prototype of the house in Barnard Eldershaw's *A House is Built* (it is 'Merimbah' in Alexandra Street as Marjorie Barnard later told me).

In the late thirties Gertrude Scarlett accompanied one of her newly married sons and his wife to look at a house for sale in Hunters Hill, and put her foot down. 'You can't live here,' Scarlett said. 'Just *look* at all these run-down old empty places, and all the old people about. This is no place for a young couple who hope to have a family. You want to find a suburb where your children can make friends.' They settled elsewhere.

By 1955, although there were not many empty houses to be seen, much of 'the hill' as its residents affectionately refer to the peninsula was indubitably shabby in the calm before the storm of popularity that was about to burst upon it. Garrick Avenue had, and still has, eight houses, counting two on either side of Crescent Street. 'Avenue' over-dignifies it: it is a dead-end lane ending at a foot track that winds behind and beside the gardens of 'Passy' and lesser houses, to emerge in Passy Avenue. A century earlier Passy's grounds covered the whole area from the grand mansion down to the Lane Cove River. Excluding the two Crescent Street houses and number 3, the other five were built during the thirties. Number 3 was a vacant block until after World War II — a very useful dumping ground for its neighbour's garden rubbish. It retains a legacy of more, and more varied and ineradicable, weeds than, I swear, any other Sydney garden. It was built directly after the War by a builder as a wedding present for his daughter who sold it to Mr Jones. It was said to be the first dwelling constructed on the hill after the War and the Misses Budden, who conducted their long-established kindergarten nearby—one of their early pupils was R. D. FitzGerald—used to take the children for walks to see the novelty of joists being sawn and bricks being laid. (Henry Budden, their architect brother was for a time in partnership with my father's firm.)

After the War there were stringent restrictions on the sizes and construction of new houses and many materials were in short supply. 'Our' builder used stock he'd had in store since before the War; hence number 3 had dreadful lavatory cisterns that were virtual museum pieces but good quality, and generous doors and windows.

At first sight the house was unappealing. I'd sworn never to live in a house with stairs but this was a four-square, red-roofed, two-storey building. Despite weeds and neglect the lawn in front, and a grassed bank sloping from the house, were not too bad. There were some good trees.

Indoors Mr Jones showed us through to a litany of: 'That stain is where she threw a cup of coffee at me; that one is where I threw a cup of cocoa at her.' Every wall, upstairs and down, bore witness. He had been baching for some weeks and hadn't cleaned anything much. He had contrived to burn out the oven of an old electric stove that must have been pretty grotty before the mishap. The kitchen was painted in an awful combination of bright red and cream. But, and deservedly, his asking price was reasonable *and* (he offered expansively) he would throw in all those very good garden tools in the outside shed.

We said we'd think it over and arranged to meet him again within a few days. He was late for that appointment, the house was locked and one of us wished to make an urgent telephone call so we went to the house nearly opposite number 3 on the corner of Crescent Street because we could hear signs of life behind the door to its back porch. And so we met Jean Travanner, a slightly scatty looking woman wearing an ancient cotton dress. She had no telephone but said that Kylie, at number 5, would surely let us use hers. 'Kylie Tennant, the author, you know.' So we went next door and introduced ourselves to Kylie—expansive, ebullient, generous, of the cooing, crooning voice.

Mr Jones arrived. We bought his house—the only one we ever looked at. We were probably mad but we did wish to be settled before Margery was born.

'Oh,' said an affected young mother I knew, 'you're lucky to be going to Hunters Hill. Mr Rodd, the headmaster there, is a *marvellous* man; he gave a talk to our parents' group. His ideas for children are *so* creative. Quite marvellous.'

When I first met Lewis Rodd (Roddy), Kylie's quietly spoken, quiet-mannered husband, I remembered those words with some incredulity; but as we got to know him better I understood their truth. Dear Roddy, always neat, always it would seem, composed within the chaos of his house. Often invisibly working or reading out of sight.

We started to paint our rooms. As we finished each one we said gleefully, 'That's another de-Jonesed!' We had a card table, a few chairs and bed. Most of our furniture had yet to be delivered. We put in a new electric stove. There were no carpets and the Jones bit of green rug in the hallway fortunately didn't matter when we happened upon a large Aylesbury duck in the living room and found its droppings all over the floors. It was an amiable bird and left without nervousness or protest. The next day it was back. 'It belongs to Kylie,' Jean Travanner said. 'Of course she *ought* to clip its wings, but Kylie does not believe in restricting the freedom of anything or anyone.'

Kylie did not, however, object to eating her duck. 'It was due to be a dinner anyway.' A little boy of about six materialised behind her; he had a wide, perpetual smile. He'd been christened John, was known as Bimbi and privately, by me, nicknamed Smiler. His sister Benison was a few years older.

Jean Travanner had four daughters. Two were married but Jane, about eleven, and Michelle, about eight, were still at home. Soon after we moved to number 3 Michelle was old enough to return from school by herself, so Jean who was a trained Home Economics teacher took a job at a High School. She also, in the early days of TV transmission, gave a series of cookery demonstrations.

Vi Binet, Del Searley and Olwen Dill Macky made of the Avenue a lane of good cooks. Kylie professed to be uninterested in swappings of recipes, but was in fact an excellent cook and hospitable hostess. Every few weeks she attacked her housework with an energy and thoroughness that left me gasping.

Kylie's parents were separated. Her father, referred to as 'the parent', was a retired businessman who lived at Woy Woy. Mrs Tennant lived somewhere closer and often visited. Kylie's voice with its crooning quality came directly from her mother but her dashing good looks were very different. When Kylie could be bothered to take trouble with dress and grooming she could look nearly as stunning as she does in Eric

Saunders's portrait of her as a young woman. Mrs Tennant, by contrast, was always exquisitely groomed and made up—to emphasise her delicate complexion and features that much resembled the dainty face of a Dresden china shepherdess.

In 1986 *The Autobiography of Kylie Tennant/The Missing Heir* was published. Hilary McPhee, reviewing this book in *Australian Book Review* wrote of 'the voice of this kindly and gutsy old girl telling her tale' and said 'Kylie Tennant hasn't taken the task of telling the story of her life too seriously.'

Not taking life too seriously is also a feature of Kylie's fiction that has been remarked upon by critics, some with approval, some with a less admiring stance. On the whole, the later the critic the more adverse the judgement. H. M. Green had an effective cut-off date of 1950 for *A History of Australian Literature* and wrote of Kylie: 'Almost all her images are humourous, ironically humourous as a rule...outright, vigorous and highly individual.' Green considered that her 'fundamental limitation consists in her utter carelessness of structure'. Twenty years down the line Adrian Mitchell in *The Oxford History of Australian Literature* says: 'Early and late, her fiction is less than serious, even as comedy. It has the false realism, the factitiousness, of the popular fiction of the period, affirming the amorphous legendry of a working-class (or unemployed) Australia but failing to formulate a co-ordinating vision of its own.'

In the house next door Tennant life did its best to mimic Tennant art, or artlessness. No one would desire to read constantly the work of one novelist no matter how good or great, and no other books at all. To live close to Kylie was often to be too uncomfortably and constantly close to the fiction of her life. At the centre of this she existed as a montage of her female central characters: gallant, undaunted, ever eager to confront problems and disasters with a jest—or else to make light of, or appear to disregard, major difficulties.

When life at Number 5 was on a reasonably even keel her intelligence and vivacity were a delight, but from time to time most people and families (including those who live in leafy middle class suburbs) encounter major problems and even disasters. Unfortunately Kylie's family was disturbed and disrupted by Roddy's increasingly severe, and increasingly evident, mental breakdown—to a degree and in ways that caused immense concern to neighbours. If Kylie's gallant, jaunty reactions and evasions were often difficult for her near neighbours to accept—irritating and inappropriate at best and profoundly disturbing at worst—her immediate family could not and did not respond in matching ways and her attitudes did indeed cause destructive problems.

This is how, in her autobiography, Kylie describes her husband's near death and grave injury in a suicide attempt:

I had heard Roddy's threats of suicide all my married life. Whenever he was in low health he was going to end it all. 'Where is your Christianity?' I would retort. 'You are meant to live out your life however strong your masculine death wish. Don't let me hear you say such a thing.' I had moved him uneasily from Laurieton to this Jude-the-Obscure gothic school with the idea that a change of scene would restore him. For some years it did. Now I had given him the perfect excuse to load the blame of his planned demise on me.

I came home to a houseful of gas or Roddy lying insensible from the effects of cramming handfuls of tranquillisers. His iron will was now set on his objective. My will was equally iron. He was going to stay alive. His last attempt, after a deepening insanity which saw him in and out of convalescent homes, even shock treatment, nervous breakdown, doctors, psychiatrists, was to fling himself under a train at Circular Quay. He recovered with a fractured skull, the loss of an arm and a foot. 'They'll be calling you Privet Hedge Rodd,' I told him when he was semi-conscious. 'You've certainly clipped yourself all around the edges.' He managed to smile.

After that he gave up trying to commit suicide. He became my first priority and a domestic tyrant because his lightest wish was law. If it was not he would relapse. He was chained by life to a rock and I was that rock. We never slept together again. Instead I nursed him. I had become once more the mother figure giving him total attention which he had craved.

He had been told he would never walk save with two sticks. He walked in the front door without any sticks at all. He was in great pain for the rest of his life and set himself to learn to write a clear hand—with his left hand. He taught himself to type, one-handed, on an electric typewriter...

...I went on earning money. There were the children, there was Roddy. My bounds had narrowed to the pride that told me nobody should have occasion to pity me. Crowds of friends, doctors, advice, flowers, kindnesses had been pouring in on us. It should cease.

We gave a 'Put Out More Flags' party when Roddy came home from hospital and the children handed round savouries, very courteously.

Throngs of friends came and saw they had no need to sympathise. We then resumed our literary industries and saw that the children had gaiety and warmth. 'I had a wonderful childhood,' Bim once said when he too was trying to kill himself. 'Nobody had a better childhood than I did.'

That is not how we, and other neighbours of the time, recall increasing worry and anxiety on Roddy's behalf before those events, or how we remember the harrowing weeks and months that followed, during which we witnessed, and admired, Roddy's struggle to walk and to work again. Neighbours also feared for the children and the effect upon them of long-continuing trauma. These fears were far from groundless —particularly for Bimbi as *The Missing Heir*, though evasively, makes plain.

Nor in her book does Kylie mention Donald McLean who lived a mile or so away and, in his retirement, was a most devoted friend to Roddy. Don in his own youth had lost an arm and his help could be very practical; he also became Roddy's confidant and his collaborator in compiling an anthology of Australian prose, *Venturing the Unknown Ways* (1965). For some years that kind and wise friend was always on call and spent at least one morning each week with Roddy.

Roddy transformed himself into a splendid, virtually full-time editor. I think he had always advised about and helped to edit Kylie's books—now he also gave his skills to other people. The word 'gave' is deliberate. I doubt whether one or two authors of well-received factual books fully realised what they owed to Roddy. He was a meticulous checker of facts and also understood how material should best be assembled and arranged. He was gentle and tactful and, at least once practically re-fashioned and re-wrote a manuscript whose author never properly appreciated what had happened to a good idea and some detailed research buried in a disordered mess of paper.

But back to beginnings. Jean Travanner owned two thieving cats, a black-and-white one called Fill-us and a tabby called Hope-full. A later cat was called Depussy. I learned the hard way to keep the kitchen door shut and food within cupboards. George and Del Searley lived (and still do) at the head of the Avenue. Their son Jim was about four. He had a pet rabbit which escaped from its hutch when it could. My first view of Jim was a pair of plump legs sticking out from beneath our garden shed under whose floor the rabbit found refuge. Behind us in a huge garden that has since been sub-divided, people kept ducks and chooks in a wired enclosure. Old, untrimmed shrubberies harboured families of feral cats and bandicoot burrows—the bandicoots tunnelled through our lawn spreading plentiful ticks and grass ticks. Birds and blue-tongued lizards were a joy. I'd never expected so much wildlife in an inner suburb.

Indirectly through Mr Jones we met other neighbours who called to enquire whether, by any chance, he'd left behind 'a mattock I lent him' or 'a lawn mower I lent him'...The splendid garden tools Jones had donated were soon back in the hands of their owners.

Hunters Hill, like Darling Point, is a peninsula. It, too, had a delightful population of elderly eccentrics. Where did Miss F buy the high-buttoned boots she wore till the day she died? Who were the pair of dotty sisters, twins perhaps, one of whom outside Mr Mussett's newsagency approached Mark to ask, 'Pardon me sir, but have you, by any chance, a lemon in your pocket?' Perhaps she'd vainly tried to buy a lemon from Mr Mussett whose remarkable shop stocked just about everything. (Reta Grace once told me of two children in Passy Avenue who caught a tame budgerigar that had obviously escaped from its cage.

Their mother contrived a temporary residence for the bird and sent the children to buy bird seed from Mr Mussett; for once he could not meet their request and was most distressed.)

Opposite the newsagency Mr Taniane and his sister lived above their fruit shop in what had been the Garibaldi Inn, built by Italian stonemasons whom early French settlers imported to fashion most of the beautiful sandstone houses for which the suburb is famous. Mr and Miss Taniane were peculiar, grudging shopkeepers who really only wanted to serve old, long-known customers.

Another phenomenon of that vanished era was the Hunters Hill Hat. Every woman between fifty and ninety-seven seemed to own a high-crowned, wide-brimmed hat of either straw or felt whose trimmings varied with the seasons. One day all the Hunters Hill Hats would be trimmed with sober-coloured ribbons and a few judicioiusly placed clusters of artificial fruits and dried seeds as they'd appeared during winter. Then Spring sprung and the brims supported a riot of fresh ribbons, artificial field flowers and bits of wheat. Come high Summer and neat arrangements of grosgrain ribbon, tucked and with a huge bow at the front, were *de rigueur*.

The large Sydney ferries no longer visited the Lane Cove River wharves, most of which had been demolished. But each morning and evening the *Radar*, owned and operated by Mr Rossman, put in at the jetties at Alexandra and Mornington Streets and took workers to and from the city. When Mark first boarded the *Radar* he realised that every passenger had his or her place, and knew it; a newcomer had to brave glares and stares to settle on a seat anywhere. Poet R. D. FitzGerald to the rescue. Few residents of the hill were longer established than Fitz who, like Mark, preferred to sit outside. Mark's place beside him was assured. Apart from general conversation their shared passion for mathematical puzzles beguiled many ferry trips. Fitz also told Mark much local history. Long before this time a great number of lawyers and judges from virtual legal dynasties had lived on the hill. Fitz's relatives, the Windeyers, still did; and so did Ruth Manning, daughter of a judge and friend of my great-aunt Dal. Consequently legal shop-talk dominated ferry conversations. One day Mr X, a young barrister, pleaded in court before Mr Justice X, his father. He made his submission until the judge interrupted: 'No, no, my boy. This is *not* what I told you to say on the ferry this morning!'

Kylie coined 'word factories' for the sound of our adjacent typewriters; factories in production were not to be interrupted. We had a sensible agreement about visitors whom we both knew. One of us might ask the other in for a cup of coffee or a drink or, depending on the reason for the visit or turn of conversation, we might not. For both of us our homes were our offices and we respected the confidentiality of each other's projects.

In 1961 Kylie was appointed to the Advisory Board of the Commonwealth Literary Fund; the outward and visible sign of her new job was an occasional huge Commonwealth car in narrow Garrick Avenue, a splendid coach by contrast with the battered utility truck, and later her Holden, both of which she drove with enormous verve.

CLF work meant for her a vast amount of reading of manuscripts which no doubt she discussed with Roddy, but never with me. For that I was grateful because a few writers, almost invariably ones I scarcely knew, used very improperly to ask me to put in a word for them and their applications to Kylie or, occasionally to Doug. I could firmly say this was not a thing I ever would or could do.

I knew Kylie and Doug did not always agree in their CLF deliberations and gathered they sometimes found each other tiresome. But, again, neither of them embarrassed me with details.

Kylie became NSW editor for Macmillan. More reading for her. She also established a popular and successful series of books for older children called 'Great Stories of Australia'. The idea governing the series was that each book should deal with persons and events that had some importance to Australia without being necessarily central to its history. In order of publication the first three titles were written by Mary Durack, Donald McLean and George Farwell. When Kylie invited me to contribute to the series and write the fourth title I was delighted. I was not able to spend long periods in libraries when the children were young but it so happened I had an abandoned, though well-researched, project that fitted into the spirit of the series. This was an opportunity to rescue from oblivion Sarah Musgrave's story as told by herself in a long out-of-print book called *The Wayback* (Cumberland Argus Press, 1925), which had interested me since about 1948 when Una Gault had lent me this rare small paper-bound volume. Una acquired her copy in a curious way. She was born in Young, a town and district pioneered by the family of Sarah Musgrave nee White, who was, in the eighteen-thirties, the first white child to be born in that district. Close to a century later the headmaster of Young Public School ordained a major spring-cleaning. Cupboards and desks were scoured for 'rubbish' to feed a bonfire in the school yard. At the back of a seldom used cupboard he found stacks of mint copies of *The Wayback* that had apparently been stored there since they were printed in 1925 and forgotten. He instructed Una and other sixth-class children to dump these books on the fire. Una protested but was told not to be silly. She did, however, rescue a copy for herself.

After I read it I found all sorts of interesting material about Sarah Musgrave in the Mitchell Library—not least that, in 1934, then being the oldest living woman in Australia, she was introduced to a royal visitor, the Duke of Gloucester, at Parramatta. I'd obtained baptismal certificates for Sarah and her sister and had interviewed two of Sarah's by then very old nieces. I listed archival and other material to read, and hoped to write a full biography. Then I made an unwelcome discovery within the papers on my desk. Certain dates and fixed points simply did not accord with Sarah's own accounts and beliefs or with those of the charming, proud, helpful old people I had interviewed. I made an informed guess at the reason for the discrepancies: if I was correct a family event that was hurtful and possibly scandalous had been hushed up in the late eighteen-thirties. Why should I even attempt to bring it to light some hundred and twenty years later? The matters and people concerned were interesting but of no central importance to general history. So I abandoned my book.

As Kylie and Roddy spoke about the 'Great Stories' project I saw how to tell Sarah's story now. The requirements of a book for older children would not make it necessary for me to speculate about, or document, my discovery. However, for my own integrity I did, in my book, include clues that might lead a later researcher to the problems I had noticed. Not even Roddy, that assiduous careful editor, spotted debatable material nor, among the hundreds of young people who have written and spoken to me about the book had anyone ever queried its one peculiarity until...a couple of years ago, a collateral descendant of Sarah's family telephoned. She was attempting a family history. She had read my book and was puzzled. Could I explain? All the old people who knew Sarah must have been long dead so I gave this woman what information I could recall and left it to her to decide whether to investigate further.

The name of the book I wrote was in my own mind, and on the manuscript, 'Girl of the Goldfields'. Oh, sexist days of yore! 'You cannot,' said Roddy, 'have the word "girl" in a book title for adolescents because no boy will read it.' I was annoyed. I think names and works often truly belong together. I argued, to no avail. I had used a verse of *Young Horses* by E. R. Murray as a chapter heading to Chapter 10. It begins: 'Over the river by gravel and gum/To a thunder of hoofbeats, hard driven they come.' Crossly and flippantly I said, 'OK, there's your title, *By Gravel and Gum*.' In a fit of madness Roddy, Kylie and Macmillan accepted this ridiculous name. My children refer to the book as 'By Bubble and Gum' and I can't blame them.

Enter Mrs Mann, mother of my house-cleaner Mrs Haynes. They lived nearby at Boronia Park. Mrs Mann came one day a week to look after the children while I went to the Mitchell Library to research for the book that became *Gold Fever* (Angus and Robertson, 1967). It was reissued as *A History of the Australian Gold Rushes* (Angus and Robertson, 1976).

I always have and always will pay someone to do the greater part of my housework, which I detest. I like to cook, but not to clean. I thought that even if, from my writing, I earned no more than enough to pay these women, at least I was using my talents a little and they were doing work they seemed to like and did well. It was not only a matter of keeping my hand in for the time being; I wanted to remain in touch with people in the fields of general writing and publishing and to continue reviewing books, chiefly at that time for the *Bulletin*. I was also writing poetry. I expected when the children reached school age to have time to plan projects again.

So each Tuesday Mrs Mann arrived and in two minutes flat, it seemed, stood in a clean apron in an orderly kitchen and put Margery and John firmly into place too. Mrs Mann had boundless patience watching by swings and slippery dips or taking the children for expeditions by bus, ferry and foot. I ransacked the goldfields, and so did Mark who, through the Battye Library in Perth, found some splendid manuscript material.

When we came to the hill Zoe Benjamin lived in her retirement at 'Figtree', a circumstance that delighted my father who, on his expeditions from Roseville by train, bus and foot to see his grandchildren and me, often called on Zoe along the way. They had been friends since their youth when they belonged to the Hebrew Debating Society. Father admired Zoe's pioneering work in training teachers of young children, and counselling parents. He made her a legendary figure in our family. In my childhood she lived not far from our Darling Point house, in a small two-storey terrace. Zoe was tiny, a dwarf. I thought she was some sort of good fairy, and was not far wrong.

In old age she was lame and increasingly blind, so one morning each week I went to read to her, though as often as not we spent much of the time talking. Lydia Pender, a fine writer for children who also lived on the hill, was another of Zoe's readers.

One day I must have described to Zoe some mischief of Margery or John (they loved her dearly), because she exclaimed in outrage: 'Surely Nancy you do not smack your chidren!' 'Oh yes I do,' I said, 'and what is more I always make certain it hurts them more than it hurts me!' She decided to laugh, bless her.

Barbara Jefferis and I first became acquainted when I joined the management committee of the Australian Society of Authors (ASA), but I'd admired her novels since 1954 when I had reviewed *Contango Day* for the *Bulletin*. Then Barbara and her husband John Hinde, the film critic, moved from the North Shore to a house at Woolwich on the tip of the peninsula, and we became good friends. We have worked together for the ASA, on judging panels and in other ways. Barbara's keen judgement and good sense are admirable. So is her writing. She comes within a category of writers who are 'unlucky' because for one reason or another their works do not fit within the guidelines of chief Australian literary awards. *If* her later novels had had Australian themes, characters or settings, or if they had been published in Australia (rather than overseas) she would probably have been a major prizewinner.

Betty James, a writer, lived near the FitzGeralds. She was also a good friend of Kylie's and an ardent worker for causes, like many Hunters Hill people—to whom, I fear, I am a disappointment. There are limitations to the amount of jumping up and down that one can perform and to the style of one's jumping. I've usually preferred the pen to the march or to the physical confrontation. FitzGerald was very active in his opposition to Australian involvement in the Vietnam War, as were many writers. I supported his stand. To an extent during the sixties one walked on eggshells in conversations and dealings with people and I relinquished a couple of old and good friends who were hawks to my dove. But I think I lost no writing friends. During that tragic, divisive period people, if possible, avoided contentious topics.

Kylie introduced us to Nancy Phelan, an elegant stylist whose best books, like Barbara Jefferis', do not fit into the moulds of major awards. Kay Brown, who lived in the mountains in those days but often visited Kylie or attended English Association events, is also a writer who has not had the recognition she merits; she is an interesting, creative painter, too. Her 'heart's country' remains Mount Isa—the setting for her novel *Knock Ten*—and western Queensland. Her letters are a delight. Later Kay revealed that she was stockman–novelist Tom Ronan's sister. Elizabeth Harrower, who had just written *Down in the City* and Kylie were close friends and colleagues in publishing and, for several years, shared a weekend house in the mountains. (Elizabeth's cousin Margaret Dick wrote a perceptive study, *The Novels of Kylie Tennant*.)

Donald and Thelma McLean lived at Woolwich. Don had had an arm amputated during his boyhood but he was the kind of man who could do more with one arm than most people might achieve with three. He is chiefly remembered as a distinguished educationalist and educational writer but he also wrote some good novels. He was one of the chief initiators of the ASA. Thelma was a school librarian. Donald visited Roddy at least weekly—no doubt they enjoyed educational shop-talk. Together they compiled a fine book of Australian Essays, *Venturing the Unknown Ways*, in 1965. I am sure that Don's example and counselling, based upon his own conquered disability, were factors in Roddy's recovery from his fall beneath a train. I greatly valued Don's good sense; he was helpful to me when I began editing *The Australian Author*, and he was a generous contributor of articles, 'fillers' and comment to whom I could confidently turn in emergencies. Don and Thelma had a long friendship with Desiderius Orban and there are some fine examples of his art in their home.

Writers apart, good neighbours have always been a part of our small street, and of the hill itself. Reta Grace has been my secretary/typist since, we think, 1973. She lives within walking distance of my house. Like me, Reta is a *nearly* infallible speller—we cherish each other's rare spelling errors and have amiable arguments about grammar and English usage. Once she typed a first novel for a young poet who was also a lecturer in the English department of a university. His spelling was amazingly frightful and I've often thought that her care and precision may have helped him to find a publisher easily. It was, justly, a much-acclaimed book.

My dear Olivia: on one day a week she has kept my house shining and tidy for some ten years, and has vastly entertained me too, for Olivia is a great raconteur.

To a substantial degree Mrs Mann, Olivia and Reta Grace *are* my books.

Except for having lived in New Zealand when I was four, I had never travelled overseas, or further than Brisbane and Melbourne in Australia. Perth in 1956 was my first experience of a place that in some ways seemed another world.

We went there at short notice in August, supposedly for about a month but in the event the factory installation with which Mark was involved was troublesome, and we did not return to Sydney until mid December. I blessed the fortunate intuition that had persuaded me to accompany him with Margery, our first child who was then some three and a half months old. Behind us we left our newly furnished and furbished house, and nearly all the necessities I'd acquired for Margery, like a convenient table and light bath, a borrowed perambulator and clothes for her to wear as she grew older and larger.

We travelled to Fremantle none too comfortably by a crowded P & O ship bound for the UK and noticed one difference almost immediately after we arrived at Fremantle: we found ourselves the parents of a bubba —that is how everyone from the most pedantic of speakers to the most casual referred to Margery. I had never lived in a place that was quite so flat as Perth, though it was not till we reached Adelaide on our return journey that I realised how very much I had missed visible hills, even distant ones. The sun rose over the land and set over the ocean so, for a time, my sense of direction suffered. The soil was sandier than any I had experienced, even in sandy Sydney. One barely had to wash green or root vegetables—the sand simply rinsed away. And what was it that made our street, and most streets away from the highway or city centre look so indefinably peculiar? After a few days I realised—there was no kerbing or guttering. The bitumen surface of the road ran directly against a mown grass verge growing in sand, and rainwater simply soaked away.

Whale-meat, which I had never seen or smelled before, was the standard pet food as we discovered because, with the semi-detached house that we rented in Claremont, we acquired a huge sleek tabby tom-cat called Monty. His owner was overseas and as soon as *his* house was tenanted he refused to eat anything offered by my next-door neighbour who was supposed to be feeding him.

In shops hard vegetables like potatoes, carrots and onions were priced by the stone. Constant efforts to divide prices by fourteen were a trouble to this 'eastern stater' or 'other sider'. I quickly grew accustomed to being referred to in those terms. The garbage man ran through the garden to the back of the house, collected the bin, emptied it onto a truck and returned it to its place. It was a marvellously honest city. On a bus I left a bag containing a few nappies and some baby oil—also a letter addressed to me. That very afternoon a woman drove across Perth to return it.

The morning newspaper carried daily reports of magpie attacks on people, especially on children, and most often on those with red or fair hair. This hazard accounted for occasional sightings of small primary-school children, in that pre-plastic-utensil era, wearing aluminium basins on their heads.

Our street ran beside the garden and some buildings of the Loreto Convent whose music room was directly opposite my front garden where, each afternoon, Margery kicked and gurgled on a rug while I tried to read against the distraction of a constant stream of little girls who endlessly played 'Charlie is my Darling', very squeakily on violins. I suppose they practised for an exam.

When it became obvious that we were destined to be in Perth for longer than we had planned, I had to shop for the bubba. I bought her some simple cotton dresses and a sort of canvas hammock in which to carry her. It had straps for me to wear around my shoulders but after a Saturday morning trudging through acres of Kings Park admiring wildflowers, with Margery kicking and squirming and the straps chafing my neck, I smartly bought a folding stroller in which she could recline and later, when old enough, sit.

We had no car, but CSR people and new-found friends were generous with lifts in city and suburbs and expeditions to see wildflowers at weekends. Our house was close to the Stirling Highway down which buses travelled to the city, and I could walk to shops at Swanbourne.

Tom Collins House at Claremont was also within walking distance. Joseph Furphy ('Tom Collins'), whose book *Such is Life* was almost venerated in Perth, had moved to Western Australia in 1905 and lived in the cottage at the time of his death in 1912. In 1949 his surviving son, Samuel Furphy, presented the house and its grounds to the Western Australian Fellowship of Australian Writers as a memorial. The FAW used it for meetings, lectures and afternoon events and receptions. A caretaker's flat in this fairly small house meant that much of its useful space was its garden; but Perth can bank on fine weather for many months of the year, which is why the splendid outdoor theatre at the University of Western Australia is also an asset.

The bequest however, had placed financial and curatorial burdens upon the FAW and the success of the cottage as a venue was chiefly due to the generosity of many members who donated time or money or both to its care. What I observed then persuaded me that gifts, bequests, endowments and like initiatives that do not make provision for managerial and administrative costs and expenses can be troublesome white elephants. That is why I foresaw, unfortunately correctly, nothing but trouble for the National Book Council when it acquired Book House in Melbourne in 1981. Down the years I have opposed comparable suggestions made to or by organisations ranging from small local historical societies to the insufficiently planned enthusiasms of larger groups.

It was chiefly at Tom Collins House that I gained an unexpected impression of Western Australia. In 1956, considering its relatively small population, a quite disproportionate number of leading writers lived there mostly, but not only in Perth. Paul and Alexandra Hasluck (he was Minister for Territories at the time but not then a knight) were absent from the city. Katharine Susannah Prichard was unwell. T. A. G. (Tom) Hungerford was overseas. But otherwise at Tom Collins House and elsewhere we met many people who were household (or bookshelf) names to me. There were Sir Walter Murdoch and his daughter, Catherine King, a well-known broadcaster. Mary Durack Miller, Henrietta Drake Brockman, J. K. (Jack) Ewers and Olive Pell would become good friends of ours. Randolph Stow was not yet widely known or published in Australia but once, at Mary Durack's house, we met him: a shy, intense man of twenty-one, not then long back from his time as a cadet patrol officer in New Guinea. Mary had read a good deal of his poetry and prose, in manuscript, and rightly prophesied for him his major career in letters. I remember Donald Stuart, his sister Lyndall Hadow and F. B. (Bert) Vickers. Dorothy Hewett was then in Sydney but, although her work was as yet relatively little known, Perth was discussing her poetry and early drama and spoke of it with, as a rule, high praise, though some people regarded her as a contentious figure. In the sixties she returned to Perth for some years—I think I first met Dorothy at an Adelaide Festival. Olive Pell was active in FAW affairs, and most hospitable to us.

One writer I'd long admired for his books of short stories and contributions to the *Bulletin* was Gavin Casey who had returned to live in Western Australia where he was born and had spent his youth. His first wife has written about her marriage with Gavin in *Casey's Wife* (1982). His friends spoke so fondly of her that I am sorry I did not know her. In 1956 Gavin was married to an American whom he'd met when he administered the Australian News and Information Service in New York.

I knew a number of ex-Western Australian writers in Sydney: Peter Hopegood, Leslie Rees and John Thompson among them. I did not ever meet Kenneth (Seaforth) Mackenzie. W. S. (Wolfe) Fairbridge who died so tragically young had, briefly, been a Sydney friend and his wife Dorothy remained one. Some Perth people still claimed these writers as their own.

Aboriginal writers like Colin Johnson and Jack Davis had not published as yet.

On a later visit I met Vincent and Carol Serventy who later on 'came east' to live near us at Hunters Hill.

This is not and cannot be a complete list, but the names I give of writers of poetry, fiction, factual books and drama who were notable in Western Australia before, during, or soon after 1956 are impressive. So it was puzzling to find that many of them, including well-known and successful authors, believed they were disadvantaged because they lived and wrote in Western Australia.

I listened to many envious comments about the supposed advantages enjoyed by 'eastern staters' and 'other siders'. This attitude persists. About four years ago an author of great seniority and high reputation, who spent much of his life making a distinguished career as an Australian government press officer in many countries, grumbled bitterly to me about his alleged raw deals from the east despite the fact that his books, some published overseas, some in Sydney and some in Perth have, since the forties attracted major notices and reviews and tertiary study. Certainly at the outset of his career a Sydney publisher behaved disgracefully to him but that was long ago. It is a paradox I cannot explain.

If one tried to dispute some debatable beliefs people cited names like Peter Hopegood, John Thompson, Leslie Rees or Dorothy Hewett who 'went east'. They brushed aside my counter claims of their colleagues who had 'come west'. 'But,' I would argue, first in 1956, and on later visits, 'if, from the holdings of Australian books in any major library, one were to remove *every* Western Australian name and title, the gaps left on the shelves would be so great that, very likely, most of the other volumes would fall down!' I would point out that I was meeting in Perth, for the first time, people whose writing I already knew well in Sydney.

Complaints might be understandable if they were limited to poetasters and would-be writers, or even to raw beginners. In fact, in 1956 Western Australia had a considerable range of freelance outlets including newspapers that published contributed material, the local ABC and other radio. Local books were well and widely reviewed. As to drama venues and available theatres and audiences Perth was very well off.

It was all the more puzzling in the fifties to note that many New Zealand writers preferred to publish overseas (including Australia) although some local New Zealand publishers were available. I did not hear complaints of disadvantage in New Zealand a few years later. The emergence of the Fremantle Arts Centre Press in 1976 might, indeed, be the envy of writers in other regions, for instance, North Queensland. The press gave initial publication to authors of the calibre of Nicholas Hasluck, Elizabeth Jolley, Phillip Salmon and A. B. Facey; it also, with some Western Australian government assistance, publishes excellent short memoirs, local histories and other works of regional interest and importance.

Mary Durack and her sister Elizabeth were two women I hoped to meet. When I was about twelve I was greatly affronted once by someone's gift of a book called *All-About*. A children's book! When one is more mature one realises that fine books for children are never outgrown. Eventually I deigned to open its covers and crashed, rather than fell, under its spell. The sub-title is 'The Story of a Black Community on Argyle Station, Kimberley'. It appeared in 1935 when, I discovered, its author Mary Durack, and illustrator, her sister Elizabeth, were only respectively some ten and twelve years older than I. Aspects of *All-About* may seem out of date now but I recall no sensation of reading a patronising account. It was my introduction to Aboriginal Australians.

One seldom saw Aboriginal people on the streets of Sydney in the thirties. Several times we'd been taken to watch 'the Abos' who made, sold and threw boomerangs at La Perouse. We spent our summer holiday at Jervis Bay each year—once a week there was a movie night in the store and black people from the settlement at Wreck Bay, some miles away, would file in to a few rows of chairs placed far too close to the screen, at the front of the room. An empty aisle separated them from the white audience. My father was no more racist than most men of his background and generation, which is to say that he usually referred to black people as 'niggers', including the negroes, he encountered when, as a young student he lived in New York. A few like those at La Perouse and Wreck Bay he considered 'good types' but most were not good types at all. Good types were mostly jolly negro actors in the movies who usually played the parts of servants who knew their places and were greatly beloved of the families (who might include Shirley Temple) whom they served.

Paul Robeson was a good type in his early days before Dad heard he was a Communist, and so was the black groundsman on the Jervis Bay golf course who became of immense interest to Father after he saw this man pick up a large snake by its tail, crack it like a whip to break its back, and toss the carcass over a fence to dry out beside other snakeskins. After a long conversation about snakes the man invited Dad to accompany him to the beach one evening to witness a fascinating feat that he called 'tickling for fish'. My father was a keen fisherman and waded through the shallow surf with his companion who trailed a line of string to which a chunk of extremely rotten meat was tied. Each of them carried a landing net. When fish came to the bait, and quite a number were attracted, they swooped and caught a tidy a lot of bream and whiting. Unfortunately Father could never reproduce this mode of fishing because while the Aborigine waded he also chanted a curious very monotonous song that he repeated constantly. He said it mesmerised the fish and, more than the smelly bait, drew them into shallow water. Anyway, Dad said, it wasn't the sort of mumbo jumbo a white man would be bothered with.

Sometimes Dad hired ponies and we rode along beaches and through bush to Wreck Bay. One Christmas morning, when the water-meadows either side of the track were thick with Christmas bells, a shabbily-dressed black mother with two children strolled towards us. Dad reined in to call out 'Merry Christmas'. 'Thank you sir,' she replied in a refined voice 'and may I reciprocate your good wishes.' For some time my father puzzled over that exchange.

So. . .I'd accepted Bet Bet, though with reservations. I had sensed the patronising attitudes of Jeannie (Mrs Aeneas) Gunn's *Little Black Princess*. As to Uncle Tom and his cabin, I'd wept over an early edition with heart-rending illustrations. . .But *All-About* exploded the lot. And now in Perth, I met Mary Durack who, with Henrietta Drake Brockman and Gavin Casey, was a leading figure at FAW occasions. Mark and I went to dinner at Mary's house and met her husband, H. C. (Horrie) Miller, a pioneer hero of aviation during World War I in France and also later in Australia, and one of the founders of MacRobertson Miller Airlines. One of their daughters, who would die tragically young, was already married to a flying doctor. I had never before met a family who travelled vast distances in little planes as casually as I might take a tram. Margery, asleep in her basket, was put in a room where a small Miller son slept very soundly in his cot, crouched on hands and knees with his bottom in the air.

As Horrie and Mary talked I realised we were fortunate to meet them in Perth because they both spent a great deal of each year in other parts of the State. Mary, just then, was involved in writing simple plays for the primary-school chidren of Broome. A nun at a convent school had told Mary how difficult it was to cast plays, including nativity plays, for children of every imaginable skin colour in that mixed-race pearling port. Some children themselves, in a class where Aborigines predominated, had objected to her choice of a part Japanese girl to play the mother of Christ—they thought the part should have gone to one of the few white girls in the group. Mary was energetically responding to this challenge.

She spoke of the days during the Depression when she and Elizabeth, for a time, managed the Durack station, Argyle (setting of *All-About*). They often visited Argyle in the fifties, before it drowned beneath the water of the Ord River scheme. I looked with some disbelief at Mary's pretty face and dainty person as she quite casually recalled how impossible it was to keep blowflies away from stored meat which had to be scraped clean of maggots before it could be cooked.

By then I had abandoned the racism of my father's generation. I had black friends in Sydney, among them Faith Bandler who was to become a notable campaigner for Aboriginal rights, although her own descent is from a New Hebridean islander black-birded to work on the Queensland canefields in 1883. When I was a social worker I'd had several contacts with Aboriginal families. But Mary was the first person I knew who had day-to-day, taken-for-granted friendships with, and knowledge of, Aborigines.

Years later, in 1974 the Literature Board and Aboriginal Arts Board of the Australia Council combined to conduct a writing workshop/seminar in Darwin for Aboriginal writers. Participants came chiefly from Broome and Mowanjum in Western Australia and from Darwin and the Northern Territory. For the first time I saw and felt at first hand some part of the love, trust and plain friendliness Mary inspired. She, and other people of her age and provenance have been accused of Uncle and Auntie Tomism, often by activists who have never met those they castigate. Two southern Aboriginal writers who also took part in the workshop did not gain a fraction of the rapport and goodwill that Mary established with the students who were of all ages from elderly to their twenties. One of the southern men was rude to Mary and several angry black students physically ejected him from the meeting room and prevented him from taking further part in the proceedings.

Henrietta Drake Brockman was beautiful, stately and had blue eyes like searchlights. Her husband Brigadier Geoffrey Drake Brockman was a distinguished engineer, soldier and public servant. From his first-hand experiences he wrote about the development of the north west of Western Australia. His autobiography *The Turning Wheel* was published in 1960. The Drake Brockmans had lived and worked in many areas of Western Australia. At this time Henrietta's novel—*The Wicked and the Fair*, which tells of the 1629 wreck off the Western Australian coast of the *Batavia*, a Dutch ship bound for Java, and of its tragic aftermath—was a year away from its publication. Doug Stewart's verse-drama, *Shipwreck*, was also based upon these events. To acquire background knowledge and atmosphere Henrietta twice visited the Abrolhos Islands, once with special permission on a regulation RAAF coastal survey flight, once with a party of crayfishermen. In 1956 the precise site of the *Batavia* wreck was not yet known, but there was a general flurry of wreck-searching up and down the coast partly because the introduction of scuba apparatus made the sport, and indeed profession, of skin-diving accessible to many adventurers.

An expedition of the Western Australian Museum in 1961 at last discovered the *Batavia* wreck on Morning Reef in the Wallabi Group of the Abrolhos. Henrietta was invited to inspect the discovery. She was then sixty but she practised skin-diving, and made an underwater inspection of the *Batavia*. I treasure a small lump of coral that she broke off from a plank and gave to me.

She then wrote *Voyage to Disaster/The Life of Francisco Pelsaert*, a definitive book 'covering his Indian Report to the Dutch East India Company and the wreck of the ship *Batavia* in 1629 off the coast of Western Australia together with the full text of his Journals concerning the Rescue Voyages, the mutiny on the Abrolhos Islands and the subsequent trials of the Mutineers'. The translations of these documents were made by E. D. Drok, a Dutch-born war hero who had migrated to Australia and worked as Senior Language Master at Christ Church Grammar School, Claremont.

Henrietta Drake Brockman was, then, intrepid. She was also a commanding, stately woman. She was justifiably proud of her mother, Dr Roberta Jull, who was an early woman graduate in medicine from the University of Sydney and the first woman medico to practise in Perth.

Henrietta invited me to lunch and to meet a few people, among them her mother. She and her husband lived in a large apartment on the Esplanade. The somewhat formal invitation was rather like a royal command. Margery was then nearly six months old, very active and accustomed to a long wakeful period each afternoon which she spent kicking and playing on a rug in the garden. It was one thing to take the baby to Tom Collins House or to Mary Durack's home where there was a young child, but the prospect of her spending an afternoon in a drawing room alarmed me. I voiced my qualms, and said I'd try to find someone to mind Margery. In her firmest, no argument voice Henrietta said: 'That beautiful child will come to see *me* and she will behave *beautifully*.'

Margery wore her prettiest dress and lay in her bassinet basket decked with a pretty frilly cover, with matching pillow, that I'd brought from Sydney and never used. She certainly *looked* sweet and content after her own early lunch. One of the guests picked us up in her car because the basket and my usual bus were not compatible. While she parked her car I hoisted my hefty daughter to the front door which Henrietta opened. She helped me carry the basket, not to some quiet back room but to a space on the floor at the centre of a group of chairs where her guests would sit. Her blue eyes bored into Margery's brown ones. Firmly and distinctly she said: 'Of course, Margery, you will be *perfectly* good.' Margery enjoyed being a centre of attention and *was* good. Henrietta that day was disappointed because two people she'd have liked me to meet could not be present. Dear Katharine Susannah was still unwell; and her dearest friend, Alexandra Hasluck, was absent from Perth, a circumstance that had a curious sequel.

I later met Alexandra Hasluck many times (she is now a Dame of the Order of Australia), but first set eyes on her at an early Adelaide Festival. Writers Week was officially opened at a function held on a large enclosed lawn, probably at the University. Distant across the grass from where I stood I noticed, side by side, two women's elegant shady hats, both of shiny black straw. When the speeches ended and the listeners moved around to speak to friends, I identified Henrietta under one of the hats and went to greet her. Beneath the other was a pretty, stately, middle-aged woman of about Henrietta's height. We smiled at each other, waiting to be introduced.

'But of course you already know each other,' Henrietta said firmly. 'Nancy, you met Alexandra at a luncheon I held in Perth.' 'I think not,' said Alexandra and, having established the date concerned said she was not in Perth just then. 'Nonsense. I planned my party especially to introduce you to each other. Surely you remember.' Our failure to do so was almost offensive to Henrietta so each of us smiled warmly at the other and mendaciously agreed that, how silly we were, and of course we recalled our meeting...

J. K. (Jack) Ewers and his wife Jean had a charming house in a garden with many native plants. Jean, a potter, was experimentally decorating her pots using large native seeds, or sections through them, which she pressed onto damp clay, to gain very interesting and beautiful effects, particularly from the huge local gumnuts. It was there we met David and June Hutchison. David's fine drawings of native plants and flowers decorated their Christmas cards. He later became a notable museum curator and was responsible for many of the excellent displays at the Maritime Museum established at Fremantle in 1970. The interest and excellence of this museum is not sufficiently recognised in Australia or overseas. Its exhibits of artefacts that have been salvaged from wrecks of Dutch ships and other shipwrecks, and the conservatorial skills that have made these displays possible, are of a high order.

When we lived opposite the Loreto convent in Claremont Mary Durack introduced me to a couple of the Sisters. It was her old school. She also kept in touch with two elderly nuns who had transferred to Loreto at Kirribilli. On her Sydney visits she would go to see them. I mentioned that my father had designed some new buildings at Loreto in about 1920, and that I'd always wanted to see these. He had been working with an architect called Hennessy who had designed many buildings for the Catholic church. Among the first books I remember were two large volumes called *Belgium the Beautiful* that were inscribed to my father by Loreto's Mother Superior.

Mary remembered my wish and one day when she was to come to our house at Hunters Hill for dinner, she phoned to say she'd be spending the afternoon with her friends at Loreto from where I could pick her up in the car, and that she had arranged for me to see the building. A friend would collect Margery from kindergarten, but our second child, John, would accompany me. It was about a month away from his third birthday and he was a very active, self-willed boy who would not have been my choice for a convent companion. But I had no choice.

In the garden near the entrance gates Mary waited with one of her ex-teachers, a very old nun called Mother Dolorosa. She belied her conventual name for she was friendly and jolly and instantly won John's heart. She was also very lame and, for this reason could not conduct us over the 'new' buildings, but had arranged with another Sister to do so, a little later. She could, however, show us the level part of the garden. We strolled along a gravelled pathway, an unwontedly patient John being charmed by her jokes and attention. Her long skirts, veil and wimple fascinated him. After a while we paused to admire some feature of the garden and, for a short time, talking with the two women, I failed to watch John. Then I could not see him. Where could he have got to? Oh horrors! His fat legs are all that is visible—the rest of John has crawled beneath Mother Dolorosa's ample black skirts. While I wondered how on earth to cope with so outlandish a problem the good Mother noticed John's presence and bellowed with laughter:

'The dear little man has noticed my caliper. He's curious. I like an inquisitive child. Come on out of there my little man and I'll show it to you properly.' John emerged. Mother Dolorosa rested her lame leg on the top of a low brick wall, pulled up her skirt to her knees and demonstrated how the caliper fitted her leg, was attached to her shoe, and how its spring helped her to walk. She insisted on keeping John in the garden while Mary and I inspected the old and some new buildings.

In the car driving to Hunters Hill Mary and I talked non-stop while John in his safety seat at the back was strangely thoughtful. At home he made a bee-line for the linen cupboard, grabbed a white hand towel and draped it around his head. He would not relinquish his 'veil' for a waking moment and his days of unabated vocation became a couple of weeks. We made a new rule: a Jewish boy can be a nun until his third birthday but not a moment thereafter.

X

Hearing Voices

ON a summer day in 1984 Kate Llewellyn and Susan Hampton sat on rugs in the shade of our lemon tree and perused books of poetry they had selected from my shelves. I had met them recently, and wished I were a painter to record the auburn and the dark heads in dappled light. Long before we met they had been working on the material that became their *Penguin Book of Australian Women Poets*. Their research was almost finished but the inevitable loose ends of obscure biographies and possible omissions remained, and I had suggested that my fairly extensive collection of Australian poetry might be helpful. For one thing most of my poetry volumes (unlike most library copies) remain in their original jackets which are often excellent sources of biographical and other information that is hard to gain elsewhere.

One discovery was Mary Durack's long lovely *Lament for the Drowned Country* which I had kept from a *Bulletin* Christmas issue where it was illustrated by Elizabeth Durack. The poem is the lament of 'Mad Maggie! Mad Maggie! Poor old *Jilligan, Numbajina*' who is a laughing stock for young people because she spends all day talking to herself and fishing, but lets the fish go. She is not mad:

> I sit along river coming down from my born country.
> That heart place! I got to talk to that water.
> I got to tell that fish: 'You go back—go back now—
> talk strong to my country. You tell him that spirit can't leave 'em.
> You tell him—Wait! Hang on! *This is not the finish*...

It is a long powerful threnody—and was not easily added to the anthology at that stage but Kate and Susan found it as moving and as beautiful as I do and made a place for it. It is one of the glories of their fine book.

That day I reflected that one of the pleasures of books is that through them, lifelong, one constantly makes friendships. When I was eighteen my Melbourne great aunt Dal and I began writing to each other though neither of us had news that was of much mutual interest. Dal decided we would write about books and discovered I had not read any of Henry James' novels. She had known the brothers Henry and Williams James (a pioneer of psychology) in Europe in her youth. Dal embarked on a project of re-reading and sent me a cheap copy of each James novel that she wished to re-discover. I introduced her to some recent Australian writing. We exchanged lively letters for years.

Today I share books with Phyllis Bryant, my one-time headmistress who, in her eighties, reads adventurously. My son-in-law Greg Sproule browses and borrows from my bookshelves and his discoveries often lead me back to volumes that I always meant to read again—a common vague intention that often needs the prodding of a motive. New friends are often school children who live nearby and ransack my shelves for projects, like Anna who was asked to imagine herself a woman born in 1900 and to write her 'biography'. Together we filled a box with women's histories; I added a collection of Australian cartoon art whose illustrations were a useful guide to changing fashions in dress and furnishing, some poetry and a few novels. Anna then began her own research into her mother's family history and acquired a number of family snapshots. All of this she wove into a document that is not only a valuable short history of a family; it also details the background of its time and describes a region that is now a densely populated eastern suburb of Sydney where, early this century, her great grandfather worked on a dairy farm and for its extensive milk run. She carefully listed all her sources of information and reading. Achievements like this make nonsense of the perennial complaints of some ultra-conservative educationalists. It is more important for people to make their own discoveries in a worthwhile way than to be able to rattle off the lineage of the Plantagenets and the bare outlines of the expeditions of Burke and Wills and Leichhardt—requirements that bored me silly in my youth. Certainly it is a bonus to read a manuscript whose spelling is accurate but some excellent writers, and some very senior academics, spell atrociously. I recall two women who were in the same form at the same school during their school days and therefore had identical teachers and instruction. One spells infallibly; the other, a successful lawyer, peppers every page she writes with spelling mistakes. One is accurate and fast at mental arithmetic; the other, with good reason, blesses the invention of the pocket calculator.

No amount of education substitutes for innate ability and determination. I met a most successful author in a prison whose cultural group I sometimes visited. Years of repressive formal teaching in a country school failed to discover his defective eyesight or his partial deafness. In jail these defects were treated; the prison library and an enlightened visiting teacher transformed him from a frustrated bitter criminal into a truly educated and creative man. Albert Facey whose book *A Fortunate Life* became an instant best-seller and undoubted classic suffered a dreadfully deprived childhood and youth. He could not read and write until he was in his mid-twenties. That book, among its many splendours, tells its stories with the unaffected directness of people who belong to oral, rather than written, traditions. Facey's detailed memory of people and events and his exact eye and ear may remind us of the rich story-telling and poetry of countless generations whose heads were not cluttered by masses of, sometimes useless, information.

Behind many books one hears, or thinks one hears, the sound of the author's own voice. When first I heard a record of James Joyce reading from *Ulysses* it sounded exactly as I expected (or perhaps exactly as James Meagher read Joyce); T. S. Eliot's parsonical delivery was a devastating shock. I fancy, but cannot prove, that if I could meet Eudora Welty or John Cheever I would recognise their voices.

E. O. (Eric) Schlunke was a superb writer of short stories and his wife, Olga, published poetry in the *Bulletin*. In the early 1950s they invited me to stay for a couple of weeks on their farm, 'Rosenthal', at Reefton near Temora in southern New South Wales. Eric's forebears were German Lutherans who came to Australia under the sponsorship of George Fife Angas in the mid-nineteenth century. Most of these migrants settled in the Barossa Valley of South Australia but a cluster took farms near Temora and some went to Queensland.

The Schlunkes lived within the immensely thick walls of a pisé house that Eric's grandfather had built. Eric grew wheat and ran sheep and cattle. He detested pretentiousness and scorned words like 'grazier' and 'pastoral property'. He firmly called himself a farmer and his wide acres a farm.

Olga's hens scratched in and out of disused stables and laid eggs on and below the seat of an abandoned sulky. Eric drove a utility truck to get around the paddocks of that very flat country. Having mechanised his farm as soon as large wool cheques after World War II made that possible, he used a tractor for most of the heavy work. He kept no horses. He loathed horses. I, like most Australians, even city dwellers, was brought up on noble legends of horses and was shocked. 'There's nothing romantic about horses to anyone who worked with them as long as I had to,' said Eric. 'A man working all day with a horse team comes in cold and wet and tired and hungry and he has to unharness the brutes and rub them down and feed them before he can make himself comfortable.' He added a few hair-raising tales of rogue horses he had known.

During the Depression, life on 'Rosenthal' had been spartan and frugal. When I was there electric power had come to the area only recently and Olga, who had cooked for shearers and other seasonal workers on a fuel stove for most of her married life was enjoying an electric cooker, refrigerator and other appliances. In their new prosperity Eric installed an elaborate sound system to play recorded music in several rooms of the house and Olga, during her visits to Sydney, bought many fine Australian paintings. Their son David became a good painter; his picture *Hawk and Prey* on one of my walls reminds me of 'Rosenthal' but the place chiefly lives for me in Eric's stories. Ray Mathew sometimes stayed with the Schlunkes and had great friendship and encouragement from them. When I spoke with Eric, and with some of his German descended neighbours, I *heard* his stories. I only have to pick up a tale of his to hear him still.

By contrast Kenneth Slessor's hurried jerky speech was *not* the voice one hears in his poetry or prose. Long before I met Kenneth Slessor or realised how very much he was 'a man of Sydney' I knew his poem *Country Towns* by heart and would say it to myself as I travelled in trains rattling towards holiday destinations:

> Country towns, with your willows and squares,
> And farmers bouncing on barrel mares
> To public-houses of yellow wood
> With '1860' over their doors,
> And that mysterious race of Hogans
> Which always keeps General Stores...
>
> At the School of Arts, a broadsheet lies
> Sprayed with the sarcasm of flies:
> 'The Great Golightly Family
> Of Entertainers Here To-night'—
> Dated a year and a half ago,
> But left there, less from carelessness
> Than from a wish to seem polite.

During a dinner party at the Stewarts' house surrounded by their glowing paintings the talk turned to Australian artists and I quoted a verse I'd noticed somewhere:

> Mister Mister Lister-Lister
> Seeing that times are hard,
> Will you paint us a line
> Of Norfolk Pine
> At seven-and-six a yard?

'I wrote that,' said Ken.

I shall not labour my point about voices except to comment on an increasing enrichment of books written in English that allow foreign voices (I detest and avoid the word 'ethnic') to be heard. Once it was usual to edit foreign voices into 'good standard English'. Dialogue (and Australian vernacular) was tortured into absurd spellings of the order of 'Vere vas you goink and vy vas you goink there?' If an author in his text wrote 'it was late already so he...' it would be altered to 'it was already late so he...'

Opportunities increase for writers to publish in languages of origin or preference though these are limited by the relatively few buyers for such books. In the Americas it was chiefly the second and third generation of emigrant families that became writers, painters and entered professions. There are American exceptions like Isaac Bashevis Singer; and here, where the pattern is proving similar, there are exceptions also. The journal *Outrider* whose first issue appeared in 1984 'aims to extend the concept of Australian literature by presenting works of multicultural writers... Poems may be printed in the original language as well as in translation; all other material must be in English. Translated works are welcome.' By 1986 its list of authors includes some well-established 'old' Australians; some well-known writers from migrant communities, and significant numbers of 'new' authors. Dezsery Ethnic Publications is a publishing house founded in Adelaide by András Dezsery, a writer and scholar who was born in Hungary. Dezsery has published an impressive list of books both in English and in European languages. The Literature Board subsidises *Outrider* and a number of Dezsery titles and Phoenix publications—publishers of multicultural literature—and has made grants to multicultural authors some of whom write in English, some in other languages.

In the mid seventies I compiled an anthology of Australian Jewish short stories called *Shalom*. I showed my original selection to several people in New South Wales and Victoria and accepted a couple of suggestions about writers who should be included, but, to my regret omitted a few authors who were then virtually unknown. A 1988 edition of *Shalom* will include a story by Serge Liberman, a very fine writer indeed, and a man who has worked immensely hard to publish and publicise multicultural literature. It is a truism that if you want something done you ask the busiest person you know to help. Serge, a busy medical practitioner with a wife and family, as well as being a fine and prolific author was the editor of the English section of the *Melbourne Chronicle*, a journal that publishes half of each issue in Yiddish. I consulted him after I received letters asking about Australian Jewish books and writers from a European library and an Israeli diplomat. Together we compiled some reasonably accurate replies. Serge then set to work on a venture that was published in 1987 as *A Bibliography of Australian Judaica*. Compiled by Serge, it is edited and indexed by Joy Ruth Young.

I was about eighteen and literally running uphill from George Street to Macquarie Street because I was late for an appointment. At Elizabeth Street my run was halted by a dense, noisy procession of protest on its way along the roadway to a mass meeting in the Domain. I could not cross the road. If you can't beat them, join them. I slipped into the ranks and marched among angry men and women edging further across their files until I got to the opposite pavement and dashed away. The whole episode must only have lasted a few minutes but it introduced me to the feeling of being in a mob and I found the experience horrible. I make protests in my own ways but I do not join protest meetings or marches. Nor do I belong to political groups and parties. Mark and I opposed Australia's involvement in the Vietnam War and I supported the poet R. D. FitzGerald in his anti-Vietnam War activities. I lent my name to books and letters. I lost three close friends whose views were hawkish.

Rightly or wrongly I fear a march is a mob is a rabble. To the guillotine. To the gas chamber. To mindlessness. Not always, but often enough.

Many of my friends do not share these views. Some of them were communists like David Martin who resigned from the Party after Russia invaded Hungary in 1956; some like Judah Waten retained their commitment. I first heard Judah Waten's name from Doug Stewart who had a review copy of *Alien Son* in 1952 and was tremendously admiring of the book. So was I when I borrowed his copy. 'Mind you,' Doug said, 'the man's a Commo. Come the revolution he'll be out on the barricades and he'll shoot us all.' I found that prophesy hard to believe as I read for the first time those fictionalised first-hand stories that told of authentic migrant experience in Australia. When, some years later at an Adelaide Festival I met large, genial, affable Judah, and listened to the slight Yiddish lisp of his conversation, I could even less fear this compassionate wise man as a threat.

Neither David Martin nor I can recall how or why we first met but it was in Sydney and not long after 1949 when he settled in Australia. David Martin, beyond any other Australian novelist of the past forty years has deliberately used his talent to explore and dispel prejudice both in his adult fiction (*The Young Wife* and *Where a Man Belongs*) and in his popular and exciting novels for young people—*Hughie*, which has an Aboriginal boy in a country town as central figure; *Frank and Francesca*, whose chief characters are an Australian girl, an Italian boy and a London-born youth; and *The Chinese Boy*, which has an historical goldfields setting. David dedicated *Hughie* to Radka and Jiří, the children of the Czech woman who translated *The Young Wife*:

> My dear young friends, I give this book to you
> In equal portion as is right for twins.
> And though your Prague is not like Merringee
> Here in Australia where my tale begins,
> I rather think you'll find what happened there
> Won't be too hard for you to understand.
> Hughie does not speak Czech. But there's no need,
> Since courage is the same in every land.

Long before those books, or that tour de force of a novel *The Hero of Too* was published, David's elegant poetry made me laugh, and cry.

Walter Stone was in the truest sense a 'bookman'; a collector, bibliographer, printer and publisher of books. His wife Jean shared his interests and his generosity in allowing people to visit and use his library in his home. One saw them both at meetings of the English Association—his press, Wentworth Press, published the English Association's journal *Southerly* for many years. He was devoted to the causes of the Fellowship of Australian Writers, the Friends of the Fisher Library, the Australian Society of Authors and the Book Collectors' Society. Walter was a smallish, quiet, wise and unassuming man and although everyone knew Walter, consulted Walter and valued his attainments and advice I do not think his full contribution to Australian letters, his long memory and accurate understanding, have been fully appreciated as yet. When I hear Sydney dismissed as Tinsel Town, even in jest, I think of Walter and feel irritated. Few people are unique or irreplaceable. He was both. His widow Jean has written his biography *Walter Stone: The Passionate Bibliophile*.

I am sure Walter, and Wentworth Press, must have lost money on many of the books they published—for one thing because small presses could not afford adequate budgets for promotion. I am certain that many of their books will be re-discovered and eventually regarded as minor classics. I think of Kay Brown's novel of mining life at Mount Isa in the thirties, *Knock Ten*. I met Kay in Kylie Tennant's house, and a good friend she was to Kylie and to Benison. She calls North Queensland 'my own country': she lived in Mount Isa and other mining towns—her husband was a miner—when her children were young. Many of her widely published short stories have won awards. She writes stories and letters in an expansive, unfettered way that speaks with one of the unmistakable voices of an Australia that is vanishing. She paints landscapes and still life subjects and very well. As I have already mentioned, for most of their lives she and Tom Ronan kept it a secret that they were sister and brother, but she proudly records the relationship now.

Television came to Australia in 1956. Woe cryers were certain TV would spell the doom of book reading and cinema and theatre. It did not do that but, in about five years, it put paid to the heyday (or heynight), of the informative public lecture. If a decision had to be made between a comfortable evening at home watching a dramatisation of the best stories of Saki or Guy de Maupassant, or *Z Cars*, and an expedition to the city to listen to a discourse on *Tristram Shandy*, or the documentary background to Eleanor Dark's novels, TV tended to win, no matter how good and distinguished the lecturer and important the topic.

Audiences then, as now, would make exceptions for very famous speakers or sometimes for contentious topics if it seemed that interesting discussion would not be covered by the eventual printed version of the lecture in one or other of the small magazines and specialist journals that began to proliferate. Groups whose members shared narrow, special professional or esoteric interests managed to attract reasonable audiences— some still do. Some old-established organisations faltered during the 1960s and some of them failed and finished. Others, like the English Association, found new roles and bases for activities within the spirit of their charters. (Geoffrey Blainey averred that one venerable Melbourne literary society, whose membership down the years had became geriatric, finally ended its life when the last few regular attenders at its programmes became too old to climb the flight of stairs to its meeting rooms.)

I had joined the Workers Educational Association (WEA) when I still worked on Garden Island. An excellent lending library in its rooms close to the Quay was very convenient for me while I travelled from work by ferry. Many of its lecture programmes, especially those on literary topics, interested me greatly and its lecturers were first rate. I chiefly remember H. M. Green's discourses on Australian Literature, and Donovan Clarke's on contemporary poetry. Several times I enjoyed class weekends at the WEA's Newport centre. By present-day standards the accommodation was spartan and the behaviour sober, but, and very cheaply, we had a lot of fun.

I made many long-lasting friendships through the WEA—Maurie and Eva Isaacs who later I often met at Tommy's rooms and Joyce Shewcroft who also belonged to the English Association were early ones; and Hig (Esmee) Higgins, a brother of Nettie Palmer, who lectured for the Association and his wife Joy. They used to give splendid parties at their house.

Most lectures, like most TV, tended to wash over me. I remember a good deal of what Donovan Clarke said about W. B. Yeats and Christopher Fry and the 'death wish' which for Don informed much recent writing, but precious little of what less inspiring speakers said about other things. For me, and perhaps for other people, part of the attraction of evening meetings of groups like the WEA and the English Association was that they provided an informal meeting place. Later in the evening groups of friends would stroll off to one of the King Street coffee shops that, unlike Repins with its fixed pew-like seats and tables, had tables and chairs that could be pushed together to accommodate large groups.

The English Association had a monthly speaker and a consistent audience of thirty or forty people. It met in the Lyceum Club in a fine old Bank of NSW building at the corner of King and George Streets. There were modest kitchen facilities sufficient to serve tea and biscuits after the talk and before the questions, and to wash up afterwards. To the English

Association I delivered my first-ever public discourse in all innocence, for if ever someone was set up, it was I!

To explain: the Association was the virtual preserve of R. G. Howarth—in direct line of descent from Professor Mungo MacCallum, who founded the NSW branch in 1923. Its secretary when I first joined was H. M. Butterley, my father's friend who had long taught English at the Edgecliff Preparatory School, a once-famous, long-vanished institution that chiefly, but not only, prepared small boys for Sydney Grammar School. (Butterley's son Nigel is a distinguished composer of music.) Mr Butterley for a long time tried to persuade me to join the English Association but I, wrongly, supposed it would be an immensely learned society and very much an extension of the University. (There was only one University in all of NSW in those days and it was familiarly known as 'the Varsity'. Only cads and lesser breeds spoke of 'the Uni'.) My resistance crumbled when I became friendly with James Meagher who added his persuasive voice to that of H. M. Butterley.

I confided to R. G. Howarth my newly acquired passion for Robert Burton's *Anatomy of Melancholy*. I first came upon this curious classic in the library of Frensham. Now I'd bought the Everyman edition for myself and read the whole, becoming intoxicated especially with some of its dottier elements: 'Cabbage. . . causeth troublesome dreams, and sends up black vapours to the brain'; 'Cornelius Gemma. . . related of a young maid, called Katherine Gualter, a cooper's daughter, *anno 1571* that had such strange passions and convulsions, three men could not sometimes hold her; she purged a live eel, which he saw, a foot and a half long, and touched himself; but the eel afterwards vanished; she vomited some twenty-four pounds of fulsome stuff of all colours, twice a day for fourteen days; and after that she voided great balls of hair, pieces of wood, pigeon's dung, parchment, goose dung, coals. . . and again coals and stones, of which some had inscriptions, bigger than a walnut. . . besides paroxysms of laughing, weeping and ecstasies, etc. *Et hoc (inquit) cum horrore vidi*, "this I saw with horror". They could do no good on her by physic, but left her to the clergy.' (And what the clergy did for the poor girl Burton does not say.)

The hooded eyes of Guy Howarth and his wife Lilian regarded me enigmatically, as I raved on, suspecting no mischief. It happened that at a recent lecture evening during question/discussion time, I *had* rather outshone a protégé of the Howarths—a brilliant English Honours student. Someone, later that night, told me that Lilian was furious but I, a stranger to academic squabbles and favouritism, did not realise that I'd done something outrageous or unforgiveable. Indeed the bright young person concerned had enjoyed the verbal give-and-take as much as I had, and accepted his 'defeat' with good humour.

Actually, what I had done was peculiarly threatening to the Howarths. I did not then know that, a few years before this time, Howarth had ruined his chances of ever being offered a Professorship at the University of Sydney. He'd had an affair with a woman that resulted in a University scandal. I doubt I ever heard, or wished to hear, the whole story. He was now a Reader in English Literature and, no doubt, fully as powerful in his field as if he had owned the title Professor, but the disappointment rankled. Through his editorship of *Southerly*, the journal of the Association, and through the Association itself, he was able to foster his outstanding students—one might be invited to give a talk to the Association, another to publish a long, important, and sometimes pretty dull article in *Southerly*. Guy and Lilian valued these spheres of influence very much; a blow at a Howarth protégé or pet project was a blow at themselves.

And so, and no doubt at far too much length, I talked on about Robert Burton's great book, and the strange eyes of the Howarths' exchanged glances. (They each had fleshy, drooping eyelids—this surely cannot have been an instance of married couples coming to resemble each other, but of like's attraction for like.) Then why, said Guy sweetly, don't you give a lecture to the Association about *The Anatomy of Melancholy*? Oh, I couldn't, I said. After all, I said, I had no degree; I was not an academic; I was a poet and general writer at the very beginning of my career. I knew nothing about composing learned discourses. Oh, go *on*, they said. You can and you must. Everyone has to start somewhere.

So I wrote my lecture—which copiously quoted my favourite bits, some of which were grand and sonorous and many, funny.

Enough people in the audience laughed at the funny parts to give me heart as I delivered. I'd also attempted to relate some of Burton's work to certain present-day psychological theory and no doubt the result was pretty pretentious and silly. It began to worry me somewhat that Thelma Herring, sitting in the audience, looked worried. Thelma, a Senior Lecturer in the English Department was one of the nicest women in the world and very, very scholarly. It was not always easy to judge her facial expression because she had a pronounced squint and her wayward eyes gave misleading messages. Nowadays a fine scholar and capable woman like Thelma would be at least an Associate Professor and even then, some forty years ago, many people considered she should have more seniority. Why did she look worried? Was it because Guy, sitting behind me on the platform, was busily taking notes as I knew from the squeaking of his pen? But then, he was to move the vote of thanks, was he not? An honour for me.

I finished my talk. The audience clapped. While we drank tea before question time several of my friends and a few other people said it had been most interesting, what a *fascinating* book, etcetera, etcetera, etcetera. Tea finished, everyone sat down again, I answered a few questions. Then Guy got to his feet smiling his accustomed agreeable smile.

Oh what a vote of thanks! How refreshing it was to listen to an enthusiastic young speaker notwithstanding that, perhaps, a young speaker might get carried away by her enthusiasms. (Merry tinkle of Lilian's laughter.) Nor was it either fair or appropriate to evaluate a non-academic young speaker entirely according to academic principles. However, he was certain Miss Keesing's appreciation of Burton would be enriched if she would read more widely and more comparatively among Burton's contemporaries: he had in mind, he said, those other great Elizabethans X, Y, Z and W. Was Miss Keesing aware, he wondered, of the splendid commentary on Burton published by the eminent Doctor ABC of Oxford University? Etcetera, etcetera, etcetera.

A very polished assassination indeed.

I was quite sure I would never open my mouth in public again but being resilient, vain, and above all increasingly good and furious, as my initial humiliation abated I was on my feet again before long.

In my own writing career or because of my involvements with writers' affairs I have met mercifully few people for whom I have felt dislike, distrust or antipathy; when I can I avoid them but occasionally they have to be confronted either in the flesh or in print. There are other people who, for various reasons, are disagreeable or boring. There are nuisances who try to influence reviewers and critics. The world of Australian letters was comparatively small and avoidance was often impracticable; fortunately most of the men and women in that world were and are likeable and congenial.

Guy Howarth was someone I could not avoid meeting quite often. I respected his attainments and achievements but deplored his deviousness and petty intrigues. No doubt he disliked me. However such good friends as Doug Stewart and Tommy and Maxine were friendly with Guy and Lilian, so at least when we met socially, and also in our professional dealings, ostensible cordiality prevailed. Twice Guy did me a truly bad turn; I had no effective remedy against these deeds so it seemed wisest to disregard them. The second occasion concerned the first *Penguin Book of Australian Verse* (1958), edited by R. G. Howarth, Kenneth Slessor and John Thompson. One morning a journalist I knew telephoned to ask if I was pleased with my selection in this new book. Taken by surprise I said I'd heard nothing about it. The journalist leafed through her copy, stuttered with embarrassment and said oh dear, she was dreadfully sorry, I was not represented in its pages. Would I comment? No.

A few days after that, at a function Ken Slessor sought me out and apologetically said that, as one of the joint editors he felt impelled to explain the omission of poems of mine. I tried to prevent him from continuing. No, he said, I must surely be hurt and he wanted me to know that he and John Thompson had selected certain of my poems, but Guy had flatly refused to include them.

Guy by then was a Professor of English at the University of Cape Town so I was spared a confrontation. I declined to talk further about the episode with Slessor and, indeed, had private doubts about his propriety in telling me anything at all. I often discussed quesions and problems with Doug Stewart but did not do so this time. Doug was a close friend of Slessor's and I had no wish to make difficulties, though the affair was, of course, a snub to Doug himself since he had published and sponsored most of my poetry. Some time later he told me he had made a protest to the trio of editors.

In 1973 Guy Howarth returned from South Africa to Sydney. On New Years Eve in 1973 he dined with friends in an outer suburb and took an electric train back to the city. During the journey he was assaulted by louts and died of his injuries early in January 1974 in Sydney Hospital.

The first Adelaide Festival of Arts in 1960 incorporated a Writers Week, an innovation so popular and successful that it has been a feature of all the Festivals since then. I think I attended the first one and certainly went to all Writers Weeks from 1962 to the late 1970s, and several thereafter.

For the content of speeches, important and otherwise, I have an excellent forgettory; to me the attraction of these events is meeting and talking with writers and other people connected with literature and books, and especially Australians. I offer no apology for being parochial in this context. Of course it is interesting and sometimes stimulating to meet celebrities and visitors from many countries; in doing so I am seldom disappointed because I do not have high expectations from short encounters during crowded gatherings. The kind of polite pleasantries expressed during most brief encounters are seldom of importance; the positive benefits of inviting distinguished overseas visitors arise chiefly from their meetings with a few people who have relevant matters to discuss.

Moreover I am convinced that as a rule the way one should *know* writers is through their books. Those who become friends or prove to be congenial as people are a bonus. Literature, and to some extent film, are indeed perhaps the only arts that can be explored and enjoyed at high levels without a need for travel either overseas or within Australia. (To an extent this is now true of music because of recent technology in recording and reproducing sound, though for most people the best machinery is no absolute substitute for attending first-rate live performances that may have the added and inspirational ambience of great concert halls and theatres.) Anyone in Australian cities and all but the remotest places who wishes to read the very latest books and greatest authors can do so either by purchase or through libraries. I can never own a Rembrandt or a Picasso or, through travel, see more than a part of their great works; but I can easily own a Complete Works of Shakespeare and every book published by Douglas Stewart and all but two or three out-of-print early books by Patrick White. If I were fluent in other languages my range could be wider.

Hedley Brideson, the State Librarian of South Australia, was active in organising pioneer Writers Weeks, and the State Library mounted excellent displays for these occasions. He had a pet phrase for speeches of welcome that amused participants: he was certain that one benefit of writers' gatherings was that they were invaluable 'safety valves' for authors whom he envisaged as, year in and out, holed up in solitary attics generating explosive steams of frustration and loneliness.

Brideson and his committee were efficient in booking reasonably priced accommodation, which is how during the week in 1964 I, Margaret Trist and a male author I'll call Brendan stayed at a small hotel near the railway, most of whose rooms were taken by the Black Theatre of Prague. I don't know how those splendid Czechoslovakian mimes, actors and dancers got on; perhaps their manager had a special key to the front door which was firmly closed early of an evening. We three writers had to ring a bell and wait for the night porter when we returned as early as about eight-thirty p.m. Mark, having CSR work to do in Adelaide, had arranged to be in the city during part of that week. He stayed at the Australian, North Adelaide, a much grander establishment.

One evening Mark and I returned to my hostelry after the theatre, and decided to have a drink in my room. Two respectable persons of forty had a problem convincing the night porter that Dr Hertzberg was Miss Keesing's husband. Reluctantly he at last admitted Mark but gave us a disapproving look when he later had to unlock the front door for Mark to leave.

Margaret Trist, Brendan and I shared a table each morning at breakfast, a time of day when she and I were marginally alive—unlike Brendan who was alert, talkative, keen to air theories and to criticise theatre seen the night before. Margaret and I dreamed up a book title *Breakfasts with Brendan* but decided the contents of the work were too horrible to contemplate. This was an instance of the ambience of Adelaide. Margaret and I had served together on committees and had met at social gatherings over some fifteen years but had never really got to know each other before.

Long before the splendid Writers Week tent was pitched beside the Torrens near the Festival Centre with its excellent facilities, the Royal Admiral Hotel in Hindley Street became a sort of writers' club where people met informally in a pleasant upstairs lounge that was partly open to a roof garden. There I first saw George Johnston who had recently returned to Australia from Greece, his craggy features distinctive beneath the digger's hat he wore. It was also in Adelaide that I really came to know Judah Waten and Stephen Murray-Smith from Melbourne and Bill Scott from Queensland. Some memories are less happy, like the evening when an interstate author whose books I admired and who was friendly, even effusive, when we met in Sydney, got drunker and drunker and made increasingly anti-Semitic statements and jibes which he directed at me. I'd have left the bar where this was happening except that I'd arranged to meet several people there a little later. Clem Christesen, poet and founder of *Meanjin* tried to muzzle the man but he was too far gone.

Mary Durack, Henrietta Drake Brockman and other writers I'd met in Perth came to Adelaide sometimes and, because the CLF usually held a meeting during Writers Week, Kylie Tennant and Doug Stewart would also be present.

The poet Robert Clark and his wife lived in the hills behind the city and had some memorable dinner parties, where most of the guests were poets. Ian Mudie and Renee lived near the beach at Glenelg and they too entertained many visiting writers. I recall a day when Renee took me for a long walk at low tide along the beach which, washed by the waters of the Great Australian Bight, displayed shells and seaweeds unlike those of my eastern coast. Ian's conversation about poetry and his knowledge of South Australian history and personalities made his conversation one of the major pleasures of the place.

I first met Colin Thiele and Rosemary Wighton at an Adelaide party. Rosemary Wighton, who was closely associated with the Adelaide Festival of the Arts, especially Writers Week went on to chair the Literature Board of the Australia Council. Colin Thiele was a writer I was especially keen to meet; he and his wife Rhonda were hospitable and interesting.

Geoffrey Dutton, a leading organiser of Writers Week, lived at Kapunda near Adelaide on his family property, 'Anlaby'. His wife Ninette, an artist, was also much involved in Festival affairs and entertaining. They were tall poppies who infuriated the kind of people who can't endure tall poppies. To hear some of these bores holding forth you might have supposed the Duttons to be some sort of celebrity-nappers when all they were guilty of was hosting overseas VIPs at 'Anlaby', bringing them to Festival events and taking them home afterwards. No doubt they protected some visiting celebrities from suffering states of exhaustion.

In 1976 at 'Anlaby' the Duttons entertained all members of the Literature Board—the body which superseded the CLF—who were meeting in

Adelaide and many other overseas and local people. I recall Sidney Nolan, Max Harris, Jean Battersby, Randolph Stow and J. J. Bray, poet and Chief Justice of South Australia.

Max Harris' Mary Martins Bookshop was a welcome oasis in the city and well-stocked with books by visiting authors.

There were romances. The poets Suzanne Hunt and Brian Ridley married not long after their first meeting in Adelaide. There were extraordinary events as when, in 1976, a posse of editors of some of Australia's 'little' magazines who had been attending a seminar arranged by UNESCO staged an unannounced 'walk-in' to a Literature Board meeting and demanded that the Board forthwith deliberate some resolutions they had just drafted. During a poetry reading on the Museum lawn, David Campbell who always fortified himself for such occasions with a pocket flask of whisky, insisted that I, sitting beside him, should share his Dutch courage. I did, despite a disapproving glare from a woman who, with her schoolgirl daughter, left the reading. This reminded me of an incident years before at the New South Wales Art Gallery which had mounted a splendid exhibition of drawings and paintings by William Blake. A girl of about eleven was absolutely entranced by one of the prophetic pictures. Her mother, a large woman, rushed into the exhibition room, grabbed the child by the collar of her school shirt and exclaimed, 'If I ever catch yer lookin' at them 'orrid naked men again I'll lam the 'ide off yer,' and bustled her out of the gallery. Later Campbell brought down the house, or lawn, when he read, I think for the first time, his satirical poem *The Australian Dream*:

> The doorbell buzzed. It was past three o'clock.
> The steeple-of-Saint-Andrew's weathercock
> Cried silently to darkness, and my head
> Was bronze with claret as I rolled from bed
> To ricochet from furniture. Light! Light
> Blinded the stairs, the hatstand sprang upright,
> I fumbled with the lock, and on the porch
> Stood the Royal Family with a wavering torch.

> 'We hope,' the Queen said, 'we do not intrude.
> The pubs were full, most of our subjects rude.
> We came before our time. It seems the Queen's
> Command brings only, "Tell the dead marines!"
> We've come to you.' I must admit I'd half
> Expected just this visit. With a laugh
> That put them at their ease, I bowed my head.
> 'Your Majesty is most welcome here,' I said.
> 'My home is yours. There is a little bed
> Downstairs, a boiler-room, might suit the Duke.'

He thanked me gravely for it and he took
Himself off with a wave. 'Then the Queen Mother?
She'd best bed down with you. There is no other
But my wide bed. I'll curl up in a chair.'
The Queen looked thoughtful. She brushed out her hair
And folded up *The Garter* on a pouf.
'Distress was the first commoner, and as proof
That queens bow to the times,' she said, 'we three
Shall share the double bed. Please follow me.'

I waited for the ladies to undress—
A sense of fitness, even in distress.
Is always with me. They had tucked away
Their state robes in the lowboy; gold crowns lay
Upon the bedside tables; ropes of pearls
Lassoed the plastic lampshade; their soft curls
Were spread out on the pillows and they smiled.
'Hop in,' said the Queen Mother. In I piled
Between them to lie like a stick of wood.
I couldn't find a thing to say. My blood
Beat, but like rollers at the ebb of tide,
'I hope your Majesties sleep well,' I lied.
A hand touched mine and the Queen said, 'I am
Most grateful to you, Jock. Please call me Ma'am.'

On the whole Australian poets, myself included, read our work poorly. Good readers like Campbell and Roland Robinson have a certain flamboyance. Yevgeny Yevtushenko at the 1966 Writers Week remains in my memory as the best poetry reader I ever heard. 'Poet of Passion and Intellect' said the *Telegraph*, and of fire. He began one Adelaide reading on the Museum lawn and then rain fell so poets and audience adjourned to the large front hall of the Museum. The listeners sat on marble stairs to hear the Russian's splendid declamation delivered in front of the articulated skeleton of an enormous whale.

At one Writers Week, as an experiment, poetry readings were held in factories and workplaces—my fate was aboard a ship at Port Adelaide before breakfast. I can't recall what I read to a receptive audience with whom I later ate fried eggs.

For twenty years we owned a cottage at Moss Vale in the Southern Highlands. 'Carrowmore' once belonged to an aunt of Banjo Paterson and I liked to think he may have visited her there. I associate it with many authors. Doug and Margaret Stewart spent a few days with us; Maslyn Williams has lived in the Highlands area for years and is one of our friends. Nancy Cato stayed for a few days and David Martin and his wife

Richenda, who is a writer for children, visited. At nearby Bundanoon the novelist David Foster, his wife Gerda and their children live in a house surrounded by a magnificent vegetable garden that reminds me of my father's Pennant Hills acres. Since David published his novel *Dog Rock* I view Bundanoon and the Southern Highlands with an altered eye and hear its speech with a quickened ear.

Rachel Roxburgh lives about a mile from 'Carrowmore' in 'The Barn', a welcoming, beautiful house that she converted from the original warm brick barn of 'Throsby Park' which is the stone house that Dr Charles Throsby built in 1834—he was the chief early explorer and settler of the region. Rachel and I, however, first met in early 1942 in an unlikely way. We both embarked upon a wartime job as probationer nurses at Sydney Hospital. I lasted about six weeks and abandoned nursing. Rachel, who was already a good painter, became a nursing sister. After the War she trained in England as a potter and had a pottery and kiln at 'The Barn' for many years. Her pots are distinctive, imaginative and elegant. She has a wide and deep knowledge of New South Wales history and has written chiefly of the history of its early houses and furniture, and farming and other buildings. She is an intrepid walker and dedicated conservationist. She is a most meticulous and reliable researcher, not only in libraries but by car and on foot. She was a leading spirit in making of 'Throsby Park' a gracious, authentically restored and furnished house which is open to the public at regular intervals and is under the wing of the National Parks and Wildlife Service, and administered with the advice of a local committee. *Early Colonial Houses of New South Wales* is perhaps the most important of Rachel's books. It is enhanced by her careful drawings.

In the sixties I tutored summer-school writing classes conducted by the Department of External Studies of Sydney University, despite my doubts—and I still have doubts—as to whether 'creative' writing has ever, or ever can be, actually taught. True, many admirable American authors are products of writing schools and colleges. Certainly talented imaginative people often need an audience who will read or listen to their work before they achieve publication, and they do need mentors to offer advice about technical and editorial matters. But I doubt anyone taught them how to write creatively and with flair.

Summer-school classes were a challenge. I felt impelled, as best I could, to provide value for the fees the students paid. Some of these people vaguely wanted 'to write' but what or why seemed mysterious. Others knew precisely what and why, but 'how on earth' was their problem—and *my* problem. Some were disarmingly frank in confessing that they had applied for other categories of classes—Painting, or Music or Drama—but those quotas were filled so they ended up in 'Writing'. One woman came only to keep her shy niece company.

In an early class there was a Chinese gentleman in his seventies who was born in Australia where he had some schooling. He then returned to mainland China with his parents and joined a business firm. As a comparatively young man he came back to Sydney and established a prosperous business. He lived in Sydney thereafter but for some years often visited China. He had numerous children and grandchildren and for them he wished to write his own life-story and some of the history of the family. He also hoped to describe and discuss historic events that were part of the background fabric. He was bilingual in Chinese and in English, which he spoke perfectly—but on paper he seemed unable to express anything.

Perhaps oral history aided by tape recorders was in its infancy then but I had no knowledge of it, did not think to enquire and have often regretted my ignorance—because what he hoped to record was valuable and perhaps unique. He was a rich old man so I suggested he might, within the Chinese community, find a person who could act as amanuensis/ghost-writer. No, this was a thing he, and only he, must do. Disappointed, unfailingly polite, he resigned.

One modest, hard-up young man showed me a couple of short stories that were so excellent and original I told him straightly he was unlikely to gain anything from me or the group. I arranged for his fee to be refunded, and put him in touch with a couple of editors. Most of his stories were published. Then he obtained a journalist's job in a South American country and has become a senior and distinguished editor of an English-language newspaper.

On the first day of a course I would confront about twenty expectant faces and twenty pens or pencils poised over notebooks. I would ask what their desires and problems were. A few had work to show me. Very often they would say: 'If only I could think of a plot I know I could...' or 'I have these wonderful plots in my head but...'

'How,' I would ask, 'did you travel here this morning?' With some puzzlement they would itemise cars, buses, trains and ferries. 'Very well. As it happens I am not in the least interested in knowing all this. *You* make me interested. Tell me what you saw, who you spoke to, what you thought. Why did you notice the girl with brown eyes? etc. etc.' Pencils flew. 'OK. Now add something that did not happen. The dear old couple on the train seat opposite suddenly have a blazing row; or a lump of masonry falls off a building and clobbers the person in front of you on the footpath. Tell me about that...'

On the first morning of a class in 1962 an alert old woman with mad eyes and the expression of an inquisitive bird sat in the front row. The secretary had 'warned' me about Miss Carew who was a pensioner, so she did not pay fees; she was well-known in adult educational circles—a nuisance but harmless. She wore a straw hat almost always.

Uni Tutorial and WEA classes I attend
On World Affairs, Science and Philosophy
Without end.
International Affairs seem a great game
With Mr Harries and Dr Alsop competing for fame.
Mr Mander with glee
Talks on Roman History.
Mr Rose, too
On Mod. History's more subdued.
The Plays that are great
Does Dr Tulip and Mrs Eddy take.
With the good Rabbi
Jewish Literature I explore
And Mr Crown on Old Testament lore,
Messrs Dash and Jenkins on Psychology
And Joss Davies on Anthropology.
Mr Ginnane to be sure
From Aristotle to More
And Rev. Stuart-Watts on Plato to Shaw.
To Messrs Conn and Carmichael it is no trouble
With High Finance and Banking to juggle.
With Messrs Mohan and Bryson Taylor on words
And Donovan Clarke on Art and Literature
Is about as much as I can endure.
With Mr Bonney on Logic and Dr Kerr on the stars
I don't know whether I'm on Earth or on Mars.

Elsie Muriel Gweneth Carew was indisputably a writer and a poet and the group acknowledged it. She was eccentric and gallant and I told her story and displayed her works in *Elsie Carew/Australian Primitive Poet* (1965) and *The Passing Pageant/Poems and Prose* (1970). In 1963 I published an article about her in *Southerly*. This was her response:

Write-up and write down

When Nancy Keesing gave me a good
Write up
A certain critic got his spite-up
Primitive Australians with no education
Except what they can get through
Public subscription (or donation)
Shouldn't measure themselves against
Eton Erudition
They live in butter-boxes with
shelters of thatch
And only live where the wild birds
hatch

And walk a track beside the
Kangaroo
Pooh! Pooh!
P.S. Someone told me there was something said in the
'N————' about Primitive Australians writing, so this is
my answer to him.

Readers enjoyed Elsie Carews's tart, sardonic view of the world and her
eccentric mysticism too, for, granted the existence of primitive or naive
poets, why not naive mystics? Barry Humphries included six of her verses
in his *Innocent Austral Verse*. Elsie, or as she sometimes called herself in her
recording of events, Gwenelda, had an extraordinary life-history which is
too long to recount here—it is told in my two books. However I shall
record the manner of her death and burial.

Her Sydney address was the People's Palace which was conducted by the
Salvation Army. The manager phoned me one morning to say that Miss
Carew had died during the night. It was not as simple as that! She had
stumbled from her room to a hallway, shrieked, 'I've been poisoned!' and
then fallen dead. Because of that shriek and the suddenness there would
have to be an autopsy and inquest.

The officer said the Salvation Army could arrange a cheap funeral of the
sort once called 'a pauper's funeral'. Walter Stone and I decided to
farewell our friend more adequately. Because of the inquest there was no
urgency, so I rang around several undertakers and accepted a quote from a
North Shore firm that was, even in 1970, some $200 less than the
amount quoted by another company. I told the man about Elsie's writing
and mentioned that she'd died just before she could see *The Passing
Pageant*. 'We could put a copy of that book in her hand in the coffin', he
suggested. Religion? Walter and I had no idea but thought she was probably a Protestant. The undertaker would ask a retired Anglican clergyman to read a non-denominational service.

At the Northern Suburbs Cemetery in Ryde, Walter and I were the
only mourners at a dignified service where nothing was skimped or rushed; the clergyman gave a carefully prepared address garnered from Elsie's
books. She lies next to the grave of a Knight and am sure would have an
amused appreciation of eternal rest beside a Sir.

My first meeting with Judith Wright, her husband J. P. McKinney and
their very small daughter Meredith had an odd outcome. I had long
admired Judith's poetry but scarcely expected to meet her, for she lived
then at Mount Tambourine in Queensland. In the late forties I was on
holiday in Brisbane. Val Vallis, the poet, whom I'd met in Sydney, said
of course I must meet Judith and made a day for us to drive to Mount
Tambourine with his friend Peter Brookes who had a car.

Judith has long been deaf. At that time she did not use an efficient hearing-aid. Conversation with a stranger was obviously tiring and, after lunch, Mr McKinney took Val, Peter and me for a long walk into the rainforest of the mountain. He explained that the rough track we followed twisted through what remained of a long-ago eroded volcanic crater and that almost every foot we descended took us into older and older eras of vegetation. From the pathway I collected a few dried-out shells of giant snails. (Later I placed them conspicuously on the outside leaves of Dad's cabbages. Terrible consternation. Joke! 'Well, if you think that's funny!')

When we were about to depart Judith gave us what Val regarded as an almost sacred trust, a wriggling bandicoot in a hessian sugar bag. No, it could not be put in the boot, it might stifle. It had become a nuisance burrowing in the McKinney vegetable garden and had to be removed, but not exterminated. Val was to release the animal far from the garden at some suitable location on the way home that Judith described in detail; it was near water, and there the bandicoot could make a new life for itself in the bush.

I sat on the back seat of the car. The bandicoot was beside me on the floor behind the driver. A mile or so along the road I noticed a tick crawling up Peter's collar, and another on Val's shoulder. Bandicoots are hosts to ticks. Peter stopped the car quickly at a very barren spot. We examined ourselves. We picked up and squashed ticks by the dozen. No sign of a creek but we bundled the bandicoot out of the bag there and then and drove home scratching at imaginary ticks crawling all over us. We did feel we'd betrayed the trust of a poet, but that did not stop us laughing.

The incident reminded Val of the time when he was returning to his home on leave during the War. He bought some sea-food as a treat for his parents, and decided he'd better let his mother know so she would not expend precious coupons on un-needed meat. So he sent her a telegram: 'Arriving Friday. Have live crabs.' Rural post offices were gossipy places in those days, and Val did wonder about the askance looks he had from old friends during his few days at home. ('Crabs' are Australian slang for lice.)

Sometimes I remember precisely how, when and where I first met a person, but many of my friends seem to have been a part of the background of my life almost for ever. David Martin, for instance. I am sure I'd read and admired his poetry before we met because I do perfectly recall the shock of his voice. David speaks with a heavy Hungarian/German accent, so that I have puzzled as to how in his head he manages to 'hear' and use the English language so perfectly and with such precision.

This led me to wonder how Joseph Conrad spoke, or how Arthur Waley sounded to Chinese people.

By contrast two weirdly unforgettable meetings were instigated by a Melbourne friend and editor. Some time in the early fifties he wrote to say that a visiting Indian journalist whom I'll call Mr Das would be coming to Sydney, and could I arrange for him to meet some Sydney writers? As good luck would have it, at the time concerned my cousin Lindsay Parker was on holiday away from Sydney, and had generously offered me the use of his bachelor flat in Elizabeth Bay. There I could invite guests to a meal in much greater comfort than what the studio afforded 'but,' I told them firmly, 'there will be no alcohol because I know many Indians do not drink it—it's against their religion.' I also, with my guest's possible dietary laws in mind, shopped for fish, not meat, and the ingredients of hearty vegetarian fare.

By telephone to his hotel I arranged with Mr Das to meet him on the long flight of steps outside the old *Sydney Morning Herald* building at the corner of O'Connell and Pitt Street. In daylight, at five o'clock, I stood at our meeting-place realising that other people also found it convenient. Two matronly middle aged women in tweeds and velour hats stood near-by. Some young office girls awaited boyfriends, and several brillian-tined young men awaited their girls.

On the curved side of the steps most distant from me a tall, bearded turbanned man was impatiently looking at his watch. Could *he* be Mr Das? I went across and asked him. He gave me a curt no. So I returned to where I'd been standing and after a minute or so a business-suited man who in fact looked more like a negro than an Indian came to stand nearby. It was now almost five-fifteen—Mr Das was late—or was he the chap in the suit? I went up to him. 'Are you Mr Das?' He gave me an affronted 'no' and moved several feet away.

I then became aware of two pairs of eyes beneath velour hats boring into my back. I half turned. They glared. Just then a nimble, chocolate-brown young man bounded up the steps, and stood at the centre of the topmost one. He peered about him, obviously looking for someone. I climbed to where he waited. Yes, he was Mr Das. So, together, we descended the steps and as we passed the tweeds and velours one said most distinctly:

'How digusting! But they say some of them *prefer* black men!'

In Lindsay's flat we had, I thought, a successful evening. Maurice and Eva Isaacs arrived, Tommy and Maxine, Tom Inglis Moore (down from Canberra), Dorothy Fairbridge, and several other guests.

Fairly late the Isaacs offered to drive Tommy back to his flat, and Tom and the guest of honour to their hotels which were near to Tommy's place.

I heard about the end of the evening later. Tommy invited the people in the car up to The Room for a cup of tea. All but Mr Das declined. At three a.m. Tommy finally got rid of his guest who was not teetotal at all and finished a whole precious bottle of Scotch while they talked.

An American comedian coined one of my favourite parodies. A and B met in the street. 'I know your name, it's your face I can't remember,' said B to A.

My Melbourne friend wrote and asked me to contact an English journalist who wanted information about young writers in Sydney. I phoned the man and arranged to meet him in the foyer of the Australia hotel—I'd carry a copy of the *Bulletin* in its distinctive pink cover, and by that he'd recognise me. The day came. I couldn't find the letter or recall the man's surname. Never mind, in a *Reader's Digest* I'd acquired a splendid solution to this predicament. If you can't recall a person's name you confess. 'Mary Smith,' replies the person. 'Oh, of *course* I remembered the Mary—it's the *surname* I couldn't recall' or vice-versa you lie.

So we met at the Australia, and the very nice man insisted on taking me to Repins Quality Inn for coffee. From the instant he spotted the *Bulletin*, along Castlereagh Street and until the waitress set down our cups of coffee, he talked or asked questions non-stop, and continued to do so for the hour of our meeting. As we got ready to go our separate ways I promised to write down some information he wanted and post it to his London address which he gave me. There had been no opportunity to use the *Reader's Digest* ploy and it was far too late to confess ignorance of his name, so I tried a variant. With pen poised over my notebook I asked: 'Just how do you spell your name?' 'J−O−N−E−S,' he replied, 'how else *could* one spell it?'

Meetings with overseas authors, no matter what their nationality, tend to be unpredictable. Michael Costigan poet and reviewer, now with the Ethnic Affairs Commission but Director of the Literature Board at the time, and I had a morning coffee meeting with a Russian contingent at one Adelaide Festival. This appointment was arranged so that we could discuss a few serious Literature Board matters with the two writers concerned and their 'minder'—a huge, intimidating fellow. However a Festival organiser asked us to keep the Russians talking for a good hour beyond what we had planned or they expected, the reason being that, in the Writers Week tent, a posse of Australian authors intended to put some highly uncomplimentary anti-Russian resolutions. Our fund of sensible conversation ran out and delaying tactics became harder and harder. Absentmindedly I took a cigarette pack from my handbag and offered around black Balkan Sobranies that Mark had brought in duty-free from an overseas trip.

'Ah! Sobranies! Do Australians like Sobranies?'

I invented a remarkable account of the literary associations of Balkan Sobranies. Oscar Wilde, I said, smoked nothing else. Sobranies were part of the background of the Naughty Nineties. Sobranies, I practically suggested, were a prime cause of the glorious revolution...on and on I stumbled. At long last it seemed safe to let them go.

An odd experience in early 1983 seemed like an embodiment or emanation of Elizabeth Jolley's fantastical imagination. She visited Sydney to promote *Mr Scobie's Riddle* and Penguin, her publishers, gave a luncheon for her at Doyles on the Beach at Watsons Bay, a restaurant that always makes me nostalgic because its building was once the boatshed from which my father often hired a rowing boat to take us for a day's fishing.

Marie Richards and other Penguin people from Melbourne in glorious weather admired the harbour sparkling like a tourist poster. We talked of the Watsons Bay background to some of Christina Stead's novels. I said: 'We're so close to The Gap we ought to walk up and see the view from the cliffside walk.' Blank looks on interstate faces so I recounted some of the history of South Head, the Macquarie lighthouse, the wreck of the Dunbar and the sad tally of suicides who have jumped from The Gap cliff to the rock platform below.

Elizabeth had an afternoon radio engagement so we decided against leisurely coffee and strolled up through the park to the cliff-top fence. 'There's a better view a bit further along past the Dunbar's anchor. You can see the iron steps that rock fishermen use—and police rescue squads too.' Absolutely on cue around a rocky corner an elderly man staggered towards us, his head and face streaming rivulets of blood, his shocked elderly wife trying to support him. No suicide; a bad fall.

Elizabeth, an experienced nurse, took charge with no thought for her good dress. I scrambled down the low sandstone cliff to the road and providentially found myself opposite the Post Office. The Postmaster grabbed his first-aid kit, 'Always keep it ready,' and his wife phoned for an ambulance.

As we drove back to town the party declined to hear more of my recollections of amazing scenes from Sydney history along New South Head Road. 'We've conjured up enough for one day,' someone said.

Another occasion, comparable in its strangeness, was a meeting with Indira Gandhi to which Sir Paul and Lady Hasluck invited Mark and me when Sir Paul was Foreign Minister. At intervals throughout the luncheon people in the Arts were asked to sit at Mrs Gandhi's table and speak to her for some five or ten minutes. What could one say to Nehru's daughter, herself the Prime Minister of India? She recounted a shopping expedition to a department store that morning where she had bought lovely woollen cardigans for herself, her friends and family. Then, for some reason I forget, we reached the topic of tigers. India, she explained, was trying to preserve its increasingly threatened population of tigers in their native jungles. This was difficult because villages existed near jungle borders and, to prevent tigers eating villagers, and thereby prompting villagers to retaliate against disappearing tigers, it was necessary to provide an optimum number of tethered goats on the outskirts of the jungle to satisfy the ravening beasts. 'Optimum' was the key word and difficulty. Too many goats and the tigers became lazy and no longer hunted in natural fashion; too few—bad luck villagers!

Most Australian conservation problems began to look ridiculously simple.

Princess Margaret and her husband on a visit to Australia had asked to meet 'people in the Arts'. Mark and I went to luncheon at the Opera House where we joined forces with Doug and Margaret Stewart, and then came upon Frank Moorhouse and Michael Wilding wearing suits and with very neat hair-does. 'Do tell me the plot of your new novel,' asked the princess of one or other of them, who manfully did his discreet best to answer the question in terms of Balmain's mores and ramifications filtered for royal ears. 'Ah I *see*' the Princess beamed satirically. 'A *menage à trois*.' She moved on serenely.

XI

The Writing on the Wall

1963: I was involved with the affairs of the English Association (NSW Branch) but did not belong to any other writers' group. Some good friends of mine were active in the Fellowship of Australian writes including Ella Turnbull and Walter Stone, its President; both of them worked hard for the English Association too. I avoided the Poetry Society which had taken twists and turns that I considered distasteful, if not disgraceful. (Apropos the Poetry Society: 'Those who write poetry are the salt of the earth,' said Doug Stewart. 'But those who *love* it...!!!')

At English Association events I met as many writers, poets and academics as I needed or wanted to add to established friendships and contacts. The children were young (seven and six respectively). Mark frequently travelled interstate and overseas. Evening engagements, whether in his company or by myself, necessitated arranging for and paying baby-sitters, so we picked and chose what we would and could attend. Perhaps I was intolerant and a bit of a snob, but I preferred the good conversation of friends in their houses or my own to enduring uncomfortable meeting-places and the often futile comments, questions and opinions of amateurs, would-bes, lonely hearts and other bores.

Predominantly for these reasons I missed my chance of becoming a foundation member of the Australian Society of Authors (ASA). I can forgive myself for this mistaken decision, but do regret it. On 15 May 1963 Walter Stone chaired a meeting of almost one hundred writers at Federation House in Sydney, which resolved 'that the Australian Society of Authors should be established'. Several days before that Jill Hellyer, who became the ASA's first secretray, phoned and invited me to attend. I declined and truthfully explained my main reason: that I supposed foundation members might be expected to work for the new organisation and I had no time to spare. In the event I joined the ASA in the following year (on 18 February 1964), but did no more to support it than pay my subscription until 1969, when Dal Stivens, the foundation President, spoke to me about a proposal that the Society should publish an anthology of writing by ASA members which might achieve good publicity and some financial gain. It was hoped that in its 'themes, styles and general treatment [it would] reflect society, thought and literary craftsmanship in Australia at the end of the sixties' to which end the chosen theme was 'transition'; and *Transition* became the name of the book that was published by Angus and Robertson in 1970. I was invited to compile the anthology, and agreed to do so. A few ASA members objected to some aspects of the project but on the whole it was well-received and, when published, a critical and financial success. In 1969 I was co-opted to the ASA management committee and was elected thereafter.

Barrie Ovenden who had created a most successful quarterly journal, *The Australian Author*, for the ASA was appointed editor of *Identity* in 1970; she then had to relinquish her editorship of the *Author*. At very short notice I agreed to edit the journal and did so for thirteen issues. This task, and my five years on the management committee, vastly enlarged my understanding of many concerns and problems not only of authors but of publishers, booksellers and the book trade generally. I had support and assistance from the ASA membership and from many people like lawyers, librarians and academics from whom I was able to commission authoritative articles. I believed that the journal should, as much as possible, debate matters of interest by displaying a variety of points of view and opinion. Once my good friend Colin Simpson, whose Public Lending Right crusade was at its height, was greatly annoyed because I printed some anti, as well as pro, PLR material.

Inevitably a few narks and knockers were disagreeable and contentious. One was an interstate member who persisted in submitting short stories though the journal had a firm policy of not publishing 'creative' writing. Later he became a considerable nuisance to the Literature Board. I am told that, whenever he referred to me he spat out: 'Tha*t* la*dy* poe*t*!'

Since 1968 an Australian Council for the Arts had advised the Government on funding and distributed its subsidies to performing arts organisations. On Australia Day 1973 the Prime Minister E. G. Whitlam announced a 'new' Council which would have responsibility for other arts, including literature. In 1975 this council became a statutory authority, The Australia Council. From Jean Battersby, the Council's Chief Executive Officer, I obtained a description of the new organisation and this appeared in the *Australian Author* of April 1973:

> A new Australian Council for the Arts was announced by the Prime Minister in January. Like the earlier Council it will be under the Chairmanship of Dr H. C. Coombs. In many respects it will be similar to the Canada Council and the Arts Council of Great Britain.
>
> By the time this issue appears further details of the Council, and of the seven Boards which it will administer, will probably have been announced. Meanwhile, we understand that the functions of the central Council will be primarily to co-ordinate:
>
> (a) Relations with government departments and agencies.
> (b) Research for the Arts.

(c) Over-all staffing for the whole organisation.

(d) Over-all finances (i.e., the Council will apply for finance to the government, and will then allocate moneys in consultation with each Board).

Policies for the support of the individual arts will be the responsibility of the various Boards, each with its own Chairman. Each Board will have its own budget and its own permanent executive staff.

Council and Board Members will be appointed for varying terms to allow for rotational membership. Board Members will include both people connected professionally and directly with the arts concerned, and people with other skills and interests; indeed, right through the whole structure it is planned that there should be "generalists" of various practical and professional skills, (i.e., legal, economic, etc.)

Within the old CLF Board and also among some sections of the literary community there was resistance to the concept of an umbrella arts organisation. It was thought that funding of literature was bound to suffer in competition with some other art forms. Some people regarded the CLF's long history of patronage and subsidy virtually sacrosanct. It was feared that loss of independence would result. However to many people the projected changes looked more appealing. The Parliamentary Committee to which the CLF Advisory Board reported had at least twice, in recent times, overridden and disallowed CLF recommendations. It was received wisdom that applications from certain well-known writers who had Communist or Socialist affiliations were almost automatically rejected. Because there were no fixed terms to CLF membership, unsuccessful applicants, who might suspect or believe themselves victims of prejudice or wholly subjective judgement, had little hope of their work being viewed from new perspectives. There were no Ombudsmen or formal review procedures then and undeniably people, no matter how distinguished and fair-minded, can and do make mistakes.

Another contributory factor to CLF and other unease was that the 1972–73 CLF budget had been very much increased (to $300,000) enabling the Advisory Board to implement some long-standing initiatives and plan further improved and adventurous kinds of funding. Now, at almost the moment of triumph plans and achievements seemed to be under threat.

It is worth noting that in 1971 only nineteen novels were published in Australia. In the event the Literature Board's first budget allocation (1973–74) was about four times that of the CLF's final year, some $1.2 million. Due to inflation and budgetary constraints such palmy days have never returned but the Board has managed to retain reasonable flexibility.

The members of the first Board were: Professor Geoffrey Blainey (Vic.), Chairman, and Mr Geoffrey Dutton (SA), Professor A. D. Hope (ACT),

Mr Judah Waten (Vic.), Miss Elizabeth Riddell (NSW), Mr David Malouf (NSW), Miss Nancy Keesing (NSW), Mr Thomas Shapcott (Qld), Professor Manning Clark (ACT), Mr Richard Hall (NSW) and Mr Richard Walsh (NSW). Of these Blainey, Dutton and Hope had been members of the CLF Advisory Board and the new Board therefore had an invaluable inbuilt 'memory'. Blainey for one had resisted the disbandment of the CLF and was apprehensive about the new system. Those three members together with Judah Waten and Manning Clark were appointed for a one-year term, although the first 'year' was in fact of some sixteen and a half months from mid February 1973 to 30 June 1974. Of the remaining members I and perhaps one or two others had two-year terms, the rest three years.

The admirable reason for differing periods of appointment (which applied to all the Boards) was to enable a regular turnover of membership to occur in a way that would ensure a mix of experienced and new members at all times.

Unfortunately admirable reasons are not always perfectly understood, or fully accepted. The first Board itself never really believed that five of its valuable senior members, including its imaginative and experienced chairman, would serve for only some sixteen months. So it was not surprising that the new system was not fully accepted or understood by the writing and book trade communities or by some academics and journalists. Everyone was accustomed to a CLF Advisory Board of virtually permanent members. Imperfect understandings, misunderstandings and a few, regrettable wilful misrepresentations by irresponsible critics, were to lead to a good deal of unpleasantness in mid 1974 when the first Board turnovers and new appointments were made public. For some of the Boards of the Council transition was relatively smooth, but outraged journalists and literary figures castigated the Council and Literature Board, speaking of 'sackings' and 'dismissals' and hinting at conspiracies. But that was all in the future when the first Board meetings were held in March 1973. Members quickly coalesced into a friendly, constructive group. Indeed, despite later unpleasantness all but one remained interested, helpful and willing to advise when requested.

My appointment took me by surprise. Jean Battersby phoned one morning in early 1973 and invited me to accept an appointment to the Board. I asked for time to consider. She said I would have to make up my mind no later than the next day. My chief question was what effect Board service might have upon my own writing programme. The children were now in secondary schools and relatively independent and during the past eighteen months I'd at last managed to write books again—two of them, *The Golden Dream* and *Garden Island People*. I had another book fully researched and waiting to be written. Could I manage to do that? (In the event *John Lang and 'The Forger's Wife'* spent nearly five years as a reproachful box full of notes and copied documents.) Mark was overseas and I could not seek his advice. I did not wish to consult Kylie or Doug because each of them was justifiably affronted by the curt way in which their CLF memberships had been terminated.

Within a couple of hours I knew my answer would be yes. I could always resign, but I was not likely to be asked again if I refused this time. Because of my involvement with writers and their affairs and long experience in reviewing and editing Australian books I believed I could be a constructive Board member. I rang Jean Battersby and gave her my decision.

I had another reason for agreement. I knew how fortunate I was that I had no need to weigh a possible application for a grant in my deliberations. Apart from Mark's senior and secure job I had, from family sources, a regular private income and also royalties from *Australian Bush Ballads, Old Bush Songs* and other books—the good fortune and hard work of my youth. I was sad that Dad was dead and could not know and that Mother was past fully comprehending what she was told, but Mark and the children were pleased and proud.

The first two meetings of the new Board in March 1973 were held modestly in Sydney. Mrs Leehy, the erstwhile secretary of the CLF, attended but then transferred to another job; Geoffrey Blainey recorded most of the subsequent early minutes, and attended to the Board's secretarial needs, for it had no staff. However by April when meetings were held in Sydney Joan O'Donnell was secretary. Joan was a splendid acquisition. She had been private secretary to the ALP Leader Arthur Calwell. As well as her job skills she had long experience of political ropes, processes and people. Otherwise the Board had no staff. That its headquarters would be in Melbourne, Geoff Blainey's city, was taken for granted by all members. There were administrative difficulties and delays associated with the phasing out of CLF commitments and procedures and the introduction of Australian Council for the Arts methods. Rightly or wrongly the Council was often seen as a prime cause of problems. Personality clashes were involved. Most if not all Board members were bent on protecting its autonomy. The Council had plans and, indeed, visions, that often seemed irrelevant, even threatening, to the Literature Board with its inherited CLF traditions.

Geoffrey Blainey, on Judah Waten's recommendation, 'discovered' Dr Michael Costigan who, having resigned his career as a priest of the Catholic church, had been working as Literary Editor of *Nation Review*. On 14 May Michael joined the staff as a 'temporary executive officer'; it was understood that when a permanent position was approved and advertised he could apply for it. He attended his first meeting in June and by July the Board met in its own premises at 4 Treasury Place, Melbourne.

This cannot be the place for any full history of the Literature Board, but when that comes to be written its author may marvel at the sheer volume of work that was handled in the first year, and at the speed, competence and imagination with which Michael Costigan took over and handled its administration. Many good decisions were made. Professor Blainey already had the respect of the literary and book worlds. Michael soon won the confidence of members and the Board's constituency. He and Joan O'Donnell worked in friendly harmony.

As well as meeting in Melbourne and Sydney the first Board, between its inception and 30 June 1974, met in Canberra, Brisbane, Perth, Adelaide and Hobart.

In November 1973 at Geoffrey Blainey's invitation, Dr H. C. Coombs, the Chairman of the Australian Council, attended a Board meeting 'to state his views on the desire of the members of the Literature Board that the administrative offices of the Board be retained in Melbourne'. Dr Coombs stressed his desire 'that each Board conduct its affairs in its own way. There was no question of either a policy or a pattern of work being imposed on the Board by the Council.' But he also saw it as a Council responsibility 'and in a sense his responsibility as Chairman of the Council' to provide the common services that the Boards would need 'as effectively and economically as possible' and also to see that coordination between the various boards and art forms should lead to the kinds of fruitful stimuli and relationships that the Council wished to foster. If the Board were to remain in Melbourne he foresaw added costs. 'He could not see in what way physical separation was necessary for the autonomy of the Board.'

In his response Blainey referred to a draft advertisement for Board Administrators that mentioned weekly meetings between the Chief Executive Officer (Dr Battersby) and the various Directors or Administrators. (Subsequently all their titles were Director.) Blainey said he was not persuaded of the value of this plan. I recall that I could not see anything against it, but failed to say so.

Each Board member was then asked to comment on Dr Coombs' address. The minutes do not record their responses except for mine, but as I recall it everyone, often quite passionately, supported Blainey. I said 'that so many organisations are established in Sydney [I] felt that it was a good time to break away and give Literature the opportunity to establish itself in another city'. To which Coombs replied that 'he was impressed with the need for decentralisation of this kind and he accepted Miss Keesing's argument as a most valid point.'

From hindsight it seems most unfortunate that the Board did not, then, perceive the writing on the wall. By our refusal to do so we made tremendous problems for the second Board and its staff during 1974–75, but that was in the future.

Almost exactly a year after the Board's first meeting Michael Costigan was selected from an impressive short list of applicants and appointed Administrator, the title which the Literature Board alone, chiefly at Blainey's insistence, was determined to retain—rather than 'Director' which was used by all the other Boards. The Board now urgently perceived its need for a Project Officer, particularly to deal with its publishing policy and initiatives but, again it was to some extent hoist with its own petard having declined to accept some of the Council's suggestions for staffing needs and procedures.

In mid 1973 I asked Blainey to write an article about the new Board for the *Australian Author*. He decided to do this in the form of an interview between himself and an alter ego, E. F. Seawood. It read in part:

I gather the board was swamped with applications?—Yes, there were 1,147 at the latest count. That was easily three times as many as last year. Nearly three of every four applications came from NSW and Victorian writers—they totalled 828. Then came South Australia (8%), Queensland (6%), Western Australia (5.5%), Tasmania (4%), and Canberra (2%). A final two per cent came from Australians living overseas. That last group included well-known names: Alan Seymour and Randolph Stow, to name two.

Did many women apply—the old CLF was reputed to have favoured men?—Men tend to take more of the awards because invariably more men than women apply. This winter about 800 men sought grants but only 344 women. I have an idea that a higher proportion of women applied than in recent years but I have no exact figures. The really welcome change, however, was in the number of youngish writers who sent in manuscripts or publications.

Yes, but the old CLF wasn't too generous to youngish writers. There was plenty of scope for an increase.—True. The CLF occasionally supported young writers but not until 1972, its last year, did it set aside fellowships specifically for writers in their twenties. That policy incidentally, partly sparked the rush of applications this year. The board has just awarded 30 fellowships to writers aged 28 or younger. Eighteen of those fellowships are worth $5,000 each and will enable the receivers to write full-time for a year. The other dozen are half-year fellowships. These new writers (aged, I guess, about 19 to 28) have been given more fellowships than all the writers of all ages received in the previous year.

By the way, I notice that few applications came from youngish writers in some of the less populous States?—While new writers from South Australia won far more than their share of fellowships, those from WA received nothing. There could be a case, next year, for setting aside at least one for a new writer from the West.

Do you think the board was almost too generous to younger writers?—I think the board *should* be too generous to younger writers. I think the board *should* be willing to take higher risks in sponsoring a writer of 25 than a writer of 55. Certainly members of the board believe that the maximum talent should be attracted into creative writing. It may well be—and we won't know the answer for decades—that serious writing has failed in recent years to attract sufficient talent. After all, the competition from rival jobs and careers is much keener than in the past. Many of us suspect that the kind of talent which forty years ago might ultimately have been attracted into creative writing is now often diverted into advertising or is dessicated by university departments. One would like to think that some of the talent was also diverted into writing for films and TV but there is not really much sign yet of such a diversion of talent, at least in Australia.

The selection of younger writers for fellowships—what qualities did the board's members look for?—They looked for signs of imagination, for literary skills. They also looked for signs of stamina though they were often content to gamble that stamina might develop. Stamina, to my mind, is vital. Some of the youngish writers who were offered fellowships were risky selections, and obviously some won't be heard of again after 1974. A few will ultimately be distinguished writers. The prospect of some waste of money, of paying $2,500 or $5,000 to someone who may never write an impressive novel or biography, does not greatly perturb us. In every profession, in every calling, there is heavy wastage in training or in apprenticeships. Moreover, in every profession much of that wastage is undetected . . . I don't think the wastage will be higher in literature than in other kinds of apprenticeship schemes. I should add that, to the taxpayers, the cost of carrying a young writer for a few years is probably far less than the cost of carrying a trainee teacher or agricultural scientist . . .

Looking back I think the first Board failed to take into account how dependent it was upon a Chairman and Administrator who were devoted workaholics, and upon members who did not question the enormous amounts of work they were asked to do, which they cheerfully did. We set aside literal weeks of days to consider preliminary applications— indeed we were jealous of our right to see everything and do everything and reluctant, often, to employ even outside readers. We aimed to prove to ourselves, the Council and the constituency that literature, unlike other art forms, could manage without costly consultants. We were pretty naive and simply did not understand the variety of roles that good project officers might be expected to assume, or the amount of research and advice they might provide.

16 and 17 May 1974: The penultimate meetings of the first Board were held in Hobart. Geoffrey Dutton, Richard Hall, Elizabeth Riddell and

Richard Walsh tendered their apologies. I do not think their presence would have altered the following:

> Members expressed concern at the prospect of six members of the present Board being replaced. Because of the way the Board operates the hope was expressed that the Government would not remove more than three members of the Board in any year, but it was agreed that no member should serve on the Board for a long period. The Board was unanimous that fiction writers, non-fiction writers, poets etc. should be appointed rather than efficiency experts. It was unanimously agreed that Geoffrey Blainey should be asked to continue as chairman and that, as experience has shown that some continuity is needed, no more than three members should be taken from the Board at this stage. Geoffrey Blainey was asked to put the Board's view to the Chairman of the Council and to submit a short list of names (as suggested Chairman and Board members) for such vacancies as the Government deems appropriate.

We submitted a long list of names of proposed Board members, and the names of three suggestions for Chairman, headed by Blainey.

Our heads were still in the sand and, to a great extent remained so buried a month later in Canberra for meetings 28 (on 20 June) and 29 (on 21 June) which were the last of the first Board. All members attended.

As it turned out 21 June was also one of the worst days of my life.

We resolved that it was 'absolutely essential for the Board to continue to operate from Melbourne'. During the morning we noted 'substantial economies gained from the quiet style of operations in Melbourne, and the continuing tendency of some officials in Sydney to persist in squeezing literature into the administrative moulds of the performing arts'. Unanimously we carried a formal resolution incorporating that phrase because 'this issue was of such importance'.

In the early afternoon the receptionist of the motel where we were meeting called me to the telephone. Dr Coombs was on the line. Without any preamble he asked me whether I would be prepared to accept the chairmanship of the Board from 1 July 1974 to 31 December 1977. I was completely taken aback. He insisted that he had to have an immediate answer. He added some persuasive comment but in no way gave any explanation of, or reason for, this invitation. I said yes. He then told me that all one-year terms on the Board would end on 30 June. He stressed that all of this was confidential. I asked whether, in confidence I might tell Geoffrey Blainey of my appointment, because not to do so seemed to me equivocal, rather cowardly and, most of all, unkind. He said as to that I might trust my own judgement.

I returned to the meeting, and sat through the afternoon's business in a state of acute mental and emotional discomfort. There would be no opportunity to say anything privately to the Chairman until the meeting concluded, so I endured listening to conjecture about the future composition of the Board. Blainey reported, though it is not minuted, that he had no news of any decision about names on the list that had been submitted after the Hobart meeting. It was perfectly apparent to me that everyone hoped and even expected that the status quo would be preserved.

Towards the end of the meeting the Chairman said that 'as his own term of office and that of perhaps four other members was about to end' he wished to record his 'deep appreciation of the work performed for the Board, and for Australian writers, by Alec Hope, Manning Clark, Geoffrey Dutton and Judah Waten'. He thanked Joan O'Donnell and Michael Costigan 'for their devoted and constructive work'. Manning Clark and Judah Waten responded and 'spoke warmly of their experience on the Board'. Then it was four-fifteen and the meeting ended. The Chairman rushed off to make a couple of phone calls. I shared a car to the airport with several of my good friends/fellow members. Their conjectures and conversation during the drive were a torture. Geoffrey Blainey and the people in his car did not arrive. It began to seem that there would not be an opportunity to speak to him by himself before he had to board his plane to Melbourne. Then he came into the departure lounge. Now or never. I asked him for a private word and, in a distant corner, near the noisy bar, told him of Dr Coombs' phone call and of my response. Immediately I knew I had made a dreadful wounding mistake in speaking to him at that time and in that place. He was shocked and angry. He brushed past me and went directly to the queue for his flight. Any pleasure I might have felt in the honour that had been offered me that day was negated by my dismay at having been so inept.

I showed my draft of this chapter to Michael Costigan and it was only when he made his comments that I learned about the wheels within wheels of those two days. 'Until I read what you have written,' Michael says, 'I didn't know that you were unaware of your pending appointment as Chairman at the time when the Board gathered in Canberra. This throws new light on the events of the evening before the Board meeting, and it also suggests that you were being placed in a very difficult situation because of the way in which the changeover was handled "from above".'

Michael remembers that on the evening of Thursday 20 June, Board members and staff gathered at the Canberra motel where the meetings were held and drove in several cars to a dinner in a Canberra restaurant. In Michael's car a Board member said he had gained some information about the appointment of a new Chairman but would not break confidentiality by naming the person. However, during dinner and no doubt after a few glasses of wine his resolve weakened. I quote Michael Costigan:

> During the dinner [the Board member named you as next Chairman]. It
> happened at the other end of the table from where I was sitting; but Joan
> [O'Donnell] must have heard because she whispered to me later that you
> were to be the new Chairman.
>
> Later that evening most of the Board members gathered for a drink in
> somebody's room at the motel. Both you and Geoff were present for at least
> part of that bit of conviviality. By this time, most of the Board members
> had heard the news, but Geoff had not. At some stage somebody (I can't
> remember who) told him. I don't think he reacted, apart from saying that
> he hadn't been told anything.
>
> It was very bad that the information circulated in this way, and very
> unfair to you, especially as you were by then probably the only Board
> member who didn't know what was happening! I think the members must
> have assumed, as I did, that you had already been approached about
> accepting the appointment.

The contretemps was not only bad for me, but for the Board. In the weeks
that followed Geoffrey Blainey did not contact me. He did not hand over,
or discuss any of the information and documents that a Chairman acquires
and which can be helpful to a successor. When the announcement of
Board retirements and new members was made I telephoned Judah
Waten. He was a close friend of Blainey's. I wished I could have spoken
to this good wise man sooner, but that was impossible. I explained my
distress. He did not think anything could be done to ameliorate the
situation. He most warmly wished me well for my chairmanship. He
offered a Russian variant of an old saying: 'If you are afraid of wolves,'
Judah advised, 'you should not go into the forest.'

The membership of the second Board was: Nancy Keesing (NSW),
Chairman and Richard Hall (NSW), Lorna Hannan (Vic.), David Malouf
(Qld), Noel Macainsh (Qld), Barrett Reid (Vic.), Elizabeth Riddell
(NSW), Thomas Shapcott (Qld), Richard Walsh (NSW), Rosemary
Wighton (SA) and Victor Williams (WA). During its first meeting in
Melbourne I explained, as to the location of the Board, that it had been
granted a trial period of two years in Melbourne, of which eighteen
months remained. I said that during those eighteen months the Board
must prove that 'not only is it as efficient as a Board that has its
headquarters in Sydney, but that there are advantages to being based in
Melbourne'. Led by Barrie Reid the new members were, upon this point,
as intransigent as their predecessors; that being so I believed I should do
everything I possibly could to make the present system work. Because I
had not come down in the last shower of rain, it did occur to me that one
possible reason for my appointment was that, as a Sydney person, I might
facilitate the Board's move to Sydney. If, I said to myself, anyone happens
to think I may possibly yield to persuasion on this point, they have
another thing coming—I am not a cipher.

In early 1975, on Ian Turner's recommendation, Pat Healy was appointed as Project Officer specialising in publishing. She was based in Melbourne.

By now the Australian Council for the Arts had moved to its permanent quarters in Sydney in Northside Gardens. An excellent large area not far from the library that *could* have been allotted to the Literature Board was otherwise used. Michael Costigan made a time-consuming weekly visit to Sydney from Melbourne for Directors' meetings and other consultations and needed some office space in the building. I very soon realised that a Sydney presence for the Board was essential, and the only person who could provide it was myself. Therefore Michael and I shared a large office in the Community Arts area. Most Board chairmen were academics, like Geoffrey, or businessmen, or belonged to well-organised concerns. I was a freelance writer whose office was located in my suburban house. I employed a typist, Reta Grace, one day a week. Otherwise I had no secretarial or telephone answering help. Increasingly people of many sorts and kinds expected to be able to speak to some Sydney representative of the Board. For a time I attended the office almost daily and there I was available for visitors.

Gradually I became, as well as a Chairman, a stand-in for a Director and a de facto Project Officer for the Board as well. Michael and I consulted frequently by telephone. The system worked fairly well but (quite apart from the inroads it made into my time and work) it had disadvantages. Both within the Council and elsewhere my proliferation of roles, and the Board's split personality (as it were) puzzled and/or confused many people. I became far more involved with certain people and matters than was ideally desirable from the point of view of an impartial chairmanship.

My Community Arts neighbours and other Council staff were generous with help in taking messages, coping with unannounced visitors and showing me all sorts of (some quite knotty) ropes. I was especially grateful to Val Evans, who later became a full-time employee in the section administering the Public Lending Right scheme. To have a good library at hand was a bonus. Usually I enjoyed my days at the office, and making new friends.

As soon as my chairmanship was announced I resigned from the management committee of the ASA and my editorship of *Australian Author*. The ASA was a client of the Board; and the Australia Council, of which all chairmen were ex-officio members, gave financial support to the Copyright Council. As I saw it this course was inevitable—though some ASA people, and some of my fellow Board chairmen, thought I was unnecessarily strict with myself. That decision did not for long reduce the number of meetings I had to attend.

One inelegant item of Theatre Board/Council jargon was 'bums on seats'. In the mid-seventies I was appointed a Governor of Winifred West Schools Ltd. at Mittagong, and a member of the Council of Kuring-gai CAE. Whenever anyone used that phrase I reflected upon the hours, days and weeks of meetings my bum was sitting through.

By 1975 Professor Peter Karmel had succeeded Dr Coombs as Chairman of the Australian Council for the Arts (soon to become the Australia Council) and Ian Turner was Chairman of its Finance and Administration Committee. They were very concerned and active at a time when there were delays in ratifying Michael's appointment, and in getting this finalised. Ian Turner was, in many ways, an almost archetypal product and citizen of the State of Victoria...and even *he* thought the Literature Board should move to Sydney. So did three of my fellow Chairmen, who every now and then would mention the topic. I tried to avoid such discussion. I found it increasingly difficult to defend the Board's intransigence because I had become convinced a move was not only inevitable but quite urgently desirable. However until the question was properly and formally discussed again by the Board, I adhered to the opinion of the majority in a formal sense, and I continued to do my utmost to mitigate obvious problems and disadvantages.

In mid 1975 Michael circulated a letter to Board members setting out his views on the pros and cons of a move. In June Ian Turner met the Board and indicated that a move to Sydney was inevitable. The plan was ratified by the Council in July. Pat Healy would continue to work from Melbourne. At very senior levels of government everything possible was done to ensure that another senior job would be offered to Joan O'Donnell who could not move from Melbourne. In mid 1975 Sandra Forbes joined the Board as Project Officer and, after a few weeks in Melbourne to familiarise herself with the Board's work, she was based in Sydney and took over a great deal of the work I had been doing for the Board.

My greatest personal concern had been for Michael Costigan and his wife Margaret. As a CSR wife I had been fortunate and in some ways not very typical, for I had no personal experience of being moved from place to place and house to house. My children's education had never been affected by changes of schools. However I well knew of the difficulties many wives faced in CSR and other companies. For one thing paid work for many of them was virtually impossible due to frequent relocations. The Costigans had a network of family and friends in Melbourne—a real consideration for people with a very young family. Fortunately they found a very nice house in Neutral Bay and made the translation happily.

At the beginning of December 1975 the Board moved to Sydney. A month or so later in early 1976 Betty Bennell became Secretary. An era was over.

The debate about whether or not Literature suffers in competition with the performing and other arts, and under the umbrella of the Australia Council, is never-ending. In July 1986 the *Melbourne Sun* reported Ken Methold, Chairman of the ASA as having a 'personal dream to establish a writers' version of the Film Commission so the book industry [could have] the same kind of structure as the Film industry'. Methold pointed out that the book industry has nothing comparable with the Australian Film Commission and the State Film Corporations. He proposed a national book commission that might be called the National Literary Fund to be financed by members of the public seeking tax concessions similar to those enjoyed by investors in the film industry. He would 'like to see the Literature Board out of the Australia Council,' saying: 'There has been no evidence that the Literature Board has got or is ever likely to get, a fair share of the Australia Council's money while it is dominated by the performing arts people.'

XII

Times of Change

I N 1983 I addressed a luncheon meeting of women graduates. I had
agreed to speak about writing experiences, and to outline changes I
perceived in the literary community over four decades of involvement in literary affairs. For some reason during the Chairman's
cordial address of introduction, I suddenly decided to abandon my notes.
Instead I said at the outset that the greatest and most beneficial change to
Australian letters in my lifetime is the virtual abolition of censorship.
Censorship stifled generations of Australian writers of every sort and
drove many of them overseas. Censorship blinkered generations of Australian readers and made criminals, at least in theory, of those who
found ways to procure and read banned books.

The word 'censorship' calls up superficial associations of obscenity, of
books with titles like *Whips and Scourges*, of blue movies, of over-explicit
scenes in movies. We forget that censorship was applied in a political
fashion and that by 1936 of some five thousand banned titles, including
novels, the majority were banned for predominantly political reasons—
because they were Marxist or Leninist, or because they discussed
economics and politics in ways that Australian governments feared or in
ways that police and customs officials considered suspect, though these
people were in no sense educated to assess such matters.

Two examples illustrate ridiculous aspects of the system. In the sixties
a Sergeant of Police walked into the South Australian State Library and
asked to see the Librarian, Hedley Brideson. The Sergeant said the father
of a schoolgirl had complained to the police about a book a teacher had
recommended. The girl *had* read this book in the State Library. He
demanded to see the book which was called *The Rape of the Lock* and had
been written by 'Mr Pope'. That episode was merely pathetic. Far more
damaging and not in the least amusing was the fate of Marjorie Barnard's
novel, which was published as *Tomorrow and Tomorrow* because the third
Tomorrow, as planned—*Tomorrow and Tomorrow and Tomorrow*—would
not fit on the spine of the book. Miss Barnard herself gave a full
background account of 'How *Tomorrow and Tomorrow* Came to be Written'
in *Meanjin* (No. 3, 1970):

> I was, and remain a nineteenth-century liberal. This philosophy had passed
> into my blood and bones and I now [c. 1941] found it inadequate. I read
> and pondered and could find nothing between Christian pacificism and
> communism that offered me the intellectual support I needed to face the
> ominous future . . . The *fait accompli* when it came offered no release. I
> could write at the time: 'Of the War it is fruitless to say anything. When I

think of it, which is practically all the time, my heart is molten with grief and anger.

[The novel] arose out of this charged atmosphere. I transmuted my doubts from the intellectual to the creative sphere and I found a quite illogical release in stating the whole problem as I saw it in a novel instead of an ideology, creatively instead of politically. This book was to be an essay in perspective and a dramatisation of the forces at work in our society.

The novel was finished in 1944 and published after delays in 1947. One delay was due to wartime paper shortage. The other was less forgiveable:

The publisher in a fit of (now quite incomprehensible) panic submitted the manuscript to the censor. He was not required to do so and there was nothing subversive in the text, unless it was some opinions expressed in character. Thus invited, the censor heavily red-pencilled the latter part of the book. The 'opinions' were left untouched but every reference to Russia was deleted and some of the imaginary effects of the imagined future were cut down or struck out. The cuts often made nonsense of the argument and so weakened the whole fabric.

Marjorie Barnard's experience emphasises some ramifications of censorship that few readers consider. When most of us think of 'book censorship' our mental image is of a finished book banned from sale or wrapped and sealed and kept under the counter for adult buyers only. We do not take into account books that were neither written nor published for fear of being banned, or books that were so greatly censored in the writing they appear as pussy-footed apologies for what they might have been. Moreover during the thirties and forties few if any Australian publishers could afford, financially, to deliberately provoke litigation. One may question why so many Australian writers of the thirties and forties including several leading figures, were quite so evasive and bland. I find it extraordinary, for instance, that in the work of one leading woman novelist of the time, whose themes were tough enough and whose characters were warm and varied, there is not one passage describing physical passion, or even physical contact between lovers. Latterly Australian television has given new life to several of these novels; and in the TV dramas sexual passion is introduced for the first time, for you cannot on film have love scenes in which lovers for ever keep yards apart.

Any part I played in anti-censorship action was late, and more in the nature of mopping up operations after the chief battles had been fought and won by people earlier on the scene. In 1970, at very short notice, I agreed to edit *The Australian Author* for the Australian Society of Authors. The excellent and experienced foundation editor, Barrie Ovenden, gave me a crash course in the task and remarked that the new printers, with whom she had established an excellent relationship, would be helpful.

Ernest Koczkar, a very experienced magazine editor, had taught me enough about layout and pasting-up, to get an issue completed. Dal Stivens, the President of the ASA, somewhat to my annoyance wished to see all copy before publication. With his firm and experienced blessing—he was vehemently anti-censorship—I included an article by a well-known lawyer who was an ASA member. It included a phrase that had been alleged to be obscene at one of the court trials of the time of the student magazine *Tharunka*. Few readers now, would be troubled by the words complained of except, perhaps, to think them in poor taste.

Frankly, and no matter for what good reasons, I think Dal and the lawyer took advantage of my editorial inexperience. I do not think that Barrie, herself a progressive woman, would have allowed that particular phrase to be sent to that particular printer. For fear of facing legal action the printer refused to print the issue; the lawyer refused to amend his article; the ASA management committee decided the article should be withdrawn. The issue appeared rather late with a substitute item hastily written by Donald McLean. Subsequently *The Author* was removed to another printer—my old friends Edwards & Shaw, who also to my great thankfulness designed the magazine for me thereafter. The lawyer, who with his wife had been good friends of ours for years, took lasting offence.

Mark returned from America with recent poetry publications for me and his usual swag of travel-reading paperbacks. The ones I always looked for first were Perry Masons. He also had quite openly in his luggage a copy of *Portnoy's Complaint*. He had no idea it was banned. Then a Jewish friend in England posted me a copy of Roth's hot potato saying she understood it was banned in Australia but thought I should read it from the standpoint of its Jewish story. That made two copies in our house.

We did not practise domestic censorship. Books of every sort, suitable and less suitable for children, were everywhere on tables and shelves. My children, as I and my sister before them, often picked up works that looked attractive but were far beyond their years; after glancing at a few pages they would put them down again. (A few years after this, at High School, Aldous Huxley's *Brave New World* which was firmly banned in my day was compulsory reading for them.) They had plenty of books of their own, and good school libraries.

(*Correction*: Margery suddenly mastered reading precisely when the Profumo/Christine Keeler affair filled newsapers. 'Mummy, why would a lady want to whip a man?' Our rule was to answer *all* questions in terms a child might understand. That one stumped me so thoroughly I resorted to concealing the *Sydney Morning Herald* for a few weeks.)

The *Portnoy's Complaint* furore increased and permeated to school playgrounds. I had no particular wish to be 'sprung' for possession of two illicit copies so I put them in a drawer of my wardrobe. Then the legal firm of Allen Allen & Hemsley asked me to be a defence witness in the test case trial of *Portnoy's Complaint* in 1971. All pages referred to in court would be from the Penguin edition, a copy of which they sent me. Now I had three. Barbara Jefferis and I were the star defence witnesses and if that trial had not had any better result, it did initiate an enduring friendship between us. I sometimes wonder if one reason for our selection was that we are respectable, sensible housewives.

In very hot weather we sweltered in court while the little paperback book was propped up on a shelf set across the dock. As if it had been a living, dangerous prisoner, it was ritually guarded by a young constable armed with a revolver. It seemed to me that if the book was as dangerous as the prosecution alleged, it was more liable to explode in a puff of sulphur and flame than attempt to escape, so that a small fire extinguisher might have been more useful. Judge Goran looked hot. The jury looked hot and so did the very vehement prosecutor, bent on amazement that a nice woman like me could find literary merit in a torrid book like *Portnoy*. I thoroughly enjoyed the game we were playing. Once, while I was in the witness box there was a pause in proceedings, but I had to remain where I was while everyone else sought breezes and cool drinks elsewhere. And who returned to the court room with a jug of iced water and a kind word? The dreaded prosecutor.

Portnoy was declared innocent. Not long afterwards I was appointed to the National Literature Board of Review and so, briefly, was a censor myself—but the two meetings I attended were its last. Censorship was finished.

No community can afford to be complacent. Government book censorship could be re-introduced. Meanwhile the hydra-headed monster rears its head in likely places like the Festival of Light, and unlikely places like school libraries; the most pernicious censors of recent years are, of all people, certain school librarians. That well-meaning people ban books for anti-racist and anti-sexist reasons may seem innocuous, even, perhaps admirable. But no censorship is admirable or innocuous. School libraries, like any others, should as far and widely as possible offer choices and contentious material for open discussion. To deprive young readers of books like Enid Blyton's *Noddy* series is sheer arrogance. Certainly tight budgets have to be spent as wisely as possible, but books should not be avoided because this or that teacher or librarian *thinks* s/he *knows* what is good for children. Rightly we are increasingly conscious of racist attitudes and books. In our day Henry Lawson sometimes seems intolerably racist and so do *Epaminondas* and *Little Black Sambo*, but I see no need to ban them when they could be valuable bases for discussing racism and changing attitudes with young children.

The children's writer Lilith Norman and I once sat through a seminar arranged by school librarians and teachers to discuss ways in which children's authors might be steered towards writing books that accorded with their perceptions of suitability. No dirty words like 'imagination' crossed anyone's lips that morning. The assaults on our heritage of English language were blithe. A resolution was passed that said, in effect: 'Only an Aboriginal child of eight can write about an Aboriginal child of eight; only a grandfather of seventy with skin cancer can write about a grandfather of seventy with skin cancer.'

That was censorship.

At lunchtime Lilith Norperson and I amused ourselves drafting possible acceptable passages like: 'Friends, Ropersons and Countrypersons...'

Grahame Johnston's *Annals of Australian Literature* is an invaluable reference work. The first woman writer whose name appears therein was Anna Maria Bunn (1808–89) nee Murray. In 1838 she published a novel using the pseudonym 'An Australian' and her book, *The Guardian* was the first novel to be printed and published on the Australian mainland. Coincidentally her name is also the very last to appear in the *Annals* because she was a sister of Terence Aubrey whose biography, *Murray of Yarralumla* by Gwendoline Wilson (also be it noted, a woman) is the final entry for 1968 which was Johnston's cut-off date. It amused me to offer this arcane information as preface to a talk I gave during International Womens Year (1975) on the broad topic of Australian women writers from go to whoa. During question time an angry feminist from the audience described me as an enemy of the Womens Movement and 'a middle class over-achiever'.

My offence was in saying I did not believe Australian women writers had been disadvantaged, seriously or perhaps at all, by comparison with their male counterparts. I did, however, identify categories of women connected with books and literature whom I thought had been disadvantaged and particularly instanced senior librarians, academics and some women in the publishing industry. (Since 1975 there has been a marked improvement in appointing qualified women to senior professional positions.)

It has often been remarked that women novelists predominated in Australia during the inter-war years. One explanation for the imbalance between women and men writers during that period is incalculable: no one can even guess how many potentially fine male writers lie in War graves in France, Gallipoli and the Middle East. Nor can one know how many good books were 'lost' during the Depression, either because their authors could not afford time or energy for writing, or dissipated their talent writing hack work for quick cash, as did my friends Gertrude

Scarlett, Charles Shaw and Eric Schlunke—though Shaw and Schlunke wrote substantial works after World War II. I have no idea to what extent women novelists of the period realised that their major output outnumbered that of men. If they were aware of this did any of them feel that, in a sense, they carried a torch? Who knows.

I had shown the draft typescript of my talk to several women writers, including Kylie Tennant who remarked that in her youth, during the Depression, writers battled to publish their work and make a living as best they could. No one stopped to consider the gender of an author.

In this field truly objective statistics are hard to come by. Recently I attempted to assemble some from the *Annals* but it is not helpful for my purpose, although a quick count disclosed that in this century approximately two-thirds of book authors have been male and one-third female. However *Annals* is selective as to book titles and cannot be used for valid comparisons between the numbers of titles published by all the individual authors it names. It is also sobering to note that, if one used no other guide than *Annals* it would appear that there was no published work in languages other than English during this or the nineteenth century which is, of course, not so.

In *The Oxford Companion to Australian Literature* the entry for S. H. Prior has significance here. Prior was editor of the *Bulletin* from 1915 to 1933:

> Under Prior the *Bulletin* became less oriented towards the bush and more conservative, but continued to encourage Australian writers; novel-writing contests initiated by him in 1928 and 1929 drew a large response including such entries as *A House is Built* (1929), *Coonardoo* (1929) and *The Passage* (1930). The S. H. Prior Memorial Prize of £100 was instituted by the *Bulletin* after Prior's death, and was awarded, 1935–46; winning entries later published include *Tiburon* (1935), *All That Swagger* (1936), *Joseph Furphy: The Legend of a Man and His Book* (1941) and *The Battlers* (1941).

All the books listed are by women except for Vance Palmer's *The Passage*.

From personal experience I have not known any writers *in the English language*, male or female, who had publishable talent, something to say, a story to tell or poetry to offer *and who were persistent* who did not have all or most of their books or occasional writing published sooner or later. For authors whose language is not English or whose works require typefaces other than Roman (such as Yiddish or Greek) the situation used to be very bleak indeed but, both for technological and other reasons, it has improved greatly during the eighties. As 'ethnic' magazines and presses proliferate even further there will be increasing multilingual contributions to Australian literature.

Until about 1975 poets of both sexes had difficulty in publishing books but little trouble in placing poems in journals, newspapers and on radio. In this context let us not forget regional newspapers, radio and small presses. There *is* a life outside the capital cities; and regional readers often take a justifiable pride in authors who reflect localised backgrounds and interests. It must be more satisfactory to sell all of an edition of 500 books printed and promoted by a local newspaper company than to fail with a small capital-city edition. Some books that first appeared in regional settings have later been taken on by major publishers. I have already cited A. B. Facey's *A Fortunate Life* which was first brought out by the Fremantle Arts Centre Press and then by Penguin; several of Elizabeth Jolley's books also originated in Fremantle and then had national acclaim and international sales—culminating in *The Well* winning the Miles Franklin Award in 1987. These are by no means the only instances of such success stories.

Until the nineteenth century writers and other artists including painters, sculptors and musicians relied heavily upon patronage and were not ashamed to seek and receive the assistance of patrons. In prehistoric civilisations and continuing into historic times patronage was chiefly religious, princely or noble. Without patronage neither the unknown sculptor of Queen Nefertiti nor Michaelangelo could have realised their vision.

The nineteenth century produced changes that made patronage unnecessary in *some* areas of art, and particularly in literature, a situation that remained fairly stable for about 150 years. It was also a time when distinctions between 'popular' and 'serious' writing became blurred. In England, America and various European countries the emergence of prosperous middle classes coincided with far-reaching technological change. Communities became increasingly literate during a period when cheap improvements in domestic lighting made it possible for people to read after work and after dark. Improved street lighting made evening excursions safer for the many people who patronised evening lectures, classes at Mechanics Institutes and theatres (which themselves could be better and more safely illuminated). There were enormous technological advances in paper-making, printing and the reproduction of illustrations. Mass-circulation newspapers and journals followed these advances and improved transport by railway and steam boats and ships quickly disseminated printed works of all kinds to readers who lived outside large urban centres. For example the Sydney *Bulletin* gained its title 'The Bushman's Bible' because it circulated among bush people and workers in remote areas and catered for their taste and interests.

The heyday of serial fiction dates from the emergence of the popular press and successful serials were published as mass circulation novels. Reading and lecture tours either by writers themselves (like Dickens) or by their admirers, and proliferating cheap books enhanced the popularity not only of novelists but of poets as various as Tennyson, Kipling, Longfellow, Bret Harte, C. J. Dennis, Banjo Paterson, Henry Lawson et al.

The larger the reading populations that purchased the work of writers, the richer their authors became. Even in Australia with its small population some writers of books that had limited overseas appeal nevertheless earned comfortable livings from their pens well into the twentieth century and had no need of patronage. However the Commonwealth Literary Fund was established as early as 1908 to assist a few authors—Shaw Neilson was one of them after 1928—who were in dire straits.

Because of the nineteenth-century aberration a notion arose that patronage is somehow unnecessary and even morally suspect. This mistaken view has persisted long after the palmy days ended and into present time when from some quarters there is still talk of 'handouts' for writers and other artists. In fact of course, and worldwide, the sources of patronage have merely shifted from kings and nobles to private benefactors, industry, universities and other institutions and the state.

When I was Chairman of the Literature Board someone in an audience once raised the hoary objection to patronage for the arts: the argument was that the money so used is more needed by hospitals and schools, for scientific research, for road improvements. I agreed that of course that was so, and always had been. If absolute social justice had prevailed throughout history, I said, there would have been no Parthenon, no Notre Dame or Chartres cathedrals; no dreaming spires at Oxford; no Samuel Johnson or Haydn; no Sydney Opera House and, very likely, no Thomas Kenneally. It is a paradox that the lasting works of art that enrich the human spirit down the ages often arose from slave societies, amid huddles of slums, misery and oppression. Judith Wright once remarked that Australian knockers are very ready to talk about subsidies for sport, and handouts for writers.

I am thankful that nowadays Australian writers and other artists may travel overseas for all kinds of reasons, but that most of them return to add to the cultural life and store of their own country. I am also thankful that thirty years further down the track the widespread intolerance and racism that prevailed during the fifties seems, though slowly in some areas and among some people, to be receding into history.

Literature in its widest sense, both 'serious' and 'popular' and including drama, much television and some histories, not only mirrors altering opinion and belief but sometimes, like *Uncle Tom's Cabin*, *Bleak House* or *For the Term of His Natural Life*, changes community attitudes. Since

Judah Waten's *Alien Son* appeared in 1952 generations of school students have read, and often loved, some of its stories. They know that Waten and most of his characters were Jewish. Young adults who admire and enjoy Angelo Loukakis' stories in *For the Patriarch* are responding to his Greek/Australian vision. At least some of these readers will be less likely than were their forebears to categorise people disparagingly as yids, wogs, chows or boongs.

In any era and place there are practices and injustices that almost no one perceives. Until the fifties when soil erosion became an urgent problem (its immediacy made graphic in some of Russell Drysdale's widely exhibited and reproduced paintings and drawings), no Australian writers known to me spoke forcibly against the wholesale deforestation and unsuitable cultivation methods used by 'the pioneers' who were commonly praised for having 'tamed' vast acreages of grazing and arable land. G. H. Ironbark Gibson is most remembered for his famous ballad *My Mate Bill*. From hindsight it seems unfortunate that while Australian readers chuckled and argued about a contrived rivalry between Banjo Paterson and Henry Lawson as to which of them was the truest poet of Australian Arcadia, Ironbark's *Jones's Selection* had no influence:

> You hear a lot of new-chum talk
> Of going on the land,
> An' raisin' record crops of wheat
> On rocks and flamin' sand.
>
> I 'ates exaggerated skite
> But if yer likes I can
> Authenticate a case, in which
> The land went on the man.
>
> Bill Jones 'e 'ad a mountain block
> Up Kosciusko way;
> He farmed it pretty nigh to death,
> The neighbours used to say.
>
> He scarified the surface with
> His double-furrow ploughs,
> An' ate its blinded heart right out
> With sheep an' milkin' cows;
>
> He filled its blamed intestines up
> With agricultural pipes,
> An' lime, and superphosphates—fit
> To give the land the gripes.
>
> Until at length the tortured soil,
> Worn out with Jones's thrift,
> Decided as the time was come
> To up an' made a shift.

One day the mountain shook itself,
An' give a sort o' groan,
The neighbours was a lot more scared
Than they was game to own.

Their jaws was dropped upon their chests,
Their eyes was opened wide,
They saw the whole of Jones's farm
Upend itself, an' slide.

It slithered down the mountain spur
Majestic-like an' slow,
An' landed in the river bed,
A thousand feet below.

Bill Jones was on the lower slopes
Of 'is long-sufferin' farm,
A-testin' some new-fangled plough
Which acted like a charm.

He'd just been screwin' up a nut
When somethin' seemed to crack,
An' fifty acres, more or less,
Come down on Jones's back.

'Twas sudden-like, a shake, a crack,
A slitherin' slide, an' Bill
Was buried fifty feet below
The soil he used to till.

One moment Bill was standing' up
A-ownin' all that land,
The next 'e's in eternity—
A spanner in 'is 'and!

They never dug up no remains
Nor scraps of William Jones—
The superphosphates ate the lot,
Hide, buttons, boots, and bones.

For this here land wot Jones abused
And harassed in the past
'Ad turned an' wiped 'im out, an' things
Got evened up at last.

From this untimely end o' Bill
It would perhaps appear
That goin' free-selectin' ain't
All skittles, no, nor beer,

So all you cocky city coves
Wot's savin' up yer screws
To get upon the land, look out
The land don't get on *yous*.

To an Australian generation living between 2000–2030 it may well seem that much of the human energy which we expended on the Womens Movement; animal liberation; anti-woodchipping and even anti-nuclear protests was misplaced. To those as yet unborn people, it will be evident that the worst, and least perceived outrages in Australia from 1970 to 2000 were...If some poet, novelist or historian writing today or tomorrow is visionary enough to describe injustice, evil or misguided action ahead of the general community's more gradual awareness, she or he may achieve changes. More likely recognition will wait until a later age that will enthusiastically hail an 'overlooked' literary hero from that past age, which is our own.

XIII

The Ring Completed

URING the fifties, and fairly late in their lives, my parents acquired a new interest—libraries. I have forgotten precisely how and why my mother was made aware of the problems and needs of the Fisher Library at the University of Sydney, but she became a major benefactor of the Fisher and, later, of the library of Macquarie University. Librarians and other University people were good friends to my parents who greatly enjoyed both formal and less formal events at the two universities. They acquired new knowledge and ideas, and sense of purpose.

Their generosity had one unexpected consequence which led my father to researches into his family history that would become a major preoccupation during most of his remaining life. Walking through the reference section of the Fisher Library en route to a reception, he noticed several thick volumes whose spines were lettered large: *Keesings Contemporary Archives*. His subsequent excitement made me feel somewhat remorseful because I'd occasionally consulted 'Keesings' for information, but had not given any thought to coincidence of name.

My father wrote to the publishers of the work whose offices were in Bristol in England, explaining that except for a couple of chance contacts, the Australian and New Zealand branches of the Keesing family had lost touch with any members of the family who might remain in Holland. He asked whether Keesings Publications Ltd. could put him in touch with some of them. Before a reply arrived he had an unexpected and very welcome visit from 'a young professor, Roger Keesing', who is now Professor of Anthropology at the ANU. At that time (November 1963) Roger was Professor of Anthropology at an American university, and was en route to the Solomon Islands where he and Peter Corris carried out major field research described in their book *Lightning meets the West Wind* (OUP, 1980).

Roger gave Dad the address of Israel Keesing of Amsterdam. Father wrote to him. In consequence of his letters he eventually began a long correspondence with Dr Elisabeth van Tricht Keesing of Ellecom in the Netherlands. Elisabeth and her second husband Henry van Tricht were retired professors of history at Amsterdam. Elisabeth became the far-flung Keesing family's chief and devoted genealogist and a dear friend to many of us.

My father died in 1971 and his papers, in general, proved to make a considerable addition to family history. There were various documents and copies of letters, including those from 1963 onwards, and also a couple of surprises. When Margaret and I were small he enthralled us each evening with a story in the saga of Betty Spoopendike, a child whose adventures inevitably pointed a very strong moral. A number of those tales survived in his beautiful handwriting. There was also an unfinished document titled *Gregory Kent*. A quick first glance disclosed that Gregory Kent was in fact Gordon Keesing, whose initials he shared. It would seem Father wrote it during the late twenties or early thirties. It began: 'Gregory Kent was born in Auckland in the year 1888...'

Gregory Kent was my father's attempt at writing his autobiography in the third person, introducing his immediate family and other people by scrambled or fictitious names. They remain perfectly recognisable. GK probably resorted to this artifice because for one thing, he intended to alter a few facts—for instance the 'Kent' family attended 'church' most regularly every Sunday, whereas the Keesings were devout founders, pillars of, and regular worshippers each Saturday at the Auckland synagogue. A more compelling reason for his method was that he intended to get some home truths off his chest. 'Truths' may not be quite the word either: whether or not some of my father's dislike of, and scorn for, certain people and family members of his youth were justifiable assessments, what he wrote was most certainly what he believed. Fortunately those of his associates whom he liked and admired outnumbered those he did not approve. I do not know whether or not he hoped or intended to publish the document (which is frankly, in every way, unpublishable), but he certainly almost completely abandoned his deceptions after 'Gregory' became an architectural student in New York and Paris. Places, people and events are correctly described then in these sections and he sometimes forgot about 'Gregory' and wrote in the first person. I too will abandon the Gregory Kent fiction at this point. Because the latter part of the autobiography is interesting of itself, and has relevance to a decision I made in 1985, I shall summarise and quote some of it here.

After he matriculated from Auckland Grammar School my father was apprenticed to an architect in Melbourne. He was a shy young man who did not make friends easily. His sports were swimming, walking and rowing. 'His profession became a passion and what he lacked in any inherent gift he made up by sheer hard work and application. Study of [overseas] Building and Architectural journals made him decide that he must be able to do the class of work he saw illustrated and that he must go abroad. Rumours of the advantages of an American training in architecture were then being discussed. It was the invariable practice of [Australian] students who could manage it to go to London and get what experience they could from office work and night classes.' When his salary reached 25/– a week he left his Grandmother's home where he lived at first to share cheap lodgings with another student architect. By 1910 his salary was £3 a week and he had saved £80. 'The fare to Tilbury by a White Star one-class boat was £20.' He visited his parents in New Zealand and from there sailed for England with a letter of credit for £50. By June 1910 he was ashore exploring Durban and thence to London.

London was disappointing. 'The schools gave very similar lectures and instruction to that he had already received [in Australia] while the office experience he was able to get after many weary tramping miles with his roll of drawings was also identical with that of Melbourne and Sydney... Before he left Melbourne an Australian architect had advised him to go to America instead of England and he now decided to take this advice.' He sailed for New York in August 1910 and, on the ship, made friends with four middle aged American women, two of whom were teachers and two nurses. One of these women, Miss Burnett, introduced him to her own New York landlady, 'a fine motherly old lady,' and he took a room in this building at 129th St Harlem near 'a restaurant patronised by mostly school teachers and musical students as the district was handy to the Conservatorium and Columbia University' and to transport. In 1910 this part of Harlem remained a white neighbourhood. He spent weeks looking for permanent work and after several temporary jobs, joined a firm whose principals were two brothers who had taken the *Ecole des Beaux Arts* Diploma in Paris. In America a number of professors of architecture and practising architects had founded the New York *Société des Beaux Arts* which had 'satellite ateliers'. Father joined the Atelier Prevot. 'The atelier system,' he wrote, 'was started in Paris in about the reign of Louis XV and until it spread to America and other European art training centres, left Paris paramount as a training ground for architects.'

Each atelier had a Patron, who was a man recognised by his profession as having outstanding ability. The Patron visited the atelier on two or more evenings a week and criticised the work done by members on set problems. 'The problem is set on a Saturday afternoon with the students sitting, as for an examination, in a large lecture room where the subject, such as a doorway or portico for juniors; a small building for the more advanced or a museum or large scheme for the proficient, is set with its special requirements. The students have one or more hours to make a sketch of the best scheme they can evolve and hand it in... The Atelier Patron criticises [this sketch] and the finished problem is worked up from it... during six weeks or so of night work, bringing a mark towards the completion of the course.'

Father now left the office at five p.m. each day, dined with fellow students at a cheap eating house, got to the atelier at six p.m. and worked there at least till midnight or, 'when *en charrette* till three or four a.m.' The last-minute rush to submit finished problems was termed 'being *en charrette*' because in Paris in past times students who were running late to meet assignments used small hand-carts, *charrettes*, 'to rush the drawings wet from the brushes and pens of the authors to reach *L'Ecole* before the time set, by a margin of minutes.'

Father commented that the long hours affected the health of many students. One of his contemporaries 'worked for sixty hours on end without sleep. Another, after his first *charrette*, slept for twenty-six hours without a break.' Despite their onerous routine Dad and his friends explored the New York countryside and city by train and on foot whenever they had a free day. Nearby Yonkers was still largely rural. The first New York winter was 'as nothing he had ever felt', and he marvelled at the sight of a burnt-out building, still smouldering and flaming at its centre, but a mass of icicles and snow mounds about its blackened shell.

There were about thirty-five students in the Atelier Prevot.

My father had many offers of work and took one with a firm that was remodelling Coney Island's amusement park. In mid Winter this turned out to be 'three months of purgatory' but he was, by then, saving to get to Paris. 'How the far-seeing fail!' he wrote, 'I was to lose four years and upset the whole of my cherished plans fighting in France.'

By 1913 my father was in Paris at the atelier of 'the great Gromort, a smart, well-groomed little man who when I last saw him was in charge of the restoration of Arras after the holocaust. He spoke English fluently.' (This reunion would have been in about 1918 when Dad was still with the AIF in France, or perhaps as late as 1919.)

Some half of the students were French or other European and half English and Americans. The *Beaux Arts* course took several years to complete and 'the entrance exam is almost impossible for the English, but in return for scholarships granted by America, a small proportion of that country's aspirants are admitted annually.' However 'most foreign students work purely for practice—compare their work with the solutions exhibited monthly at *l'Ecole* by the lucky members, and when their funds run out, or they are sufficiently adept, they depart for their home country.' Father immediately started work at the atelier 'on the problems set by *l'Ecole des Beaux Arts* and extra ones arranged by the Master who criticised two or three afternoons a week'.

Despite the long hours and hard work he experienced both in New York and Paris, Dad contrived to have a good deal of fun and innocent student horseplay. He staunchly disapproved of men who talked about their sexual prowess and exploits and avoided their company. Meals were eaten in cheap cafés, 'forty centimes being enough for a satisfactory meal of one meat course with salad or vegetables and a sweet of the universal French caramel custard or stewed fruit'. He was introduced to yoghurt or *lait Bulgar* served in small pots with an accompanying saucer of brown sugar and that became a favourite treat. Sometimes he joined squeamish

American students at a vegetarian café subsidised from America where cheap meals were served free from 'horse and donkey beef and the universal lard used so much in the cheap and appetising restaurants'. A bath in the Hotel Notre Dame de l'Esperance cost too much for poor students and was 'not nearly as good as in the public establishment a few doors away where for twenty centimes one had a hot shower cubicle for twenty minutes. Then the water was shut off from the office control.'

Father would never willingly speak about his wartime experiences and exploits but we grew up with his tales of student days and adventures. We could almost see the fair-haired concierge of the Atelier Gromort who managed 'to be perpetually in mourning with yards of crepe hanging about her sturdy figure'. She kept a goat in a lane beside the building. It was the pet of the atelier and 'thought nothing of mounting the ladder-like steps and mealing off any papers available. That goat kept the pupils tidy or their drawings disappeared.' The students wangled sugar for the goat from their cheap cafés by elaborate monkey business with the saucers provided. In New York in a building opposite to the Atelier Prevot's large window was an architect's office where a young woman draughts-man worked by her window, and frequently licked her paintbrushes into neat points for fine work. The students believed some water colours contained poisonous substances so they lettered a sign:

> Little girl
> Box of paints
> Licked the brush
> Joined the saints.

and fixed it facing outwards from their window where she could not miss seeing it. She promptly removed her draughting table to another room and whether or not she joined the saints they never knew.

After three months at the Atelier Gromort Father, with a friend, spent the Summer vacation travelling in Italy filling sketch books with measurements and pencil drawings and taking photographs. He then went to Vienna and Germany to study 'modern work' and travelled in Belgium and Holland followed by a tour of 'the Cathedral towns of England'. He returned to the atelier for three happy final months.

After he left the atelier he explored and sketched for several months in Spain with his American friend, and sailed at last for Australia from Gibraltar. He used to tell us that he arrived in Sydney with precisely £50, the same amount he took with him when he started his travels. He joined a firm of architects in Sydney but after a few months when War was declared he joined the AIF. So he saw France and Paris again but never revisited America.

My mother, too, knew Paris well in her girlhood travels with her parents but her experiences in first-class hotels were very different from those of a hard-up atelier student:

> Miss Lavinia Kelsey, my mother's governess
> Taught her most exquisite French, and singing games.
> She, in her nineties, crazed and memory-less
> Twists her fleshless fingers into frames
> And flickering signals from her schoolroom time,
> Caricaturing childhood with jingle and rhyme.
>
> *Six sous ci*
> *Six sous ça*
> *Six sous sont ces*
> *Saucissons là!*
>
> Miss Kelsey instilled stiff manners and self control.
> Oft-quoted Miss Kelsey was *our* despair. Forbidden
> Were temper, loud voices, soup slopped round a bowl,
> Uneaten crusts, et-cet-era. Overlaid, hidden
> By layers of life, house, children, our eccentric father
> Miss Kelsey has re-emerged, or her spectre, rather.
>
> Mad grey creatures widdershins shriek for food.
> Eat spoonsful of sugar, pinch morsels from a neighbour's plate.
> My mother reproves: 'Sit up! Be quiet! Be good!
> No pudding for you if you carry on this rate!'
> The nurses applaud and approve. I pity her most
> When she speaks with the voice of Lavinia Kelsey's ghost.

Father had considerable scorn for the Hart family's comfortable travels and averred that Mother really knew nothing about Europe because she had seen it in luxury and had never lived close to ordinary citizens. Whether he was right or wrong, I sided with Dad. I never doubted that I, too, would travel and study in Europe and America—not architecture because I was too innumerate to contemplate that profession, and certainly not music having been born virtually tone-deaf to the consternation of a background of musical families. My father offered the princely addition of 3d. per week to my pocket money on condition I refrained from singing under the shower and averred that 'Nancy only distinguishes *God save the weasel* from *Pop goes the King* because everyone stands for the National Anthem,' So I dreamed of being a painter or. . .and of living somewhere where the concierge kept a goat and students had high times in cafés, and of seeing the marvels and histories of great cities.

War cheated my father of his cherished hopes and expectations, and so it happened to me. Except for several visits to New Zealand my first overseas experience was in 1970 when I was forty-seven, after which I accompanied Mark on several of his business trips in circumstances that more resembled my mother's modes of travel than anything my father ever knew. In all my life so far I have spent five days in Paris, two weeks in London and a fortnight in Italy. The European city I know best, but not well, is Amsterdam, thanks to my cousin Elisabeth who, one memorable day, led Mark and me to many of its famous places and to other sites that had Keesing family associations. We also met her brother Leo Keesing who was a friend of Ann Frank's father Otto, and a trustee of the museum established in the house where she spent her hidden, tragic youth. We have been back to Amsterdam and have explored it further, and travelled by train to Ellecom, the village where Elisabeth lives. Indeed, from trains I have seen a good deal of the Scandinavian, Dutch, French and Italian countrysides but I have had little opportunity to explore at leisure. I always longed to visit cities in Spain that Father described but have not seen much more than Barcelona and the mountainous road to Montserrat. The Alhambra remains a dream and so do the Goyas in Madrid's Prado museum. Mark and I managed a few free days to visit Carcasonne, a medieval fortified city which my father adored and often spoke about, and we had a brief holiday in Amboise and saw some of the Loire valley. I have explored far more of Japan and China than anywhere in Europe, and have spent more time in America than in the old world.

That elephant of mine obstinately takes its own directions, but it has given me some marvellous rides, and I'm not complaining.

Gordon Samuel Keesing died in 1971 when he was eighty-three. Margery Isabel Rahel lived until 1983 when she was in her nineties but, as I have told in my poem, during her last years her mind deteriorated and, sadly, she lived beyond what she would ever have wished for herself. In 1977 I first had to realise how greatly she had changed over some twelve months. In that year Angus and Robertson published my anthology, *The White Chrysanthemum* which was subtitled *Changing Images of Australian Motherhood*. (It was re-issued as a paperback with the title *Dear Mum* in 1985.) I had compiled this book while I was Chairman of the Literature Board and was too involved with writers' affairs to contemplate sustained and demanding work of my own. The theme of the book was suggested by Sue Phillips, wife of Richard Walsh who was then the publisher of Angus and Robertson. I had much enjoyment in re-reading books from my own shelves and in discovering new books and writers, and illustrations and paragraphs. The anthology's name, as I explained in the introduction, arose from a fancy of mine that the white chrysanthe*mum* which is *the* Great Australian Mothers Day Flower, resembles nothing so much as 'a pristine dish-mop ready for months of work among the greasy dishes and disgusting slops of a domestic sink'. The dedication appeared in the final paragraph of the introduction:

My paternal grandmother was one of fourteen children; my maternal grandmother had ten brothers and sisters, but they had two and three children respectively; my mother produced two. They were all Australians, all great mums. I dedicate this book to them, and especially to my own mother Margery Keesing.

As soon as I received six advance copies I inscribed one for my mother who sat in her sunroom pretending to be pleased with the book but in fact puzzled and confused. When I pointed out the dedicatory paragraph she said, 'That's my name printed there. Why?' It was one of the saddest moments of my life.

Death was a blessed release for her. After a while we, her family, were able to remember her again as she was when her mind was whole. Letters from the university libraries she had supported, and from friends she made because of her generosity, helped this process of renewal. Many of these correspondents recalled and praised my father too.

There were no conditions or requests attached to the legacy my mother left me in her will, but I greatly desired to find some way of perpetuating my parents' concerns and generosities with some of this money. I thought, though, that I would prefer to support a project or cause that, while in the spirit of their interest in libraries, was more directly connected with my own preoccupations and career as a writer. A Literary Award? Nowadays there are a number of literary awards both private and governmental and some of them are substantial. There is support for writers and writing through the Literature Board. In any year few, if any, excellent books or their authors fail to receive one or other of the prizes, and recognition through one or other of the competitions. Talented writers, both those who are established and those newly on the scene, may buy time to write because of cash prizes, grants and fellowships.

In 1985 I discussed my wish with Tom Shapcott, the Director of the Literature Board and with Professor Di Yerbury, the General Manager of the Australia Council. They told me that the French Government was building a complex of studios in Paris to be known as *La Cité Internationale des Arts*, and had offered two of these studios to the Australian Government on 75-year leases, until 2060 AD. The Australia Council had been given carriage of this offer. The Visual Arts Board had already agreed to lease one studio. The second could be available to the Literature Board, but its budget was committed and it was doubtful whether it could accept the offer within the fairly short time allowed for a decision.

Here was the way in which I could do something constructive for Australian writers and also honour my parents in the city that meant so much to them when they were young. I donated the money to pay for the studio and asked that the Literature Board and/or the Australia Council should deal with applications and decisions about occupants for the duration of the lease. My only request was that, if suitable young writers applied they should be given preference over older people provided the quality of talent was comparable. It was not my fate to attain a dream of living and working overseas in my youth and it would please me if other youthful dreams could become reality.

Australian publishers have made generous donations of books for a library within the studio. The first occupant was Robert Carter whose novel *The Sugar Factory* was published shortly before he left Australia. The second is, as I write, Alan Wearne, whose remarkable verse novel, *The Night Markets*, was published in 1986. *The Sugar Factory* was short-listed for the 1986 NSW Premiers Award, and *The Night Markets* won the 1987 National Book Council Award.

One of my cousins who insists on anonymity wished to be associated with the studio because of admiration and love for my parents, and made a donation which has enabled a fund to be established that can assist, when needed, with living expenses for a studio occupant.

The project gives me much joy and not least because Mark, Margery and John have been keen on the idea from its inception, and remain very interested in its development. We look forward to the reports and reactions of writers who use the Keesing Studio.

'Because of your gift,' said a young man who had read the first chapter of this book, 'you are still riding the elephant!' One day soon Mark and I hope we may travel to Paris, rather more quickly and comfortably than by pachyderm, and see the Keesing Studio for ourselves. But I still hope and intend to be an elephant rider.

Index

Numbers in *italics* refer to photographs.